Your Home Mortgage

THE ICFP PERSONAL WEALTH BUILDING GUIDES

YOUR HOME MORTGAGE
Michael C. Thomsett

YOUR PARENT'S FINANCIAL SECURITY
Barbara Weltman

YOUR RETIREMENT BENEFITS
Peter E. Gaudio and Virginia S. Nicols

Your Home Mortgage

Michael C. Thomsett

JOHN WILEY & SONS, INC.

New York • Chichester • Brisbane • Toronto • Singapore

Library of Congress Cataloging-in-Publication Data

Thomsett, Michael C.
    Your home mortgage / by Michael C. Thomsett.
      p.   cm.
    Includes index.
    ISBN 0-471-54828-6 (cloth). — ISBN 0-471-54829-4 (paper)
     1. Mortgage loans—United States. 2. Mortgage loans—United
States—Refinancing. I. Title.
HG2040.5.U5T48 1992
332.7′22′0973—dc20   91-37900

Printed in the United States of America

10 9 8 7 6 5 4 3 2 1

Printed and bound by Malloy Lithographing, Inc.

Contents

Introduction: The Homeowner's Dilemma

You have probably heard or read all of the arguments for and against home buying. It's the biggest investment you will ever make. Interest rates today are low—or, they're high. Property values will be rising in the future—or, they will be flat, or falling. The arguments are many and confusing, and invariably end up in a comparison of numbers and rates, with everyone trying to make decisions based on an uncertain future.

The fact is, no one really knows what the future will bring, in real estate or in any other market. We can know for certain, however, that, historically, buying your own home has proven to be a sound and profitable investment *for those who stay in their homes for many years*.

Note the important qualifier. Home ownership is profitable in most cases when people do not move frequently. You could lose money by turning over your investment every few years, if the market didn't rise quickly. The cost of financing and selling your home is too high to afford rapid turnover in a slow market. This is the key point. It is actually difficult to lose money when you buy your own home, *unless* you move too often and in the wrong market conditions, or borrow too heavily against your home's equity, or fail to take good care of your home through maintenance and insurance.

When the market for housing slows down, everyone becomes afraid. There is widespread confusion about what it means. Articles begin to appear in national magazines, announcing that the "free ride" in real estate is over. In other words, prices won't be going up any more. This conclusion is reached every time the real estate cycle hits bottom. And it's always wrong.

You do not need to fear changes in the real estate cycle as long as you don't need to sell your home and move on. You should plan to be in your home for the long term, as a homeowner and not as a speculator. You're not looking for a fast profit; instead, you want a place where you can raise a family and fix your housing costs over the long term.

Confusion about real estate cycles comes about largely because those cycles occur regionally, not nationally. This point is overlooked in the financial press time and again. The housing market in New York may slow to a grinding halt; at the same time, it may be booming in Seattle. Those were the actual conditions in those two cities during 1988 and 1989. New York's market was flat, and there was a glut of properties on the market. But 3,000 miles away, the Pacific Northwest was going through an amazing real estate boom. Many homeowners saw their properties rise 25 to 50 percent or more per year, for 2 years running.

You need to make a clear distinction between your home and your other investments. The distinction—regardless of what is going on in the market—is based not on paper profits, but on the purpose behind the investment. You might buy stocks, bonds, or shares of a mutual fund in the hopes of turning a fast profit. When the profit comes, you pocket it and then move your money into something else.

That's not the way it works with real estate. Your home is purchased as a personal asset, not as part of a portfolio. If you were to take profits, you would have to find a new home. You might also have to change jobs, find new social contacts, put your children in a new school, and otherwise disrupt the continuity of your life and the lives of your family.

You need to view real estate as a long-term investment. The day may come when you will want to move to a new community or a larger house. On average, first-time homeowners stay less than 5 years in that first home. Given the long-term nature of real estate, you need to manage your personal home investment just as wisely as you manage a portfolio of stocks and bonds. You need to make good selections and then manage your home intelligently, with an awareness of some of the alternatives available to you. The cornerstone of wise financial management in real estate is your financing. By knowing where the best deals are and how to reduce the cost of your mortgage, you will drastically change the true overall cost of buying your home.

For example, the day may come when that attractive mortgage you signed isn't so attractive any more. Perhaps rates have come way down, and refinancing would make sense. You need to know how to determine whether the cost of refinancing is justified by the savings you'll achieve. That decision can be made only when you know what costs are involved, and how your decision will affect your monthly payments and interest costs. These are the types of issues you will learn to master by reading this book. For wise money managers, mortgage management is only one aspect to consider. As a long-term homeowner, you enjoy a number of advantages, even without exercising any management or financial skills. These include:

▶ *Fixed long-term cost.* Your housing costs become fixed, once you buy. This is true whether you commit to a fixed-rate mortgage or an adjustable-rate mortgage. With the fixed-rate contract, your payments won't vary at all. With an adjustable-rate contract, you may experience increases each year, but your contract places a ceiling on how high the interest rate can go during the life of your contract. Within that range, even the adjustable-rate mortgage is relatively fixed.

▶ *Equity building.* As a homeowner, you build equity in several ways. Each time you make a payment, part of that payment goes toward principal. The longer this goes on, the more your equity grows. Market values may be increasing, over the years you own your home. If you improve your property, that will increase its equity even more. Adding a bedroom or putting in a remodeled kitchen will add market value and appeal to your home.

▶ *Personal security.* Because you and your family live in your home, your investment gives you much more than financial value; it gives you personal security and safety. You have a place to *live.* You cannot discount the value or importance of this benefit. In fact, its importance should carry greater weight than your home's investment and financial value—at least until you have decided to sell and move on.

▶ *Investment value.* Even though your home is primarily a personal asset, you cannot ignore the fact that, eventually, you will cash in on a profitable decision. When you sell your home, in most cases, you will realize the profits that come from making a sound investment decision. Your home, like many forms of real estate, has investment value. At the point when you decide to sell, you will want to get the most for your home and to close the sale on a time schedule that is convenient for you.

▶ *Insurance.* One feature of home ownership makes it unlike any other investment. You will carry homeowner's insurance, which is protection against fires and other catastrophes. As long as you have a mortgage, your lender will require this. However, even if you own your home free and clear, you should always have homeowner's insurance. As long as you do, your investment is protected against the consequences of unexpected loss. In addition, the fact that you're there every day adds investment quality to your home. Few other investments can come close to the risk-reducing features of insurance and on-site maintenance, while offering the same return on your investment dollars.

In this book, you will see how the value of your investment can be maintained and improved through smart mortgage management. In some situations, this means replacing one mortgage with another. At times, it could mean paying off your debt more quickly than is required by the contract. Often, you will have a great deal and should simply leave things alone.

The tricky part of mortgage management is knowing when to act or not act. Taking action is not always the best policy or alternative. Smart investors know that timing is important and picking the moment to act is critical, but they also know that there is a time to *not* act, a time when doing nothing is the best course of all. With the information we provide here, you will be better equipped to make informed decisions concerning your home.

Investment information is collected at the back of the book, so that you can compare the costs of financing your home with various options, and can see approximately what portion of your mortgage remains unpaid from one year to the next. By understanding how lenders calculate your interest, you will be better informed on the real cost of home ownership. By seeing how your mortgage balance changes from year to year, you will be able to select the debt repayment plan that is best suited to your financial goals.

The book gives you the information you need to take charge of your mortgage and to plan your future so that you will own your own home when you want to, not when the bank says so. You'll learn the basics you will need, to execute and then to control your financial plan. With this knowledge, you will enjoy the greatest of all privileges of planning: financial freedom and the knowledge of how to keep it.

1

The Real Bottom Line

What does your house really cost you? Depending on how you manage and plan your mortgage, your house might cost a lot more than you think. An encouraging secret, however, is that *you* can decide, years ahead of time, how much your house will cost you. There's nothing too complex about your decision, either, if you understand exactly what factors are involved in the price of a house.

The cost of your house is really determined by two things: your monthly payment and the interest rate you pay. The payment is important because you have to be able to afford a certain amount each month. The interest rate counts because *that* is what determines your housing costs, over the period of a mortgage loan. *The purchase price you see advertised in the newspaper is not what you pay for your house.*

WHAT YOUR HOUSE REALLY COSTS

To examine why this is true, let's use the example of a house for which, we'll assume, you paid $120,000. You make a down payment of $20,000 and finance $100,000. In shopping for a loan, you narrow down your choices to two options. One bank wants to lend you the money at 10 percent interest and will give you 30 years to repay it. Another bank will charge only 9 percent interest, but only if you agree to repay the loan over 15 years.

The payments will be much different with each loan. The 30-year loan will cost you $877.58 per month; the 15-year contract will be

$1,014.27. The difference between these two loans is $136.69 per month. That's a lot of money if you're on a fixed income and have been renting for a lot less than either of these monthly amounts.

The payments are higher for the 9 percent loan even though the interest rate is lower. That's because the loan is scheduled to be repaid in one-half the time. It has to be amortized, or paid down, at a faster rate than the 30-year loan.

There's another potential problem here. In order to get the loan, you will have to qualify. That means your income has to be high enough to make the payments, based on a formula the lender uses. For example, some banks want your monthly payment to be no greater than a certain percentage of your monthly income. If your lender applies 28 percent in the repayment formula, you would need to make more than $3,600 per month to qualify for the 9 percent loan. Many people who are capable of making the monthly payments don't get the loan, because they don't qualify.

The second part of this test is the total cost of your home. Remember, the purchase price you negotiate for a home isn't its real cost. This example will prove that point. The total of payments under the 30-year loan will be $315,928.80 Add on your down payment of $20,000, and your house will cost $335,928.80. On the 15-year loan, the total of payments is much less, only $182,568.60. Again, adding the down payment, the total cost of your house would be $202,568.60. Even though this is more than twice the purchase price, it is much less than the cost with a 30-year loan. With the 15-year repayment schedule, you cut the cost by $133,360.20.

Why does a $120,000 house cost two to three times the stated amount? *Interest.* The lender charges interest each and every month, and the interest is always based on the amount of your loan that's still outstanding. When you owe a lot, your interest is very high. In fact, in the early years of your loan, very little of your monthly payment goes toward principal. Almost all of it is for interest. For example, on that 10 percent, 30-year loan on which you would pay $877.58 per month, your first payment is made up of $833.33 interest and only $44.25 principal.

A 30-year loan's balance falls very slowly during the first few years. After the end of the 10th year (one-third of the way through the period), you will have paid off only about 9 percent of the total loan. Out of the $100,000, you will still owe about $90,900 to the lender. In fact, you will have paid off only one-half of the loan by the middle of the 24th year. In the last 6 years, you will pay off the other half.

As you can see from this example, the real expense of buying a house is only vaguely connected to the purchase price. Conceivably, you could decide on a house that has a much higher purchase price, and end up buying it for much less, if you knew how to arrange the right financing, or if you were able to accelerate the repayment schedule to your advantage.

It is ironic, with this higher-price/lower-cost possibility in mind, that so much time and effort go into finding the right house at the right price, but so little time and effort are invested in finding financing and the best possible terms. In other words, too many home buyers spend their energies looking for bargains that will come in $2,000 below what a seller wants; they often forget to look at what they will be spending for the house over the next 30 years. In perspective, a few thousand dollars of purchase price is virtually meaningless. The same energy could be put to much better use in negotiating a better deal with the lender.

It makes sense to shop for financing *before* going out and looking at houses. Within the range of prices for which you can qualify according to your lender's rules, it doesn't matter what purchase prices are involved. What matters is the method you use to pay your mortgage.

What is my house really costing me?

It's the sum of the purchase price plus the interest you will pay over the whole mortgage term, reduced by the tax benefits of itemizing deductions.

How do I compute the real cost?

Multiply monthly payments by the number of months in which you will repay your mortgage. Subtract the loan amount, to arrive at total interest. Then subtract the tax savings.

Exactly what are the tax savings? The reduced taxes?

Yes. For example, if your marginal tax rate is 28 percent, then your savings is equal to 28 percent of the total interest paid each year.

Will my tax savings remain the same every year?

That's unlikely. Changes in the tax law, as well as in your personal income level, will undoubtedly change your situation drastically. For purposes of planning, today's comparisons are made based on your present situation.

Does this mean that long-term planning could be wrong?

You have to plan for changes. You need to constantly review and revise your financial plan.

Would I be better off with a shorter-term mortgage?

You would be able to reduce your interest costs. But remember, you have to first be able to qualify according to your lender's rules. That might mean having to commit to a 30-year mortgage just to hold down the payments.

How can I better understand what my home costs?

Learn how lenders compute interest. Be aware of the cost from one month to another, by tracking your repayments. Plan your future with a reduction of your mortgage costs in mind.

Does the purchase price really matter?

In the long term, the actual purchase price is relatively meaningless, except to the extent that it affects your ability to qualify for a loan.

Where should my emphasis be placed, when shopping for a home?

Your first step should be to shop for financing. That will tell you how much of a home you can afford, based on the lender's qualification rules.

What if I find out that I can afford to pay more than required?

The more you pay, the lower your future interest expense will be.

SETTING YOUR RULES

One of the goals of writing this book is to attempt to cure a widespread mistake: the failure to shop for financing and to plan far into the future. For anyone who presently owns a house, the mistake has already been made, but it can be remedied. A far greater mistake would be to not remedy the failure when you recognize it. You can close your financing and planning gap in a number of ways. Set a few immediate rules for yourself, before going forward.

Take Charge of Managing Your Mortgage

Never assume that a lender's job is to "manage" your mortgage for you. The lender is in the business of renting money, and interest is the rental fee. Today, most commercial lenders end up selling your mortgage in the secondary market (a market for the repurchase of mortgage loans already contracted). The buyer in the secondary market is usually a government-sponsored mortgage pool. Gone are the days of long-term relationships between banks and their customers. Banks have become money brokers; they are not the financial institutions our fathers and mothers knew.

This new reality changes your role. Today, you need to be in charge of your own finances. It has always been that way, but many people never realized it. If you want financial freedom and success, you have to take responsibility for your future. That means *you* have to manage your mortgage, shop for the best deals, and decide whether you're on the best course for yourself and your family.

→ **ACTION ITEM** ←

Write out, for yourself, a "shopping list" of the steps you need to take to put yourself in complete charge.

Don't even think about depending on your real estate agent to act as your financial adviser. Real estate agents are not supposed to offer financial, tax, or legal advice. Most agents are not qualified to do so, anyway. They do not understand how financing works in the long term. They might know which lender has the most liberal rules for qualifying you for a loan, but that does not necessarily mean that the loan you will get will be best for you. When it comes to planning your long-term future and taking charge of your housing costs, you're on your own.

Establish a Long-Term Financial Plan

What do you *want*? You have to set your financial goals if you expect to achieve them. In serious thought about the distant future, a few issues come up over and over: retirement, health insurance for old age, living expenses, college education for children. All of these future needs share one thing in common. They require money; not just a lump sum, but a continuous flow of income to finance goals and to give protection against being forced to live life in any way other than the way you want.

One big problem with buying a house is that, at the time you buy, no one is thinking about the long term. You want to get the deal at the best price and qualify for financing. The lender wants a lot of paperwork filled out. The agent wants to get the deal accepted and into escrow, so that he or she will get a commission. Again, it's up to you to keep your best interests in mind, and to find the right loan and the right lender. For the moment, the attention-getting goal is to make the deal work, both for buyer and seller. The fact is, you have a number of other goals. Closing the deal is push-button mechanics. What you really want extends over decades, not just the next few weeks.

Regardless of our immediate goals, we all want the same thing: financial freedom. You don't want to have to keep working when you'd rather retire. You want to be in control of where you live. You want the financial freedom to pursue a comfortable and secure life-style. That simple goal is so often missed, even by intelligent and well-educated people who earn a good living. Why? Because they didn't take conscious steps to get financial freedom. One of the many ways to ensure that freedom for yourself is to own your own home, free and clear, by the time you want to retire and stop making payments.

Choose a Payoff Date

You want to ensure that you will be able to retire comfortably. Or, if you prefer not to fully retire, like so many people today, you at least want the flexibility to reduce your income without changing your life-style. One way to do that is to decide, for yourself, when your mortgage will be paid off.

A common reaction to this advice is: "But the lender and I have a contract. The lender is in charge of the contract, and will tell me when my loan is paid off." This is simply not the case. You can change the contract. You can't delay the repayment period, but there's no reason you can't repay the loan sooner.

Why pick a payoff date? Because you have to do your own math, if you want to be in charge of your financial future. A 40-year-old husband and wife who buy a home and finance it over a 30-year term will not make the final payment until after their 70th birthday. But what if they're planning to retire when they're 60? They face one of three situations:

▶ They will need a fairly large retirement income, to continue making those payments.

▶ They will have to make the payments out of assets being preserved for retirement, which will cause a more restrictive life-style than the couple had planned.

▶ They need to do some financial planning now, to meet a goal of paying off their mortgage in the next 20, not 30, years.

Calculate Your Housing Costs

This advice, usually given to first-time home buyers, most often means comparing the difference between renting and buying. That's not what is meant here. Calculate the true cost of buying your house over the coming years. With the interest expense you must pay during the contractual term of your mortgage, what is it really going to cost you?

The purchase price is only the starting point for calculating the *real* cost of buying your house. A rule to remember is: The shorter the mortgage repayment period, the lower your housing cost. You will be paying interest on a more rapidly declining balance, which reduces the monthly interest. Every dollar you use today to reduce the principal balance also reduces the interest expense every month for the remainder of the mortgage term.

WHO MAKES THE PROFIT?

You have heard that buying a house is a worthwhile and profitable investment. That's true. You will accumulate equity during the years you are a homeowner. But you should also know that, in the majority of cases, the lender makes a greater profit on your home than you do. The equity—the portion of your home that you own above and beyond the mortgage debt—is actually converted over to the lender in the form of long-term interest.

In the earlier illustration of a 30-year loan used to finance $100,000, the cost added up to more than $315,000 over the life of the mortgage. To buy the $120,000 house (down payment plus financing), you would have had to give the lender $215,000 in interest. You would have put a total of $335,000 into the house, not $120,000. The important question is this: Will the house increase in value, enough to keep pace with inflation and to justify the interest cost?

Let's say it does. Let's assume that, after 30 years, your $120,000 house increases in value and is then worth $335,000. What does that mean? Because of the payments you've made, in actual truth, you paid $335,000 for the house. Over 30 years, you paid the future value of the house, but you didn't make a profit. The lender advanced you $100,000 so that you could get your house, and you repaid the lender $315,000. The bank's profit is $215,000, and you didn't make a profit at all. If you sold your house at the end of 30 years, you would get back exactly what you paid for it!

⟶ ACTION ITEM ⟵

Calculate the future value of your house, assuming 3 percent inflation per year. What will your house be worth when your mortgage is repaid? How much will you have paid to the lender by then?

The bank makes its profit, even when a house does not rise in value enough to justify the interest expense. The bank's risks, then, are actually lower than yours. For example, what if the $120,000 house was worth only $200,000 at the end of 30 years? You would still have paid $335,000 for it, and the bank would still have profit of $215,000. But you would sell at a loss.

Some people would question how selling at $200,000 would be selling at a loss. The house cost $120,000, and it sold for $200,000.

That's a profit of $80,000, right? People tend to concentrate on purchase and sales prices and ignore the real costs. In this example, you would pay $335,000 over 30 years, and sell the house for $200,000. That's a loss of $135,000, when interest is considered. Most people compare only purchase and sale prices.

Make whatever claims of profit you want, when talking to your friends and relatives, but, for your own benefit, set another rule for yourself: don't deceive yourself by playing games with the numbers. Look constantly for the real bottom line. Count the interest in your calculations of cost.

To be completely fair, the real interest cost does get reduced somewhat, because there's a tax benefit to paying interest. You are entitled to an itemized deduction for home mortgage interest. The more you pay, the more you reduce your taxes, so interest can't be taken into account at 100 percent. You must calculate the tax savings, and consider the difference as your net cost. You'll learn how to do this later on in the chapter.

First, though, you need to develop a preliminary understanding of the way interest works. Your lender calculates amortization (a repayment schedule) for your loan, based on the time, interest rate, and amount of the loan. When you know how this calculation works, you will have a better grasp on how to plan for yourself.

LOAN AMORTIZATION

The process of calculating principal and interest breakdowns of mortgage payments is not at all mysterious. If you think a computer, or at least a sophisticated hand-held calculator, is necessary, remember that people have been buying and financing houses for many years, long before computers were in use.

How Difficult Is the Process?

Figuring out loan amortization requires a few steps, and there *are* hand-held calculators that will do all of the work for you. However, to truly understand how the process works, you should go through the steps for yourself. Doing so will remove any sense of mystery from the process.

For a number of reasons, you should know how to break down a loan payment. Here are some of those reasons.

Know the Process, to Improve Your Control

It's important that you take control over your finances. One way to achieve control is to master the math that has such a direct impact on you. The sense of knowing how your expenses are calculated puts you in direct control and enables you to face your financial task with confidence.

Check for Lender Errors

You'll make a serious mistake if you assume that the lender's numbers are always right. Even if the lender is using a computer, it makes sense to check the numbers for yourself. Errors are made, and they go uncaught because the majority of borrowers don't know how to check, or assume that they don't need to.

Be Informed, If You Use Private Lending

If you borrow or lend money privately, someone will have to figure out the breakdown between principal and interest. You'll have to know how much is to be paid each month, and how much interest should be reported for tax purposes on both sides. Instead of consulting a banker or an accountant, you can figure out the breakdown all by yourself.

There are two things you need to be able to do. First, you need to figure out the monthly payment required; second, once monthly payments begin, you will need to break them down between interest and principal.

Let's take the second part first. (A later section gets into more detail about figuring out the amount.) As an example, let's assume that you are told how much to pay each month on your mortgage loan. Using familiar figures, you have a $100,000 loan at 10 percent interest, payable in 30 years. Monthly payments are $877.58.

Interest for the first payment is based on the full loan amount outstanding, $100,000. The interest rate is 10 percent per year and, because payments are made every month, the monthly interest will be $1/12$ of the annual rate. To calculate interest for the first month, use a worksheet like the one shown in Figure 1–1(a).

Worksheet: Loan Payments

1. Enter the balance of the loan $ _____

2. Multiply by the interest rate
   (in decimal form)   x _____

3. Result: annual interest $ _____

4. Divide by 12   ÷ 12

5. Result: this month's interest $ _____

6. Subtract the monthly payment   − _____

7. Result: this month's principal $ _____

8. Add the loan balance forward   + _____

9. Result: new loan balance $ _____

———————————— **Figure 1–1(a)** ————————————
Figuring the monthly payment.

This worksheet shows the exact steps needed to break down each payment between principle and interest. A filled-in example, using $100,000 and 10 percent, would be shown in Figure 1–1(b).

This same process is applied to any fully amortized loan, whether the lender is a commercial bank or a private party. The annual interest is broken down into 12 parts and is then applied against the outstanding balance of the loan.

During the first full 12 months of payment, only about ½ of 1 percent of the loan is paid off (based on a 10 percent interest loan amortized over 30 years). The first year's payments on a $100,000 loan breakdown are as shown in the table on page 13.

Worksheet: Loan Payments

1. Enter the balance of the loan	$ 100,000.00
2. Multiply by the interest rate (in decimal form)	x _____.10
3. Result: annual interest	$ 10,000.00
4. Divide by 12	÷ 12
5. Result: this month's interest	$ 833.33
6. Subtract the monthly payment	− 877.58
7. Result: this month's principal	$ 44.25
8. Add the loan balance forward	+ 100,000
9. Result: new loan balance	$ 99,955.75

———————————— **Figure 1–1(b)** ————————————
How to break down the payment between interest and principal.

The table shows how little of the total payment goes toward principal during the first year of a 30-year term. In this example, more than $10,000 is paid to the lender during the first year, but only $556 is applied to reduction of the loan. Each year during the loan term, the amount of principal increases and the amount of interest decreases.

The monthly payment must be greater than the monthly interest, or the loan balance will rise instead of falling (negative amortization). In our example, the first month's interest is $833.33. If less than that amount were to be paid, the loan's balance could not decline. The full payment of $877.58 is required in order to retire the

Loan Amortization, First Year
10 Percent, 30-Year Term

Month	Total Payment	Interest	Principal	Balance
				$100,000.00
1	$ 877.58	$ 833.33	$ 44.25	99,955.75
2	877.58	832.96	44.62	99,911.13
3	877.58	832.59	44.99	99,866.14
4	877.58	832.22	45.36	99,820.78
5	877.58	831.84	45.74	99,775.04
6	877.58	831.46	46.12	99,728.92
7	877.58	831.07	46.51	99,682.41
8	877.58	830.69	46.89	99,635.52
9	877.58	830.30	47.28	99,588.24
10	877.58	829.90	47.68	99,540.56
11	877.58	829.50	48.08	99,492.48
12	877.58	829.10	48.48	99,444.00
Total	$10,530.96	$9,974.96	$556.00	

loan by the 30th year. Negative amortization occurs when the payment doesn't cover the interest due that month; as a result, the loan's balance goes up instead of down, because interest is accrued and added to the debt.

WEALTH BUILDING PROFILE   *Losing Ground.* Andy and Marsha's $100,000 loan is supposed to be paid in 30 years. However, they are only required to make payments of $800 per month. In this situation, their loan balance will *rise* each month.

To prove this point, note that the interest during the first month is $833.33. After applying that amount to the smaller payment, you will be short by $33.33 per month. The balance forward would then be $100,033.33, an amount larger than the previous balance.

Negative amortization can occur in adjustable-rate mortgages, if a payment ceiling (called the cap) is contracted rather than a rate cap. This type of contract was drawn in the past, but is less common today.

The point about negative amortization is mentioned to emphasize that the monthly payment in a fully amortized loan is not an arbitrary amount. It is calculated to repay the loan by a specific date in the future.

What Method Is Best?

This leads to the second part of our loan amortization discussion: the method in which the monthly amount is computed. Most of us nod agreement when a banker or a real estate agent tells us, "For that much debt, and assuming such-and-such interest rate, your payment will be so much per month."

Most people accept that answer because they don't know how to calculate the payment, nor where to look for the answer. Yet, it's available to all of us. Every well-stocked bookstore has several books, priced under $10, that contain loan repayment tables. The titles may include wording like "interest amortization," "loan repayment," or "mortgage payments."

The table you need is called "payments required to amortize a loan." It will show the amount you would need to pay each month. The amounts vary for a number of reasons:

▶ *Amount.* The amount of the loan determines the amount of the payment. The higher the loan, the higher the payment required to amortize it, or pay it off.

▶ *Interest rate.* The interest rate also determines the amount of the payment. The higher the rate, the higher the required payment.

▶ *Compounding method.* The more frequently interest is compounded, the higher the required monthly payment. Monthly compounding is more expensive than quarterly compounding. Mortgages usually are paid monthly and include calculations of interest compounded on a monthly basis.

▶ *Time.* The shorter the period until the loan is due, the higher the monthly payment. A 15-year amortization will save a lot in interest expense, but it will also mean higher payments than would be required for amortization over 30 years.

Appendix A provides amortization tables for monthly compounding and for a number of different interest rates.

Why is it so important to know how loan amortization works?

It's primarily a matter of control. If you want to be in control of your financial future, you need to know how lenders are figuring how much to charge you for borrowed money.

Am I likely to catch a lender's error?

Loan amortization is a straightforward process of math. With computerized systems, a lender error is unlikely. But you should still police your lender. Errors can and do occur; it's in your best interest to keep an eye on the computations.

Do all lenders have computers these days?

Far from it. You might get a seller to carry all or part of a loan. In that case, you will need to compute the breakdown between interest and principal every month.

If I want to pay off a loan in a certain number of years, do I have to go through a long computation?

Not at all. You only need to figure out how to use an interest amortization table.

Does a loan amortization table explain how to break out interest and principal?

No, it only gives the total payment. To break out interest and principal, you have to do a little math on your own.

Do I have to worry about negative amortization?

In that situation, the monthly payment is not high enough to cover the interest, so the loan amount rises each month. If you ever find yourself in negative amortization, you need to increase your payment, to get your principal level down.

What are the four critical elements of the interest calculation?

The amount, the interest rate, the compounding method, and the amount of time involved.

COMPARING THE TAX
BENEFIT/COST

Once you start calculating interest for yourself, you will begin to better understand how lending works. You only need to multiply the monthly payment by the number of months to see that interest adds up quickly over the term of your loan.

One of the advantages of paying interest on your home mortgage is that the interest is tax-deductible. Some home buyers have annual deductions above $10,000, which could translate to a savings of $3,000—or more, if state taxes are added to federal.

With tax deductions in mind, many people argue in favor of being in debt: "You need the deduction to reduce your taxes, so paying interest is not a problem." This tax argument is flawed, because it ignores the mathematical facts. You might need to mortgage your home, in order to afford it, but taxes should never be the sole reason for going into debt, nor for postponing paying off your debt if you can afford to pay it now.

WEALTH BUILDING PROFILE   *Needed Deductions.* John's mortgage interest expense this year will be $10,000. He can afford to repay the loan right now, and eliminate the expense. But he doesn't do so because he "needs" the $3,000 tax deduction. This means that John will continue to pay $10,000 in interest. If he paid off the loan and lost the deduction, he would still be ahead by the net difference, $7,000. He would be better off paying no interest, giving up the tax deduction, and saving $7,000. Like John, many people remain in debt unnecessarily, failing to realize that the tax argument just doesn't make sense.

The tax argument is most often made in favor of keeping a loan going, even when money is available to pay it off. For example, suppose you receive an inheritance. You could use the money to pay off your mortgage, but then you'd lose your tax deduction. Too many people, in this situation, would advise, "Don't pay off your mortgage. You need the deduction."

A better answer would be, "Pay off the debt, unless you can beat the interest rate somewhere else. For example, if your mortgage is costing you 9 percent, you might be able to beat that rate by investing the money somewhere else. If you can't get more than 9 percent elsewhere, the best thing to do is pay off your debt and give up the tax benefit."

An argument is also made to *go into debt* by taking out a new mortgage loan, just to get the tax break. This is an equally weak argument. For example, many financial advisers tell clients to borrow money to invest through their home mortgage, and to then write off the interest on the mortgage loan. On the surface, this argument might seem logical, but it has several flaws.

▸ Your risks will not be the same. The fact that is nearly always forgotten by pro-mortgage advocates is that the risks involved with investing borrowed money (as from a mortgage) may be greater than the risk of owning your own home. You might be able to find an investment that matches the rate you're paying on your mortgage, but how much control will you have? What are the risks? With your home, you're there every day keeping an eye on your investment. It provides your family with shelter and it's insured through your homeowner's policy. Can you say the same about a stock market purchase?

▸ The cash flow probably won't be there to repay the loan every month. The theory put forth by some financial advisers is that you're better off leveraging the money "sitting idle" in your home, by borrowing it and making other investments. That's fine as long as you can afford the extra mortgage payment; many people cannot. You will have a difficult time finding an investment that will produce a monthly cash flow that is adequate to cover your mortgage payment.

▸ Income from investments is taxable; mortgage interest is deductible. There may be little point to putting yourself at risk by borrowing money against your home equity. If the expense of borrowing is equal to the income from investing, why expose yourself to the risk? Remember, your mortgage interest is deductible, but any profits you earn on investments are taxable. There is no tax break in borrowing to invest.

▸ Even a currently attractive rate has to be earned for the entire period the loan is outstanding. For the investment plan to work out for you, it has to stay in effect for your entire loan period. When the idea of borrowing to invest is proposed, this is often forgotten entirely. An adviser might tell you, for example, that a particular investment has yielded an average of 23 percent per year for the past 10 years. As impressive as that might sound, your concern is more for the future. If your mortgage will extend for 30 years, you will need to beat the mortgage rate each and every year for 30 years—and you'll need cash flow every month to make the payments. That guarantee cannot be given.

CALCULATING NET INTEREST

Once you view the tax arguments in perspective, you will see that the reasons to borrow are not compelling. You should preserve your home equity for future improvements, or to save up for the day when you may want to move to a bigger home. At that time, the more equity you have, the more you will be able to afford for an upgraded residence—or the lower your future mortgage payments will be.

The interest you pay on your mortgage loan today does provide a tax benefit that is worth calculating. To compute your net interest cost, reduce your mortgage interest rate by the "effective" tax rate you are paying (the rate you're assessed on your taxable income).

You can find your effective tax rate by looking at the tax rate schedule in the IRS's annual tax booklet. Use the tax rate schedule to determine your effective tax rate, even if you don't use that schedule to compute your tax. You will notice that, in each category, the instructions call for a lump sum, plus a percentage of the amount over a ceiling. That percentage is the effective tax rate.

For example, in 1990, the tax rate schedule for a married couple filing jointly looked like this:

Taxable Income Over	But Not Over	Your Tax Is	Of the Amount Over
$ 0	$ 32,450	. . . 15%	$ 0
32,450	78,400	$ 4,867.50 + 28%	
78,400	162,770	17,733.50 + 33%	78,400

The way to read this is to add the fixed amount to the indicated percentage. If your taxable income was $35,800, your tax would be:

Fixed amount		$4,867.50
Total	$35,800	
Less:	32,450	
Difference	$ 3,350	
28%		938.00
Total tax		$5,805.50

The effective tax rate here is 28 percent. The effective tax rate can easily be used to calculate your net interest rate or your net interest cost. Your net interest rate is the rate you're assessed, reduced by the effective tax rate.

WEALTH BUILDING PROFILE   *Effective Tax Rate.* Bob and Joann have a mortgage contract with interest at 9.625 percent. Their effective tax rate is 28 percent. Their after-tax rate is the difference between 100 percent and 28 percent (effective tax rate):

$$100 - 28 = 72\%$$

To calculate their net interest rate, Bob and Joann should multiply this rate by the rate they are paying on their mortgage:

$$.72 \times 9.625 = 6.93\%$$

They are paying a net after-tax interest rate on their mortgage of 6.93 percent.

Information on your interest rate and tax rate is useful, but only if you also apply it on the income side. For example, if you are told you should borrow money to invest, be sure to apply your after-tax earnings rate to the estimated yield. The benefit or consequence of taxation applies on both sides of the equation.

─────────────────→ ACTION ITEM ←─────────────

Calculate net interest for your situation, based on:

▸ **The percentage you pay on your mortgage**

▸ **Your tax bracket.**

What is your net interest cost?

You can use the same technique to calculate your actual after-tax interest expense.

WEALTH   *After-Tax Interest.* Bob and Joann previously calcu-
BUILDING   lated that 72 percent was the difference between 100
PROFILE   percent and their effective tax rate (28 percent). Us-
                ing the same assumption, how can they calculate
their annual interest expense? They should multiply the percentage by
the amount of interest they actually paid. Last year, Bob and Joann
paid $8,512.63 to their lender for interest. If they multiply that
amount by .72

$$.72 \times \$8,512.63 = \$6,129.09$$

they find that their net interest cost on their payout of $8,512.63 was
only $6,129.09. The difference, $2,383.54, was the tax savings they
achieved by deducting interest as an itemized deduction.

You now possess much more knowledge than most consumers have
about how interest is calculated, how the tax benefits are figured in,
and what it really costs to buy your own home. With this preliminary
information, you are ready to begin controlling the financial and
management aspects of your home purchase.

What do lenders do when you apply for a loan? In the next chapter,
you will be given many tips for speeding up the review process, and
for helping your lender to make a decision favorable to you.

——————— POINTS TO REMEMBER ———————

▸ Your home does not cost the purchase price. The *real* cost is determined by how much you pay in interest during the years you make payments to your lender.

▸ Loan balances decline very slowly during a loan's early years, when most of your payment represents interest. If you sell your home before 5 years have elapsed, you will have very little equity.

▸ You should seek financing and preapproval from a lender before shopping for the house itself.

▸ You will do better for yourself by directly managing and taking responsibility for your mortgage, as part of your personal financial plan.

▸ Your mortgage should be reviewed and controlled as part of your financial plan, not as a separate issue.

▸ You should determine when you want your mortgage paid off, and then come up with the method for achieving that goal.

▸ Calculate what it will cost you to buy your home over a mortgage term. Then make plans to reduce your costs.

▸ Learn how loan amortization works. Knowing how it's done will help you gain control of your debt and will allow you to keep an eye on your lender.

▸ Learn how to compare pretax and after-tax mortgage costs. Know where you stand in terms of net cost.

▸ Learn how to figure out your effective tax rate, and how to apply that information to your mortgage.

2

Jumping Through the Hoops

*H*ere's how most people buy a home: First, they find a real estate agent and begin looking at properties. Next, they find a house they think they can afford, and they make an offer. If the offer is accepted, then they go to a bank and apply for a mortgage loan.

These steps are completely backward. They should be performed in the reverse order, so that you, the buyer, can remain in control of the process. The steps are listed in the sequence that is commonly followed. However, if you think about it, the sequence doesn't make sense.

Getting approved for financing takes time and paperwork. The faster you can get approved, the better. If your offer to buy a house rests on the contingency of financing approval, then the entire deal is in jeopardy. In fact, most deals that fall through do so because a lender turns down the loan application. The prospective buyer doesn't meet the lender's qualifications.

You shouldn't care that the process is time-consuming, because applying for financing should be your *first* step. Besides, the approval process has two parts. Preapproval, based only on your financial and credit status, takes relatively little time. The real delays in financing are related to the properties themselves. You can be prequalified by applying to the lender before you even locate a home, and prequalification takes very little time.

After your financial and credit status has been approved by the lender, your application can then be reviewed without the pressure of a deadline written into your offer for a specific property. Even though there are methods you can use to speed up the process, you have much greater leverage when you start looking at homes with preapproval already in your hands.

Next, you locate properties within your price range. That price range is not dictated by your perceptions of what is a good bargain, nor by neighborhood conditions. Your price range is what you can afford, and nothing more or less. After you are preapproved, you know exactly what you can afford, and that knowledge narrows your search considerably. You won't make the mistake of falling in love with a house that is priced far above your affordable range—and a real estate agent won't show you properties you can't afford. In fact, at this point, you probably don't even need an agent, because you can do a considerable amount of research on your own. Remember that you don't have to buy the most expensive house you can afford. With preapproval, you only know the upper limits. You can buy anything available at that price or below.

→ **ACTION ITEM** ←

Visit your lender before you start shopping for a house. As a first step, ask for a listing of the application steps needed. Begin to prequalify by gathering copies of the documents and other information the lender will want to see.

Look in the local newspaper and in publications that advertise homes for sale. Multiple listing services and independent companies, in many areas, publish books and booklets of information on homes for sale, and some even sponsor 30-minute television shows featuring listings. Identify the area where you want to buy. Look around in that area and note any "for sale" signs. Narrow down your search before you contact an agent.

Go to any "open house" in the area. Talk to the agents at each open house and tell them what you need. Write down phone numbers listed on for sale signs, and call those agents. This process will help you narrow down your choices and will probably lead you to an agent with whom you will want to work in locating your new home.

The last step is actually working with an agent. At this point, remember one key thing: Unless you retain an agent specifically to represent you, the agent you find will be compensated by a commission paid by the seller. The agent is obligated to protect your best interests, but in most situations, the agent is working for the seller.

→ **ACTION ITEM** ←

Search for an agent by making up a list of relevant questions. Interview several agents before you decide which one is right for you.

By approaching the home-buying process in the sequence of steps described above—the reverse of the usual method—you will save a lot of time and trouble with your lender. You will not be at risk of losing a good deal because the deadline passed, or because you do not qualify for the amount you need to borrow.

THE LOAN APPLICATION

The first thing a lender wants from you is a completed loan application. This is an information form listing your full name, social security number, address, number and names of dependents, income and employment, financial obligations, and other important information. The application will ask for a complete listing of your financial status: assets and liabilities.

Assets are things you own, such as your bank accounts, investments, automobile, real estate, and retirement plans. Liabilities are debts, like a mortgage, a loan for your car, or credit card balances. The loan application includes space to list all assets and all liabilities. The difference between these two totals is your net worth.

The application also asks for a summary of monthly payments against your liabilities. This shows the bank what kind of financial burden you are carrying, and how well you can afford to take on an additional commitment to repay a mortgage loan.

The lender will send away to a credit bureau for a current report on your credit standing. All of the information in your credit file will be given to the lender, assuming you signed a form granting permission for the lender to obtain the report. If you don't sign this form, the application process won't go forward.

The lender goes through a rather sophisticated review procedure; you might be required to give the lender a nonrefundable deposit to begin the review process. This deposit prevents you from putting in applications with every lender in town, causing a lot of paperwork for everyone, when only one lender will get your business.

The lender looks at your loan application and your credit report, and verifies information by calling your employer and asking for the date you were hired and the amount you are paid each month. If you are self-employed, the lender will want to see 2 or 3 years' tax returns. After your information has been verified and reviewed, the lender decides whether to take a risk by lending you money.

That decision is made on the basis of your financial strength as well as your credit history. For example, if you have a record of late payments or nonpayment of past debts, your record hurts your credit status significantly, and could result in a rejection of your application. If your credit background is clean, that's one possible problem out of the way.

WEALTH BUILDING PROFILE *Too Many Credit Cards.* Carol has 15 active credit cards with lines of credit between $2,000 and $8,000. Added together, the total lines of credit exceed $50,000. Carol has never missed a payment and she repays the entire balance used on each card every month. Her practice has been to use only one card for a period of a few weeks, and then to use a different card for a while. That keeps all of the accounts active. She believes the pattern has established a responsible credit history.

Your financial strength includes the assets you have, as well as your net worth. The higher your assets and the lower your liabilities, the better. Your monthly payment burden also affects your financial strength. If you are committed to paying out several hundred dollars each month on old credit card balances and store revolving accounts, you'll find lenders reluctant to let you take on additional debt, like a long-term mortgage loan.

Another item affecting financial strength is the accumulated debt or credit you have now. It helps to have a good record of timely payments, but it is equally important to not carry an excessive number of charge accounts or lines of credit. Even if your record is clean, lenders do not react well to borrowers who carry many credit cards. They represent too much danger of overusing credit and overextending a limited amount of financial strength.

Consistent repayment on time will establish that you are a good credit risk. But your lender will look at the past as only one indicator of risk. If you have $50,000 in borrowing power and you were to use that power, you might be in serious financial trouble. The lender would probably prefer to see you with a lot less credit and fewer credit cards.

A suggestion: To strengthen your situation, cancel all but one or two of your credit cards. Your credit report will show a pattern of good risk for a number of accounts that have since been closed. That counts as much as a good record on open accounts, but it reduces the lender's perception of risks.

→ **ACTION ITEM** ←

Before making any final decisions or canceling any credit card accounts, visit your loan officer. Explain the situation and ask for his or her advice.

Closing down unneeded accounts is a step you should take well before going to see the lender. Allow one full month for information about closure of your accounts to reach the credit bureau, so that the report the lender gets is current and complete.

Finally, the lender—usually a bank or savings and loan—reviews your income and job history. Your job history is important because it establishes your stability. If you change jobs frequently, you're less stable, at least in the eyes of the lender.

Income is reviewed because it relates to your ability to repay a new loan. Remember, the lender's job is to evaluate risk. How risky is it for the lender to advance money to you? Are you likely to be late with your payments? Can you afford the payments? Do you make enough money so that the mortgage won't be an unreasonable burden?

To answer these questions, lenders often apply a formula. The amount of a proposed monthly payment cannot be greater than a specified percentage of your monthly income.

WEALTH   *Qualification Rules.* One lender has a strict policy
BUILDING   that a borrower will qualify as long as the monthly
PROFILE   payment will not be greater than 28 percent of
monthly gross income. Pete and Wendy earn a monthly income of $2,750. Applying the lender's rule, their monthly payment cannot exceed 28 percent of that level, or $770 per month. At 10 percent, a 30-year contract could be approved for about $87,000.

On the surface, it may appear that a borrower's potential loan will be very small. However, there are many ways around the restriction of a lender's formula. The lender may offer an adjustable-rate mortgage with a much lower interest rate for the first year, for example. (In later chapters, you will see how a number of creative methods can be used to qualify applicants for a much larger loan than their income would dictate.) The important thing may be to reduce the monthly payment, at least for the first year, so that the borrower meets the payment-to-income ratio policy.

How do lenders begin to evaluate my prospects as a borrower?

The first step is completing the loan application. You should be careful to provide complete and accurate information on this form.

Should I tell the lender about my credit, even with those companies I've repaid a bit late at times?

Complete disclosure is always the best rule. The lender will order up a credit report on you anyway, so the information will eventually be revealed. You will score more points by listing everything than you will by holding something back.

Are any costs involved, when applying for a mortgage loan?

The lender will consider you a serious applicant only if you prepay the appraisal and credit report fee.

Is it a plus to have a lot of good credit?

Good credit is always beneficial. However, if you have an excessive number of revolving credit accounts or lines of credit, the lender could view it as too much exposure. It might make sense to limit your open credit lines and to close down the ones you don't need, before making a new application for a mortgage loan.

On what basis does the lender approve or reject my application?

The lender uses a combination of financial strength, income, and credit history. Each of these factors is taken into account by the lender.

Does it matter that I've changed jobs or residences a lot in recent years?

Yes. Lenders will consider you a lower risk if you can show some stability. They like to see borrowers in the same job and the same town for a couple of years. Instability doesn't mean you can't get a loan; it just makes it tougher.

Will my chances be hurt by a recent divorce?

Yes, but only to the extent that it represents a change in financial status. If you had two incomes, but now have only one; or if you are paying child support and separate maintenance; or if your assets are cut in half as part of a settlement, the lender will have to make adjustments in your risk category.

If the lender can take my house in the event that I default, why is my financial condition so important? Does the lender really assume any risk?

Yes. Lenders don't want defaulted loans. They would have to sell your house to get their money back. If the market is soft, they might not recover 100 percent of the amount loaned. Besides, it costs money to foreclose on property.

The lender would prefer lending money to those who can afford to make payments, and who have an equity stake in the property.

Is it true that financially stronger people have a much better chance of getting a loan?

Of course. The lender is in the business of loaning money. Their risk is nonpayment. They will make more profit if there are fewer defaults.

What if the lender turns me down?

You should apply to another lender. You might consider going to the Veterans Administration (if you're a veteran) or the Federal Housing Administration. Not only is it easier to get loans with these agencies than through conventional lenders, but you might also be able to buy a home with very little down payment.

MAKING THE LENDER'S JOB EASIER

You are more likely to get approval of credit if you make the lender's job easier. Getting loan approval before finding a house is the first step in this process. Most people who have borrowed mortgage money in the past know which items take the longest: appraisals, inspections, and title search. These steps all relate to specific properties. Imagine how much easier the financing phase is when these steps take place *after* your financing has been approved.

When a lender approves financing before you locate a house, there are some conditions attached. For example, the lender may grant approval on the condition that the house you select passes certain inspections and reviews. Once you locate the right house, the lender will require a title search and a title insurance policy. You will need to arrange for homeowner's insurance. Before funds will be released, the lender will want an appraisal. The appraiser may recommend that the lender ask for and review structural and pest control inspection reports. Conditions discovered in the inspections may require some repair work, or, in the appraiser's opinion, the house might be worth a lot less than the purchase price, in which case the lender probably won't approve the full loan amount. All of these require-ments must be met and satisfied before the lender will release the funds needed to buy your house.

Any preapproval will be based partly on your credit and income and partly on the condition of the house you eventually find. There are actually two forms of risk the lender wants to explore. The first risk is relatively easy: Are you capable of repaying the debt you ask for, based on your income, net worth, and credit history? The second risk depends on the house: What is its price, condition, and location? Is it worth the price the seller wants?

Requesting preapproval makes the lender's job easier: the two re-views can be separated and executed at different times. Once you have passed the personal financial and credit review, the review of the prop-erty is easier, although there are more steps and the process takes longer. With the combination of appraisal, title search, and inspec-tions, it could take many weeks to complete the financing approval for a specific house.

You cam make the first phase—your financial review—much faster and easier by preparing in advance. Before you visit your lender, make sure you know you're getting the best terms possible. Compare the terms offered by several institutions in your area. Don't limit your review to only the interest rate. Make sure you're comparing the same types of loans. If you're not sure how to do that, contact a mortgage broker and ask help in finding the best possible deal. Guidelines for researching different loans and making valid comparisons are offered in the next chapter.

When you are ready to apply with the lender you have selected, first call and make an appointment with the loan officer. Prepare all of the following, in advance, to bring to your appointment:

▶ Copies of tax returns for the past 3 years, whether required by the lender or not. (If you are self-employed, copies of tax returns are mandatory.)

▶ A listing of all current credit cards you have in active status, includ-ing the account number, issuer and issuer's address, credit limit, and current balance.

▶ A personal financial statement (preferably typed), listing all of your assets and liabilities.

▶ A summary of all your bank accounts, including each institution's name and address, your account numbers, the types of account, and current balances.

▶ A summary of all investments and retirement plans, including the name of the institution or company where funds are on deposit, your account numbers, and current balances.

▶ A business financial statement, if you are self-employed, including both the balance sheet and income statement as of the latest month and for the latest full year.

▶ A notice from your employer's personnel department, if you are an employee, stating the date you were hired, your job title, and your current salary.

Having all of these documents will speed up the preapproval process. The lender will request them if you do not supply them, so you will cut a few days out of the process by anticipating the request in advance. Your having the documents ready will make a favorable impression on the lender.

A key point: If there are any negatives about your credit or personal history, disclose them at the very beginning, before the lender discovers them through a credit report. You don't need to emphasize or dwell on the negatives, but don't try to hide them either.

⟶ ACTION ITEM ⟵

Write a letter to explain all the negative points on your credit report. In addition to giving the lender a copy, send a copy to *all* of the credit bureaus as well, and ask that the letter be added to your file.

If you have filed bankruptcy or have had a judgment against you in the past few years, explain the circumstances to the lender and demonstrate how you have rectified the problem. For example, if you are currently paying off an old debt or have restructured your finances, explain your remedies in a letter to the lender. Include this letter with your application package.

If you have had repayment problems, you already know that your chances of approval are not as good as they would be for someone who has a perfect credit record. Still, full disclosure is the best policy. When your credit history is less than perfect, it helps even more to go to the lender with all of the necessary information and to anticipate the questions the lender will ask.

LOAN AND RATE COMMITMENTS

At the beginning of the loan review process, the lender may offer a rate commitment to you. This is a written promise to grant you a loan at a specific rate, *not* a promise to grant the loan. The promise is that, in the event your application is approved, a specified rate will be in effect; you are guaranteed that rate. The simple guarantee is often given without charge, and it protects you if rates rise.

If the institution's rates rise between your application date and the date when funds are released, you will still be given the loan at the guaranteed rate. However, if rates fall, the lender may not be willing to give you the lower rate.

Lenders offer a number of variations on the rate guarantee. Some are available for a fee based on the amount of the loan. For example, you may be guaranteed the lowest available rate at the time escrow closes, and that rate may be no higher than the current rate. This guarantee may also come with an extended deadline.

The lender, upon completing a review of your finances, will give you a document called a loan commitment, which is much different from the rate guarantee. The loan commitment lists the maximum loan amount the lender has preapproved for you, the interest rate, the repayment term, the type of mortgage, and the commitment deadline. Beyond the deadline, none of the terms or conditions will continue to apply. You need to ensure that escrow on your house will close by the lender's deadline, or that you will be able to get an extension if needed.

Some delays may be beyond your control—in fact, the lender might be the cause of a delay. For example, if escrow can't close because the lender has delayed reviewing a required inspection report, that is not your fault. If the deadline is approaching and so is the expiration date for your loan commitment, ask for a fast decision or an extension, especially if you had to pay for a rate commitment and you don't want to lose it.

THE REPAYMENT TERM

As part of the financial review process, you will be given a number of choices. Some loans are available with fixed rates, others are adjustable. Some lenders offer conversion privileges within a limited number of years. For example, you may begin with a fixed rate that reverts to adjustable after 3 years; however, you can convert to a long-term fixed-rate mortgage within the 3-year term. There are endless varieties of this theme.

In making comparisons between loans, conversion privileges and similar points should be considered. They may not have a tangible value but could be worth a lot in the future. Their intangible value makes comparison difficult, but each loan's privileges should still be in your mind when you are matching up one lender's range of loan terms alongside those of another.

One point to think about carefully: Do you want to repay your loan over a very long term, or over a very short term? The 30-year mortgage means paying for your house at a much higher level, because of interest expenses and the rate of amortization, but it also means lower monthly payments. A 15-year mortgage means your house will cost less, but your monthly payments will be much higher.

Remember, if your lender applies a ratio between your income and your monthly payments, you might not qualify for a shorter-term loan. You might have to go for the longer term, even if you would prefer a shorter one. The payments on the 15-year mortgage will be higher than any longer-term loan at the same rate of interest; the lender might not be able to approve your application except with the 30-year loan. This dilemma has one possible solution: you can still repay the contracted 30-year loan, but at an accelerated level that will retire the debt sooner. By agreeing to a 30-year repayment term but having the flexibility to repay the loan sooner, you take control of your financial future.

→ ACTION ITEM ←

Agree to repay your loan on as long a term as possible, then repay on an accelerated basis.

That strategy could be the best way to go. Your contract calls for 30-year payments, but you actually pay at a much higher rate, saving a lot in interest. However, if you lose your job or experience some other temporary financial emergency, you can revert to the lower payment schedule until you're back on your feet. If, on the other hand, you start out by agreeing to higher monthly payments, you cannot adjust the payment level to suit your own convenience.

Your repayment term should be based on the goals you select as part of your personal financial plan. For example, if you want to retire in 20 years, and that goal calls for living on a lower income, then it doesn't make sense to commit yourself to a 30-year loan. However, you can contract a 30-year loan and then accelerate payments so that completed repayment coincides with your retirement date.

Think of the repayment term as two separate plans. First is the contractual plan, the document you sign with the bank. That involves commitment to a minimum monthly payment that will retire the loan in 30 years. Second, and more important, is your personal plan. This part is within your direct control. *You* decide when that loan will be repaid, not the lender.

How can you identify the amount needed to repay a loan within a specified number of years? Refer to Appendix A, "Mortgage Amortization Tables." These are repayment tables. Find the interest rate for your loan and the number of years involved. Then study the various rows for different numbers of repayment years for the same amount of borrowed money.

WEALTH BUILDING PROFILE

Using the Tables. Mark has a $100,000 loan and the interest rate is 10 percent, payable over 30 years. Find the 10 percent table and refer to the column where $100,000 is listed; then find the row for a 30-year repayment term. Mark's monthly payment is $877.58. However, by moving to the left, a declining number of years can be found. Monthly payments are shown in 5-year segments. The first column to the left indicates $908.71, the amount Mark would need to pay each month, to retire the mortgage in 25 years. As the number of years declines, the required monthly payment rises.

It is fairly easy to identify the amount needed to retire a loan within any number of years. You need to coordinate the desirability of more rapid payoff (and lower interest expenses) with the size of payment you can afford. By paying off your mortgage more quickly, you exercise control over the cost of your home; you obviously need to do so in a way your budget will allow. The concept is one thing; the practice is another.

In some cases, you may need to compromise. For example, it might be most desirable to pay off your mortgage in 15 years, but your budget won't allow for payments that steep. Instead, you have to settle for a 20-year schedule. Keep a few points about this compromise in mind when you do your planning.

▶ Any planning beyond the immediate future is difficult at best. Chances are, your plans will change drastically before your retirement deadline. Plan today according to what you want to achieve, within the limitations of what you can afford.

▶ You can always change your schedule later. The limitations under which you have to operate today may be temporary. As your income level increases, you can and should revise your plan.

▶ You might not be in the same house by the time you retire. Even if you believe you will never move again, a number of circumstances could change your planning—divorce, a death in the family, a change in jobs, an inheritance, or transitions going on in your neighborhood.

▶ Upon retirement, you might decide to move, in spite of today's planning. Many families assume they will retire in their present house. Then their children grow up and leave, and they suddenly discover they don't need a four-bedroom house any more. They sell and move to a smaller place.

Today's plans will probably change. You need to plan and schedule the future, and to exercise some necessary controls. But if you are unable to meet the current repayment plan goal, don't despair. Plan as far as you can, and be prepared to modify your plan later on.

THE QUESTION OF RISK

We have previously mentioned the idea of risk from the lender's perspective. Many would-be borrowers fail to recognize that risk exists on both sides of the borrowing deal. It's true that you, as a borrower and home buyer, face a number of risks. You might not have enough insurance; your income could stop suddenly, because of layoff or disability; the bank could foreclose for nonpayment, ruining your credit and putting your family on the street; the neighborhood might deteriorate and property values could quickly follow. Most of these possibilities are remote, but they can happen.

You also need to be aware of the bank's point of view concerning risk. It's naive to say that, because a loan is secured by real estate, the lending bank has no risks. On the contrary, lenders' risks could be substantial.

When a bank grants a loan with a fixed rate for 30 years, it makes a very long-term commitment. If interest rates rise far above the fixed rate level, the bank stands to lose money on its portfolio. This has occurred before and it could occur again. In addition, what if the bank were forced to foreclose on a number of houses? Chances are, those homes could not be quickly resold, either because of their condition or location, or because of a slow market. The bank might find itself unavoidably stuck in the real estate business, but without the cash flow it needs to stay in business.

Another risk is that the local economy might go sour. Real estate prices could fall at the same time that one or two major employers lay off thousands of workers. A lot of people who are suddenly out of work might just walk away from their limited equity and relatively high debt.

Risk exists on both sides. If you approach a lender with an awareness of the lender's risks as well as your own, you will have a better chance of addressing risk and reducing it. The lender-to-borrower equation is not as one-sided as it might appear. You need to convince the lender that you are dependable, solvent, responsible, and willing to put up the equity that will prevent you from walking away from the obligation.

That invariably means committing yourself to the down payment the bank requires. Most lenders would like to see borrowers approach the deal with 20 percent down. Some will allow you to enter into the agreement with only 10 percent down; and you can get a house for less, (nothing down, in some cases), if your loan is guaranteed or insured by the FHA or the VA. These agencies might ask you to put down minimum closing costs, equal to 3 to 5 percent of the purchase price; or, those costs may be financed along with the purchase price.

A government-guaranteed or insured loan does, in fact, relieve the lender from most forms of risk. In the event of default, the bank is off the hook. However, if you apply for a conventional loan from a bank or a savings and loan association, you should be aware of the risk factors the bank has to think about. If there is a limited supply of money to lend, the lender will naturally prefer to go with the least risky borrowers.

In the next chapter, the complex question of comparisons between loans and loan terms is discussed. Remember, whenever terms vary from one loan or one institution to another, comparisons are much more difficult. Beyond the question of qualifying for the loan itself, you need to identify the most affordable loan, based on your plans, the length of time you expect to remain in the house, the risk of higher or lower interest rates in the future, and the availability of flexible loan terms.

—————————— **POINTS TO REMEMBER** ——————————

▶ Shop for financing before you look for the right house.

▶ Shop for the right house before looking for an agent, unless you know an agent who understands and respects the limits of what you want and can afford.

▶ Look at the loan application process from the lender's point of view. Give the lender everything needed to complete the review.

▶ Explain *in writing* any negatives on your credit report. Submit your explanation to the lender and to the credit reporting agencies.

▶ Ask the lender for a rate commitment.

▶ If you have the choice, select the repayment term most suited to your personal financial plan.

▶ Know the lender's risks, and address those risks in the way you present information about yourself.

3

The Hidden Cost

*W*hen you buy a new car or a computer, or when you plan a vacation, you do not speak to only one person. You check out the entire market and look for the best deal. Even when you buy a house, you don't take the first one you see; you look at everything available in the right neighborhood and within your price range.

All this careful shopping is directed toward the item being purchased. Little time or attention is given to a review of financing. All loan terms are *not* the same. Some institutions charge higher rates or higher up-front costs than others. Without shopping around first, you might pay far too high a price to finance your house, and not even know it. You can't know until you do some comparison shopping for yourself.

THE DIFFICULTY OF COMPARISONS

Making a valid comparison between lenders and loan terms is very difficult. The interest rate is not all you need to consider; there is much more to review. However, interest rates are the most obvious test to apply.

The rate itself might be as distracting as the problem you face when you look at different housing prices. Similar houses in different areas may have extremely different prices. Two houses on the same block might be priced thousands of dollars apart. Just as homeowners price their homes at a given level for a number of different reasons, lenders price their loans according to a number of criteria; competition is only one factor. They might not really want a lot of business; their rates and terms will then be expensive. They may be aggressively looking for new loans; they will then be more competitive, and willing to offer more for your business.

———————————→ **ACTION ITEM** ←———————————

Ask lenders to make comparisons on a like basis—assuming the same number of points and other up-front fees. When that isn't possible, ask them to calculate the adjustment that the differences represent.

The lender might be willing to charge a lower initial interest rate than its competitors, but the rate might be adjustable and its competitors' rates might be fixed. Within a year or two, the "cheaper" loan could end up costing a lot more. As another possibility, a lower-rate fixed mortgage might be available now with one lender, but that lender may be charging more points than anyone else.

A "point"—also called a discount point or loan fee—is equal to 1 percent of the loan. For example, on a $100,000 loan, each point is $1,000. This amount is charged to the borrower and must be paid at the time the loan is funded. Some lenders add the points to the amount borrowed. If your $100,000 loan is granted with two points, you must either pay up an extra $2,000 to get the loan or owe the lender $102,000.

Why charge points? Like anyone selling an in-demand commodity, the lender wants a return on its money. The point is one way of adjusting the interest rate, based on the demand level. The more demand, the higher the number of points the lender will charge.

Many people think of points as a fee charged for getting the loan. In fact, some lenders call points origination fees or other, similar names. In truth, the points you pay affect your overall interest rate and the cost of your house. However, because the points are paid at the time the loan is granted, it is difficult to think of them as part of the longer-term overall cost.

Here's why comparisons are difficult. You might be reviewing loans offered by two local banks. One offers loans at ¼ percent lower than the other; the difference in monthly payments is about $9 on a loan of $100,000. But because that bank charges one point more, getting the loan will cost $1,000 more in up-front charges.

Which loan is better? The advantage of lower payments will take about 9 years to make up. That result is computed by dividing the $1,000 loan point cost by the monthly savings. The result is about 111 months, or more than 9 years. One way to evaluate the difference, then, is to decide whether that small savings in monthly payments is worth paying $1,000 to get.

Most first-time buyers stay in their house for less than 5 years. With that in mind, the average buyer will do better by paying a slightly higher interest rate. That makes more sense than paying a higher number of points. However, what if you think you will remain in your house for the next 30 years? Considering that your plans could change, it still might be better for you to pay the extra point and go for the lower rate on a long-term loan. Your decision depends on the circumstances in your case.

Admittedly, the comparison based on monthly payments versus the cost of a point is overly simplistic. It doesn't take into account the factors of compound interest and the time value of money. Lenders will disclose to you the annual percentage rate (APR) they charge, including the cost of points. That might be the more valid comparison, in a strict sense, but don't overlook the time factor. The length of time you stay in your house ultimately determines whether it's worth paying points to get a lower rate. You need to make comparisons on a long-term basis, not just on the basis of what your initial costs would be or what the interest rate works out to during the next few years.

UNCOMPLICATING THE COMPARISON

The comparison between different lenders' terms can get more complicated, even beyond the rate and points question. Other fees may be involved as well.

Some lenders advertise attractive rates and low points, but charge relatively high loan review or processing fees. Because of these fees, the overall costs of a loan with one particular lender might be higher than the competitors' rates.

Make a valid comparison by following these guidelines:

▶ Consider all fees and charges. Don't isolate your review to only the interest rate, or only a combination of the rate and the number of points. Ask the lender for a disclosure of all loan charges. A little market-comparison shopping might save you a lot of money in the long run. Be aware that options built into contracts have definite value, even though they can't be easily compared. For example, if you have the right, with one loan, to convert from an adjustable rate to a fixed rate, you would be gaining a valuable privilege that might be worth a half percentage higher interest or an extra point up-front.

▶ Evaluate fees based on the length of time you believe you will own the house. If you think you will trade up in 5 years or less, go for the loan with the lowest up-front fees and charges, even if that means paying a higher interest rate. You won't recover the additional costs by the time you sell, by trying to minimize your interest rate. You should be aware that it takes many years to offset origination charges, and that, if you sell before the recapture period, you will be paying more than you need to pay.

▶ Compare monthly payments and rates. A lot of emphasis is placed on the differences between lenders, in terms of the percentage rate charged for loans. Thus, in ads for two or more institutions, you might read that one charges 9.625 percent and the other charges 9.50 percent. The lender charging the higher rate might offer some additional benefits you like, but you still want the lower rate. Be aware not only of the rate, but of what other changes mean in terms of monthly payments. On a $100,000 loan, $1/8$ of 1 percent translates to about $10 per month. That's a small price for some benefits (like a conversion privilege, for example). If up-front fees are involved, compute the monthly payment difference and divide the up-front costs by that difference. How long will it take to reach a breakeven point? Making this comparison will help you to clarify what the differences really mean.

▶ Always make comparisons with two or more lenders. Never compare different programs offered by one lender, without also going to other lenders. Comparison shopping for financing means you need to look at terms and conditions offered by several different suppliers. Some lenders offer a wide variety of programs and might distract you from this important point. When you buy a new car, you probably want to compare features between two or three manufacturers. The same is true of lenders. Loans might come in a number of different models. But what is the lender across the street doing to invite business in? Does that lender offer a better deal?

Once you narrow down your initial search, you might decide to work with a particular lender, especially if that lender offers a number of different plans. One lender that has a number of plans and also offers competitive rates is a valuable contact for you.

 **ACTION ITEM**

If you just can't pin down the comparison on an "apples to apples" basis, gather up your information and make an appointment with your financial planner.

▶ Negotiate. It comes as a surprise to many people to discover one fact about borrowing money: Everything can be negotiated. Nothing is set in concrete, even though a loan officer might express some terms as though they are. For example, the loan officer might tell you that the terms today are 10.0 percent, with two points. Period. But you might be able to negotiate a lower rate, fewer points, or both. You won't know until you try.

One good way to negotiate is by comparing the offered terms to a competitor's terms. Go to the lender and ask for a match to the terms offered by another bank. In this way, you might be able to cut a final deal that is far better than either bank's initial offer. For example, you might get a lender to match rates and points, but to leave in a conversion privilege, or to include a no-charge line of credit of $5,000 with the loan. Become a shrewd shopper *and* negotiator by knowing the market thoroughly.

What should I know before comparing one lender's terms to another?

Your comparison should be on a like basis. That means you have to adjust for dissimilar up-front charges, fees, and other terms, besides interest rate.

What if terms between lenders are just too far apart? How can I make a comparison easily?

Take the information on the terms offered by one lender, and ask another lender to give you a point-by-point comparison between its own program and the competition's. This shifts the burden to the lender and shows that you are shopping around.

Shouldn't I shop for a loan with the least number of points?

Points are an up-front adjustment to interest. You might be better off getting a break on the interest rate for an additional point. Compare the monthly payment before going for lower initial costs. Determine how long it will take to make up the difference.

Would it be best in every case to get a long-term loan for my residence?

No. Your choice of term depends on how long you plan to live in that residence. Most first-time buyers sell and move on within the first 5 years.

Should I limit my comparison shopping to the loan programs offered by one lender?

No. Shop around and compare between lenders to find the most competitive overall program.

When would it be wise to pay a higher interest rate?

In several circumstances. For example, you might be willing to pay an extra $1/4$ of 1 percent for a conversion privilege from variable to a fixed rate. Depending on where interest rates move in the future, that could be a valuable feature.

Do I have any bargaining power with the lender?

Certainly. You may get a more favorable deal with a higher down payment, a shorter loan term, or other adjustments. You might also get a break just by asking for it.

LENDER PROMOTIONS

Be aware that there is a specific and unavoidable cost to borrowing money. In the case of a long-term loan—even one with an attractive low, fixed rate—interest is very expensive. The amount you have to repay can be two to three times the amount you borrow.

Even beyond this reality, lenders will entice your business with advertising programs designed to convince you that a particular loan is an exceptional deal. It might be, but the promotional claims might also be misleading.

As an example, one lender might advertise that it charges no points and no appraisal fees. However, what the ads don't tell you is that the interest rate is a half-point higher than the lender's other loan programs, and that administrative fees more than offset the cost of an appraisal.

Some lenders make a tidy profit from charges assessed to borrowers. Some closing costs and other fees are not charged at the amount the lender pays out. The costs are marked up and passed along as higher fees to the borrower. For example, some lenders use their own inside appraiser, but they charge borrowers the same amount that other lenders charge for hiring an outside appraiser. This fee may be as high as $300, even though the institution's appraiser may complete the appraisal in a half-hour or less. Another example is the charge for processing and reviewing the loan application. The fee might be substantially higher than the salary paid to employees who actually conduct the review. A credit report costing $40 or $50 might be charged to the borrower at $150 or more.

When you respond to a lender's promotions, also check with the lender's competitors. Get a thorough run-down of the fees. Find out what the real costs are, and negotiate a lower charge when appropriate. Ask these questions whenever you are shopping for a mortgage lender:

▸ "What types of loans do you offer?" The lender you meet with probably offers a number of different loans. The fact that one type of loan is currently being promoted doesn't mean you have to commit to that one. A different loan may be more suitable for you. This question also helps you to evaluate the lender's programs in comparison to those offered by other institutions.

Pay close attention to special provisions and features offered with various loan programs. Besides the obvious (fixed versus adjustable rates, for example), look for loans with conveniences like conversion.

▶ "What is the estimated total of closing costs and other fees you charge?" You can compare specific charges all day and become very distracted, especially if the lender's promotion is skillfully designed. What you really need, in order to pick the best mortgage, is a complete comparison. That means knowing the estimated full range of charges, not just appraisal fee or points. Ask questions and expect reasonable and prompt answers from the lender. If the answer is "That depends," ask to see a typical loan broken down by fees (with the borrower remaining anonymous, of course). Ask for explanations for any charges and fees you don't understand. From this review, you will get a more complete idea of what it will cost to borrow from a particular lender.

▶ "Who performs the appraisal?" Some lenders hire professional and independent appraisers who charge between $200 and $300 for their work. Other lenders charge the same fee but do only a quick visual appraisal for their own purposes. One test in comparing lenders is to ask whether the appraisal is done internally or externally. Also ask how much detail is put into the written appraisal report.

Internal appraisals tend to be very brief (and, for the lender, very inexpensive as well). A professional appraisal report includes photographs, very detailed listings and calculations, and a map of the area, showing comparable houses and their most recent sales prices. The point here is, if you're going to be charged for a full appraisal, you should get one! If the bank is going to do a budget job, then the appraisal fee to you should definitely be lowered.

▶ "Will you negotiate on the rate, points, closing costs, or fees?" If you believe the lender is charging too much for some of its fees, you should ask for an adjustment, either in the interest rate or in the fees themselves. If the lender wants your business, you might be surprised to discover that, in fact, adjustments *will* be made. If you think you'll stay in your house for many years without refinancing again, go for a lower rate. However, if you believe you will move within the next few years, give in on the rate but ask for reduced fees and charges.

▶ "How long does it take for approval?" In some cases, it's worth higher fees, or slightly higher interest, to get an approval sooner than would be possible with the competition. Some lenders offer very attractive rates and terms, but take far too long to complete approval. Other lenders may charge more, but they seem to be able to get a loan application through their system in less than 3 weeks. If you can find a lender who charges less than everyone else, offers lower-than-average interest rates on loans, *and* gets the application process completed quickly, that's the lender worth using.

BORROWING THE RIGHT AMOUNT

When you visit a lender to borrow money, it is important to establish at the beginning exactly how much you will need to borrow. If you are going to take charge of your financial future, the best place to start is when you first start the process of borrowing.

To many people, the "right" amount is obvious: it's the purchase price minus the down payment. Sometimes, however, you will have choices to make. Let's assume, for the sake of illustrating this point, that there is no problem in qualifying for a loan. Your family income is high enough for you to have flexibility in choosing from among a number of loan programs.

---------------------→ **ACTION ITEM** ←---------------------

Before deciding how much to borrow, know in advance how much you can qualify for. Make up the difference either in the down payment or in the price of the house you buy.

In these circumstances, you have to decide which option is best for you. If you were to offer a 20 percent down payment, you would lower your monthly payments and reduce your interest costs over the long term. If you were to allow the bank to lend you 90 percent, you would need to come up with only 10 percent. You could keep half of your cash for other purposes.

Either plan is viable, depending on your financial status and requirements. If you have a good sum of cash in liquid positions already, you don't need to hold cash back, and it might make more sense to commit to a larger down payment. However, if you don't have an emergency reserve fund in the form of cash and other liquid assets, this is an opportunity to establish one. Once you make your down payment, the only way to get your money back will be to refinance your mortgage and borrow against it.

WEALTH BUILDING PROFILE   *Down Payment Changes.* Paul and Susan were planning to offer a down payment of 20 percent of the purchase price. They assumed that the lender would require that much. However, because they will be owner-occupants, and because their income is high enough, the lender is willing to loan out up to 90 percent of the purchase price.

There could be yet another choice. Again, let's assume that you can qualify with no trouble. The lender offers a number of different plans, and will finance up to 90 percent of the purchase price.

WEALTH BUILDING PROFILE   *Accelerated Term.* Steve and Lynn have been offered a loan for as little as 10 percent down, because they plan to occupy their home. They are tempted, though, to put down 20 percent, to reduce their interest costs over the next 30 years. As an alternative, they finally decided to put down only 10 percent, but they elect to take out a 15-year mortgage instead of going for the 30-year term.

As a result of choosing this option, you will be able to reduce your interest substantially, build equity, and eliminate your debt much sooner.

You can also reduce the amount you need to borrow by offering a reduced price on the house. Because a price is asked doesn't mean that it's not negotiable. You could make an offer substantially lower than the asked price. If your offer is accepted, recognizing the opportunity to reduce your initial price is a good way to lower your housing costs at the onset. Failure to do so adds to your hidden costs. Make a lower offer in these situations:

▸ It's a buyer's market. A buyer's market is characterized by an excessive number of houses for sale at the same time. There are more houses for sale than there are buyers looking for housing. In this situation, you, as a buyer, have a tremendous advantage over the seller. In all probability, your offer will be the only one on the table. The seller will have three choices: take your terms, make a counteroffer, or reject your offer and hope someone else will come along soon.

▸ The owner is selling directly. Rather than using a real estate agent, some people try to save a few thousand dollars by selling their own homes. This does cut 6 or 7 percent from the closing costs, but, as many sellers have discovered, it means a lot more work. Another point is often overlooked: without a real estate agent acting as liaison, the seller gives up a lot of advantage. The agent insulates a seller from a buyer, and often prevents a big price reduction through intelligent negotiation. The owner who sells directly might save the cost of commissions, but could easily have the savings canceled by a reduced price.

What does this mean to you as a buyer? You might automatically assume that you can offer 6 to 7 percent below the advertised price. The seller might argue that the price is already reduced, to reflect the net value. That's a negotiating point. Remember that, when seller and buyer deal directly, neither has available the information that an agent can supply—comparable prices, a sense of the market, and knowledge of what the other side really wants.

▸ You are making your offer with no contingencies. Many real estate deals are complicated by contingencies and could fall through if those contingencies are not met. For example, a buyer might make a deal on the contingency of selling a currently owned home. Another contingency might be acceptance of a structural or pest report. The financing contingency is written into virtually every contract automatically.

Imagine how valuable it is, from the seller's point of view, to have a buyer make an offer with no contingencies (or with very few). For example, you (the buyer) might still require the standard pest control report. But if you don't have to wait until your present house is sold, you are a much more attractive buyer. You might get away with a substantially lower offer when few contingencies are attached to your offer. For example, coming to the table with a preapproved loan puts you in a very powerful position as a buyer.

▶ The house needs a lot of work. If the house will need a lot of work, you should consider that point when making your offer. It is true that a house could be purchased because it has potential; it might not make sense, though, to pay for potential value. Creating that value will take dollars and time. You might do one of two things: require that the seller pay for needed work, or reduce the offer price for the estimated dollar amount of the repairs. In either case, the repairs represent a real cost, and should not be over-looked.

▶ The house has been on the market longer than three months. A house might remain on the market for many months, regardless of whether it's a seller's or a buyer's market. If the average house is selling in less than 3 months, you should ask why a particular property is still for sale. Chances are very good that the price is too high. People sense value and will not make a full-price offer when the seller is asking too much. The house could remain on the market because the owner is stubborn about the offered price, even when the real estate agent is pointing out the pricing problem.

▶ The house is located on a busy street. This is an especially notable problem. Houses on very busy streets do not sell as quickly as those one block away from main thoroughfares. You should also be aware that these houses do not appreciate in value as quickly as houses on quieter streets. This is a good reason for you to reduce your offered price.

▶ The house has other notable flaws. In addition to the problem of location, the house could have other drawbacks—no garage, only one bathroom, or nonconforming style. "Conforming" means the house's appearance is about the same as that of other houses in the area. If the architecture, shape, size, number of rooms, types of additions, or other features of a house are nonconforming, they retard its future value. You can reduce the offered price when a house does not conform to the other houses in the immediate area.

▶ The owner is anxious. For a number of reasons, the seller might be very anxious to get the house sold. Usually, the seller is moving to a new job, has already bought another house (or has a contingency offer on the table), or needs the cash for some other reason, such as divorce or financial problems.

Real estate agents use a number of terms, such as "motivated," to describe an anxious owner. When you see an ad indicating that the owner is anxious for a sale, that could be a signal that an offer below the asked price might be accepted.

Is the "right amount" to borrow always easy to identify?

No. First, you must establish how much you need to borrow. The amount is affected by your qualification, your monthly income, your financial strength, the price range of homes, and the amount you're willing and able to put down on your purchase.

Isn't it an advantage to put as little down as possible?

That's the common belief. But remember, the more you finance, the higher your payments—not only from month to month, but over the long term. If you pay more interest, your house ultimately costs you much more.

Is it smart to reduce the down payment and invest the difference somewhere else?

It might be, and it might not. You have to evaluate potential income and risk, versus the cost of borrowing money to buy your home. Be aware that you might have little choice. You need to qualify for the loan based on the lender's rules.

Does it make sense to offer less than the asked price on a home?

Yes, unless that home is already being offered at a bargain price. If you're in a buyer's market, you can probably expect a 10 to 15 percent reduction. It all depends on the seller's degree of desperation and on how much of a buyer's market there is at the time.

What if the seller is not using an agent?

You might be able to offer a price that's lower, based on the elimination of real estate commission. The seller may argue that the price has already been reduced with that in mind.

Do I gain any leverage by simplifying the offer?

Absolutely. Many offers come with a package of contingencies: the sale of a present home, pest and structural inspections, homeowner warranties, and any number of other conditions. If you can make a clean offer with few contingencies, it will be much more attractive, even if the price is lower.

What should I do if I'm making an offer on a fixer-upper house?

You might be able to reduce your offer by a considerable amount, especially if you can itemize the estimated cost of essential repairs.

Can I reduce the price based on how long the house has been on the market?

Every situation is different. As a general rule, you should assume that if the house has been available longer than 3 months, it's probably priced too high.

Does the neighborhood affect value?

Yes. For example, if the house is located on a busy street, you might be able to reduce the offer because of the noise levels. Such houses don't appreciate in value as well as houses on quieter streets do.

Should I consider how anxious the owner is to sell?

Yes. If the owner is in a hurry to close the deal, he or she will consider any reasonable offer—even one with a lower price.

DECIDING ON A LOAN

If the real costs of buying a house were easy to understand, it would be fairly simple to borrow money, find a house, and complete the transaction. However, many of the costs, including the largest ones, are hidden. Finding the right lender, negotiating the right terms, and selecting the right house are all difficult.

Any shopper is more comfortable when costs are apparent. In the grocery store, items sit side-by-side on the shelves. The prices are clearly marked and comparisons are easy. The choice comes down to price versus brand preference. With a housing purchase, the issues are much more complicated. Buyers have to determine not only what they can afford, but what is a good value.

As mentioned before, because of the emphasis put on finding the right house, the real costs are often ignored completely. Finding the right house should be the least of your problems. You will save much more in the long run if you first select the best financing.

It would also be easy if the "best" loan could be described in the same way for everyone. Instead, what's best for you might not be best for someone else, and what's best for you today might not be good for you at all in a few years. The problem with selecting a loan is that it depends on your current income, financial status, ability to qualify, and individual financial goals. Those things change with time.

Begin by writing our your goals, to help you understand what you hope to achieve with the type of loan you agree to. If you want the lowest possible payments, go for a lower interest rate and a longer term. If you want to reduce interest costs, make a higher down payment, go for a shorter repayment term, and shop for rates carefully. Then plan how you can accelerate your payments to reduce the interest expense even more.

Once you have defined your goals, compare them to your financial limitations. Will you have a problem getting financing approval because of your income level? Have past credit problems prevented you from approval? What steps have you taken to remedy these problems? Know what you want, but know the inhibiting factors as well.

You should shop for a mortgage loan by making valid comparisons. This is difficult when comparing programs among different lenders, so here's a possible solution: select one lender and compare the programs that lender offers. An earlier section advised comparing between institutions; that advice still holds, at least when you first begin looking for a mortgage. After you get through that initial phase, your comparison can be reduced to the programs within one institution. You can narrow down your search by using these two general guidelines:

▶ Work with a lender that offers a wide selection of loan programs. One lender might offer a variety of programs, in the hope of attracting a wider base of business. For you, this means that, based on your current financial status, you are more likely to find the loan suited to you within that institution. The lender is being responsive to market demand by recognizing that not everyone wants the same kind of loan.

▶ Select the lender on the basis of competitive interest rates, points, and other fees. You still need to first evaluate the market as a whole. Work with a lender that goes beyond a flexible program of loan choices and offers interest rates at market rates, and a reasonable level of points, based on what others are charging. Avoid a lender that tries to make additional profits by loading up the loan application and review fees.

The next chapter gives guidelines for determining when it's worthwhile to refinance your loan. Every homeowner is eventually faced with this question. Making a smart financial decision can save you thousands of dollars, reduce your risks, and help preserve or increase your equity.

────────── **POINTS TO REMEMBER** ──────────

▶ Be very careful when comparing different loans. The comparison is not always simple.
▶ Ask lenders to make like comparisons for you. If they can't or won't, ask for help from a financial planner.
▶ Compare rates based on how long you think you will stay in the house. Most first-time buyers sell and trade up within the first 5 years.
▶ Be prepared to negotiate with the lender. You might be able to get a better deal than was initially offered.
▶ Know the questions to ask of the lender, and make sure you get satisfactory answers.

▸ Be willing to adjust your down payment to qualify for a loan or to get a favorable rate.

▸ Coordinate your personal financial goals with the type of loan, length of the contract, and other terms of the loan.

▸ Work with a lender that offers more than only one or two programs.

4

Cashing In

When you buy your home, you will probably assume that the payments you agree to make under your contract will continue for the next 30 years. However, within a few years, your attitude may change. Interest rates may be lower, and market values may be much higher. You may suddenly discover that you can refinance your home and take out quite a bit of cash.

The most commonly asked question about refinancing is: How much can I get? You should replace this question with another: Does it make sense? Ask yourself another question: Does it make sense to refinance at all? The answer to that question is: It depends. . . .

REFINANCING YOUR HOME

You might refinance your home for a variety of reasons. For example, you might want to expand your living space without having to uproot your family, change jobs, make new friends, and go through the expense and trauma of moving. Your family is growing; you need an additional bedroom, not a new life. Refinancing your mortgage might free up enough cash to pay a contractor for the renovation work. This use of proceeds makes financial sense, because the addition will increase the value of your house. Your equity is converted from one form to another, not taken out and spent.

Other reasons to refinance include paying for a vacation, purchasing a new car, and covering other expenses. Unfortunately, once you spend the money in those ways, it's gone and can't be recovered. Equity has definitely been *spent*.

————————————→ **ACTION ITEM** ←————————————

Before seeking refinancing, make a list of what you will use the money for. If borrowing for those reasons is a poor idea, don't refinance.

Another common reason for refinancing is to consolidate debts. Many lenders promote this idea by pointing out that mortgage interest is tax-deductible and consumer interest is not. Converting the debt from consumer interest to mortgage interest is promoted as a loophole. Be aware, though, that conversion could be a very dangerous trap and a bad habit that could cost you more than your credit. You could actually lose your house by going too far into debt. Consolidation might not be a wise move, unless you can also revise your spending habits and keep control of your outlay of funds.

WEALTH   *The Consolidation Trap.* Andrea has over $16,000
BUILDING   in credit card and store revolving account card debts.
PROFILE   She decides to refinance her mortgage to consolidate
                 her debts. However, within 6 months, Andrea's debts
are back up to the $16,000 level again, and she still hasn't repaid her refinanced mortgage.

If you can't destroy the credit cards that got you into trouble in the first place, consolidation doesn't work. One good thing about being at your credit limit is that those accounts can't get you into further trouble. However, when you consolidate, you are free to begin charging all over again.

Refinancing is the same thing as borrowing money. Lenders don't like to emphasize this, because they would rather have you think of refinancing as "putting idle equity to work." In a sense, the equity is your money, so the claim is not entirely false. But you can only remove the debt by selling your home. As a first step, think of refinancing as getting a new loan.

A good rule of thumb, and one that will help you remain true to your own financial plan, is this: Borrow money to increase equity, not to spend it. Be a shrewd homeowner and investor by recognizing that equity is not the same thing as income. As long as you intend to remain in your home, equity is borrowing power, but it's also net worth. Depending on your financial goals, it could be more important to preserve equity than to pull it out and use it in some way. If you are a risk taker and speculator and you seek the highest possible leverage, then borrowing the maximum amount is an appropriate strategy to employ. Most people are not in this category, and they don't want to use their home equity to finance speculative activities.

When you use refinancing money to add a room to your house, to invest in a second home or other investments, or to start your own business, you are increasing your equity. When you use borrowed money to consolidate bills, to take a vacation, or to buy a car, you are spending. Your equity is not being transferred to other investments or increased in some way; it is being used up.

Assuming that you would like to own your home free and clear one day, there must come a point where equity is allowed to build undisturbed. That will mean not increasing your debt level in the future, unless your goals change. Even if you don't intend to remain in this house, remember what refinancing means: you'll have less equity to pull out and transfer later. Refinancing now could mean you won't be able to afford the house you want, the next time you're ready to move.

WEALTH   *Using Up Equity.* Tom and Ruby purchased a house
BUILDING   a number of years ago for $40,000. Their original loan
PROFILE   after the down payment was $34,000, and was due in
                        30 years. A few years ago, the house was appraised at
$100,000, and Tom and Ruby replaced their original mortgage with a new one for $80,000.

They used the money to consolidate debts, buy a new car, and start a savings and investment plan. Over the past few years, the savings and investments were gradually reduced through withdrawals. Now, there's nothing left. The family wants to sell the house this year and buy a larger one, but their equity is minimal. It has all been used up and their debt level is high.

Your house may increase in value substantially. But if you refinance and then use the proceeds unwisely, your equity will be used up. If your family wants to buy another house, your resources are limited and, with minimal equity, they won't be able to buy as nice a house as they wanted. Payments will be higher than you would like. Chances are, if the second house increases in value, the same mistake will be repeated in the future.

Avoid making the same mistakes over and over. Break the spending cycle by setting specific goals, deciding what uses your equity should serve, and then sticking to your plan. You can take charge and plan out the equity in your home.

WHEN REFINANCING MAKES SENSE

It is financially irresponsible to spend equity rather than preserve it. To do so does a great disservice to yourself. However, it is also important to recognize that owning a home is a wonderful opportunity. Having equity available gives you the financial flexibility to move quickly, should a good investment opportunity present itself.

The greatest danger is that, because equity is so easily available, you will misuse it. Your financial success as a homeowner will depend on discipline. You have to have enough perseverance to stay well disciplined and to stick to your own goals and your financial plan. You have an opportunity to succeed or to fail, depending on how you use the equity you have available.

There are a number of good reasons to refinance. They include the following.

Lower Rates

The most common reason for refinancing is because interest rates are lower. There is no hard-and-fast rule of thumb, but many experts say that you should refinance when current rates are at least 2 percent below the rate you are paying. The truth is, you should refinance whenever it makes economic sense. Paying off the same debt in the same number of years, but at a lower cost, is nothing short of sound financial planning. Later in this chapter, you will learn how to figure out whether it makes sense to take advantage of lower rates.

---------------------→ **ACTION ITEM** ←-----------------

Check lender rates from time to time, to determine whether your mortgage is still a good idea. Remain open-minded to the idea of refinancing whenever it makes sense.

In some instances, you could refinance and achieve two different goals. You might be able to free up some money *and* reduce your monthly payment.

WEALTH BUILDING PROFILE   *Achieving Two Goals.* Larry and Theresa originally owed $45,000 on their 30-year mortgage at 12 percent. Payments have been $462.88 per month. Now, 10 years later, their home is worth much more, so they want to borrow $50,000 through a home equity loan. At today's prevailing rate of 9.25 percent, payments over a 20-year term will be $457.94 per month—less than they are paying on their original loan.

In the Wealth Building Profile above, the mortgage payments are reduced and cash is freed up. However, the repayment date is not changed. The original, 30-year term is replaced 10 years later with a 20-year repayment term. This is of critical importance. The target payoff date is left intact. Taking a shorter-term mortgage than is required also holds down interest expenses.

Investment Opportunities

Another reason to refinance is that an investment opportunity has come to your attention. You can take advantage of it if you have equity at your disposal. Be careful here, though: there is no such thing as a "sure thing," no matter what you're told. It's much easier to lose a fortune than to make one, and there are many investment hustlers out there, ready to appeal to your greed, if you get greedy.

Follow these guidelines:

▶ Never buy in response to an unsolicited offer, especially if it comes over the phone.

▶ Be aware of risk levels. If an investment is riskier than owning your own home, the yield should be substantially higher in order to justify it.

▶ Decide in advance what types of investments are suitable, given your financial knowledge and your financial plan. Don't invest outside of that defined "comfort zone," and you won't have any problems.

A Chance to Revise Your Plan

You probably already know that any planning you do today is likely to change in the future. Alterations in your marital and family status, job situation, personal maturity, and personal attitude will all affect your goals and your plan.

At some point in the future, you might want to revise your plan drastically. You might change your investment posture as the result of other changes. All your goals will then change as well.

WEALTH   *Changing Goals.* Thad was very conservative. He in-
BUILDING   vested in mutual funds, maintained his home equity
PROFILE   carefully, and planned for his retirement. Eventually, he paid off all of his debts. After living debt-free for a year, Thad drastically revised his way of thinking. He borrowed all of his equity and began investing in real estate rental properties. His new attitude was: the more leverage, the better. Within a few months, Thad controlled six properties. Two years later, the market values had grown enough for Thad to be able to sell the rentals at a handsome profit.

Your goals may change quite drastically; more likely, they will evolve into different priorities. As your career develops, for example, you will gain a different financial perspective. Maturity as an investor and as a homeowner will help round out your investment goals. In addition, reaching one series of goals leads to replacing those goals with others. Goals have deadlines and will come and go many times during your life.

WEALTH   *New Priorities.* Carl and Karen began their financial
BUILDING   planning when they were first married. When they
PROFILE   started to have children, they opened a college savings
               account. When that was in place for their children,
they began putting money aside for retirement, when they hope to eventually start their own business and to travel. As one set of priorities was met and dealt with; another set of priorities came along.

As a general rule, what is a good reason to refinance my home?

Two reasons are most obvious. First, take advantage of a significantly lower interest rate; second, increase the value of your home, for example, by adding living space.

Why can't I borrow the maximum and just add all the living space possible?

There is a limit to how much value you can add. The principle of "conformity" dictates that you won't get your money back if you overimprove to the extent that you outpace the typical similar home in the same area. You could spend too much for improvements without being able to get your money back when you sell.

With growing equity in my home, I can take out a new loan to buy a car, consolidate debts, or go on vacation, can't I?

You can, but it would be a mistake. As a general rule of thumb, avoid *spending* equity. Spend your income and preserve your equity. Borrow money only when it will be spent to increase your net worth.

Doesn't debt consolidation make sense? Payments are lowered with a new loan, aren't they?

The argument for debt consolidation is flawed. Chances are, you will be back in debt in a few months, *and* will still have a higher mortgage payment each month. Solve your spending-habit problem first; don't misuse your home equity to make the problem worse.

Isn't the equity my money? Why should I leave it sitting idle in my home?

That's what the lenders all say, too. You have to realize that "taking out equity" is a fancy phrase for borrowing money. Whenever you borrow, you must pay interest. The translation: A higher cost of your home.

What's wrong with borrowing? Can't I write off the interest on my home mortgage?

When you borrow through a mortgage loan, you are allowing a lender to convert your equity into the lender's profits. This occurs through interest payments, even *after* tax benefits. If you really want to control your housing costs and your financial plan, you need to control your borrowing and your spending habits.

Is there an advantage to having a large amount of equity in my home?

Yes, for several reasons. First, building equity allows you to cash it in one day, even if only to move elsewhere. Second, in the event of an unexpected need, the equity can be borrowed, but only if you have preserved it through the years.

Why can't I borrow the equity I have today, and let growing market values take care of my future equity growth?

That's fine, if equity does indeed grow in the future, at a faster rate than the rate you're paying the lender. You might, in fact, convert all of your equity to the lender through excessive interest.

What if a great investment opportunity comes up? Should I take out a new loan in that case?

Yes, but be careful. You should be absolutely sure about what you're doing, because many people have lost their money on a "sure thing" in the past. Compare risk levels before using your equity and putting it—and your family's security—at risk.

Does this mean that I have to keep my mortgage intact for 30 years?

No. Your plan will change at some time during the next three decades. Chances are, you won't even be in the same house by then. Set policies for yourself based on today's circumstances, and then live by your own sensible policies.

WHEN TO AVOID REFINANCING

Whether your goals change or remain the same, one general rule is worth observing at all times: if you refinance, do it when it's right for you, and not because someone else encourages you to do so.

If you have seen televised ads from lending institutions, you have already heard the chiding and the promises. "Your equity is sitting idle in your home." "You can get a loan approved fast." "You can get the money out to take your dream vacation."

Forget all of these advertising ploys. Remember, the lender makes a profit when you borrow, and home equity refinancing *is* borrowing money. Refinance only on your own terms and for your own reasons, and only when it makes sense in your overall plan for meeting your own financial goals.

When is refinancing a bad idea? Here are some reasons *not* to do it.

Higher Rates Than for Your Current Loan

It makes no sense to refinance a loan when you already have a fixed, lower rate on a previous loan. You do not have to replace your mortgage; you can simply take out a second mortgage, when rates are higher than those you already have.

Some lenders try to entice borrowers to refinance, especially when their existing interest rate is low. They may offer a no-points loan, a free appraisal, or even a prequalified approval plan.

WEALTH   *Keeping Low Rates.* Marilyn has a 7 percent loan
BUILDING   on her mortgage, on a house she bought more than 20
PROFILE   years ago. The lender has offered a preapproved loan
                 with no appraisal fee and no points, if she refinances.
Marilyn wants to take out some equity. Instead of refinancing, she enters a contract for a second mortgage. In this way, the lower interest rate on her first loan is left intact.

Excessively High Refinancing Cost

In certain types of markets, when credit and money are tight, lenders' fees rise. Points go up and so do the administrative fees associated with borrowing. At such times, it might be unwise to refinance, if only because the cost of doing so is very high.

Whenever the demand for money is greater than the supply, lenders' policies and fees will become more restrictive. Lenders who used to charge one or two points might now be demanding three or four, or even more. They will be less willing to negotiate with you, to lower their fees, or to compromise on terms.

Pressure to Borrow, for the Wrong Reasons

No financial transaction should be decided on under pressure. Unfortunately, many borrowers are under the gun when they go to see a lender. Even though it can take 3 weeks or more to process a loan under the best of conditions, some borrowers have a sense of urgency that makes it impossible for them to negotiate wisely or to know when to back away. If borrowers believe that they cannot afford to pass up the chance of getting a loan, they will agree to any terms.

Deciding under Pressure. Kevin was behind on payments to several credit card companies and other lenders. His payment lag had gone on too long, and creditors were threatening to sue. He applied for a loan and, although the fees and the interest rate were high, he didn't think he had any choice. He signed the papers. Later on, in a moment of relative calm, Kevin realized that other lenders had offered much more favorable terms. Making the decision under pressure had cost him thousands of dollars.

Burden of Risk or Poor Cash Flow

Be careful when you plan to invest the proceeds from refinancing your mortgage. You may end up with a much steeper payment than you're used to, and many investments won't yield the same cash flow on a month-to-month basis.

You could end up in a cash crisis if you commit yourself to a long-term mortgage, only to discover that you can't afford the payments. Your mortgage has to be paid every month, regardless of how your investment performs.

Cash Flow Mistakes. Eric and Evelyn refinanced to invest in a mutual fund that had been yielding an average of 21 percent per year. That return was based on reinvesting all dividends, however. To earn 21 percent, no withdrawals could be made—assuming the fund continued to perform at the same level as in the past. However, the higher payments on the refinanced mortgage were a severe burden for Eric and Evelyn. Refinancing to invest in the mutual fund was a mistake.

FIGURING THE BREAKEVEN POINT

You face a dilemma whenever the refinancing question arises. If you plan to sell your house within the next few years, the more equity you have, the more there will be to transfer to the purchase of your next house. The amount of your equity in your current house, to an extent, determines the price range and the monthly payments for your next house.

We can all use a lump sum of cash from time to time, to invest, to pay bills, and to spend for a variety of other purposes. Refinancing is a nice luxury. Whether you will use the money wisely or unwisely, refinancing is one of the more attractive features of buying and holding on to real estate.

The typical first-time home buyer keeps that house less than 5 years. If you have been in your house for 3 years, and prices have gone up, does it make sense to refinance? Probably not, if you plan to move within the near future. If you plan to stay in that house for many years to come, refinancing might make sense financially, but only if the following assumptions apply to you.

▶ You plan to use the money wisely. There is no way around this fact: refinancing for the wrong reasons is poor financial management. If you plan to use the money to pay off consumer debts (which you'll probably replace), to buy a car, or to take a vacation, then you're wasting your home equity. You might have been better off remaining as a renter, paying less each month for your housing costs, and saving the difference.

  Use the money wisely. Increase your net worth by purchasing other assets that will grow in value, such as rental real estate. Another wise use of the money is to cover an unavoidable emergency. Rather than suffer financially, use your equity for a child's college education, unexpected medical or family emergencies, and similar events that were not planned for but require large sums of money. Even though these problems don't add to your equity, you need to address them as quickly as possible.

▶ Interest rates are lower, and your new payment will be lower, too. Like most people, you may be prompted to refinance when interest rates go down. It is then possible to reduce your interest cost. (To get the lower rate, you still have to pay the lender's fees.)

If rates are lower, then your monthly payments should be lower, too. Although this is a fair assumption, the monthly payment could be higher, for a number of reasons. If you commit to a more rapid repayment schedule, your payments will rise. If you borrow more money that was outstanding on the previous loan, that will also increase your payments.

▶ You will remain as owner of the house long enough to justify the costs involved. If you plan to move within the next year or two, it probably won't save anything to refinance; it's going to cost you money instead. If your monthly savings won't absorb the expense of refinancing, then you should not refinance now.

To figure your breakeven point, first estimate the fees involved in refinancing. (The lender will estimate them for you, upon request.) Next, compare your present monthly payment to the monthly payment you'll be required to make with the new loan. Divide the estimated costs by the savings in the monthly payment. This formula is summarized for you in Figure 4–1.

An example will help to clarify the process. The lender's fees for refinancing a loan total about $2,315. The existing loan was originally written for a 30-year term at 11 percent, and the amount was $100,000. Payments are $952.33 per month. There are 20 years remaining on this loan, and the current balance is approximately $92,000. The homeowner wants to refinance at 9.5 percent with a repayment date in 20 years (same date as the previous loan). Payments will be $857.57. To compute the breakeven point, first calculate the monthly savings:

$$\$952.33 - \$857.57 = \$94.76$$

$$\frac{refinancing\ charges}{monthly\ savings} = \frac{number\ of}{months}$$

Figure 4–1
Refinancing breakeven point.

Next, divide the total of the lender's fees ($2,315) by the monthly savings amount ($94.76):

$$\frac{\$2{,}315}{\$94.76} = 24.4 \text{ months}$$

It will take about 2 years to break even from this refinancing. If the homeowner plans to keep this home for more than 2 years, it makes sense to go for the lower rate. If plans call for selling within 2 years, it will cost money to refinance now.

▸ The final pay-off date remains the same or is shortened. Refinancing makes financial sense when the breakeven test works, and when the repayment date is the same as on the original loan (or earlier). You save interest when you don't extend the repayment term. You save even more if you're able to shorten it, because interest will be reduced by two factors: a lower rate, and a shorter repayment term.

ADJUSTING THE CALCULATION

An adjustment in the financial calculations is required when the amount or the repayment term changes. If either or both events occur during the refinancing, you cannot calculate whether refinancing makes sense, without first adjusting for the changes.

Let's work out an example, to understand how to adjust the figures. A borrower currently owes about $92,000 on a mortgage, originated about 10 years before, in the amount of $100,000. Upon refinancing, two facts complicate the question of whether refinancing makes sense financially. First, the borrower applies for a loan in the amount of $100,000. Second, he applies for a 30-year term. The amount to be borrowed is higher than the current balance of the loan, and, although there are only 20 years remaining on the original loan, the term will be extended to 30 years upon refinancing.

In a situation like this, the monthly payment might still be lower, even though a higher amount is being borrowed. For example, if a current loan calls for 11 percent interest, and a new loan is at 9.5, the monthly payment will be lower on the same original amount of $100,000, because of the lower rate and the 30-year term:

11% loan payment	$952.33
9.5% loan payment	840.86
difference	$111.47

The savings in the monthly payment is substantial, and, upon refinancing, the borrower gets $8,000 (minus the lender's fees). From one point of view, this would be "found money." The monthly payment drops $111.47, and the homeowner gets to take out several thousand dollars. The cost will be high, but it's hidden. Consider the difference in monthly payments over the life of the new loan, versus payments on the older, higher-rate loan:

Payments:

30 years at 9.5 percent: $840.86 × 360 months	$302,709.60
20 years at 11 percent: $952.33 × 240 months	$228,559.20
Difference	$ 74,150.40

The convenience of lower payments, plus several thousand dollars in "found money," will cost more than $74,000 over the next 30 years. In addition, the homeowner will be committed to a repayment schedule for 10 years longer than with the original plan.

─────────────→ **ACTION ITEM** ←─────────────

Whenever you are thinking of refinancing, always calculate and compare the overall interest cost and savings. It will help you to make the right decision every time.

This argument is only theoretical, if plans call for selling the home before the repayment term expires. In many situations, it will make more sense to extend the term—accepting higher interest costs on the loan in exchange for a lower monthly payment—and plan to sell and move within the next few years. In that case, you get not only the lower monthly cost and the cash, but more of an interest tax write-off as well.

Sometimes, it makes more sense to take the money out because interest rates are lower. This is especially true if you can lower your monthly payment at the same time. Extending the payoff date isn't a major issue if you know you will sell and move up before that happens.

One point to remember: Refinancing at a higher amount than the existing mortgage reduces your present and future equity. When the house is finally sold, you will have less proceeds to reinvest in another house.

To calculate the breakeven point on a comparable basis, adjust the repayment level to what it would be if the term were the same. For example, a 30-year mortgage that is refinanced 10 years later might be written again for a 30-year term. However, calculate what the payments would have been if the repayment term were 20 years instead (tied to the original payoff date). Your lender can help you to calculate this, or you can use Appendix A to calculate your payments.

Go through the same process, if you borrow an amount above the current balance. What would the payments have been if you had borrowed the same amount as you now owe? This lets you make a valid comparison, in order to judge whether it makes sense to refinance, based on the status of the original loan.

Once you decide to change the debt level or the repayment term, you're dealing with an entirely different set of circumstances. You will have altered the financing and, ultimately, the true cost of your house. After you adjust the numbers to compare on the same basis, you then need to recognize that you're making a major revision in the plan itself. The price and the debt period change.

As you can see, the process of refinancing involves more than an answer to How much can I get? Recall the opening paragraph of this chapter: The entire question of whether to refinance has to be answered with the response: That depends. Your personal situation, the time you believe you will stay in the house, and the current rates and fees, will all affect your decision.

The next two chapters address another area that greatly confuses many people: different mortgage strategies. Fixed-rate and adjustable mortgages are the two primary types; there are many variations on those themes.

———————— POINTS TO REMEMBER ————————

▶ Ask yourself seriously why you want to refinance. Make sure it's for a sound reason that will save you money, not cost you more.

▶ Refinance to increase your net worth, not to spend it.

▶ Avoid using up equity over time by refinancing unwisely, using equity lines of credit, and making other mistakes that convert your equity to the lender's bottom line.

▶ Take advantage of lower interest rates by refinancing, but only if you can justify the costs of refinancing.

▶ Know when it is unwise to refinance, and resist temptations that could cause you to make a mistake.

▶ Never make decisions under pressure, for the wrong reasons, or without first getting all the facts you need.

▶ Evaluate the cash flow consequences of refinancing. Make sure you know where you will be after you sign the contract.

▶ Know how to figure the refinancing breakeven point. Don't refinance unless you will be ahead in the long run.

5

FRM, ARM, and UMM

*T*he concept of borrowing and repaying money is fairly straightforward. Virtually everyone understands how it works. But there are many varieties in the way a loan can be structured, and just keeping up with the abbreviations is a task in itself.

This chapter explains the differences between the two broad types of mortgages: fixed-rate mortgages (FRMs) and adjustable-rate mortgages (ARMs). With this information in hand, you should be able to untangle mortgage misinformation (UMM). In Chapter 6, you will see how varieties of mortgages are carried even further, through the use of an assortment of creative devices.

Why is it necessary to have so many different types of mortgages? A few decades ago, there was only one type: the fixed-rate mortgage, usually written for homeowners over a 30-year term. Today, that mortgage is still popular and is used widely. But the story no longer ends at FRMs. In today's mortgage market, you have many decisions to make every time you need to borrow. You now have to shop for a good mortgage bargain, just as you do when you buy any other commodity. It is important to keep in mind that the right mortgage can reduce the real cost of housing by thousands of dollars, and the wrong mortgage can add thousands to your costs. The following sections describe some of the reasons for today's variety in mortgages.

Higher Home Prices

Housing prices are now drastically higher than they were before the days of different types of mortgages. In the past, housing appreciation was a sure thing, but it did not vary significantly. It kept pace with inflation, and homeowners expected their investment to grow at a modest rate. This was generally true until the beginning of the 1970s. Since then, the pricing of houses has been erratic and unpredictable.

Today, homeowners and investors alike speculate on the value of housing. You might want to live in a particular neighborhood; you are probably aware of the area's potential for growth in value. In many areas, housing prices have not only outpaced inflation, they have become a substantial growth investment.

This change has led to the need for new varieties of financing. The 30-year mortgage is not always the most appropriate contract, especially because today's home buyer does not usually stay in one house for the entire 30-year period covered by the traditional mortgage. If you are typical, you will probably sell your first home in under 5 years.

Volatile Changes in Values

Not only have housing prices risen; they are far more volatile than in the past. Real estate is not the steady growth investment it was in the 1950s and 1960s. Today, values change rapidly and different areas gain or lose in popularity from one economic phase to another. Employment, climate, crime, congestion, pollution, and many other life-style and economic factors affect the value and perceived value of housing. Remember, with this point in mind, that housing value, like supply and demand, is a regional issue. The trends are very localized and cannot be judged on a national basis—in spite of what the national business press reports.

―――――――――→ **ACTION ITEM** ←―――――――――
Forget what you've read about national trends in real estate. Check with *local* real estate professionals, lenders, and business publications, to find out what's going on in your area.

National trends in real estate might not affect what is happening in your neighborhood. Real estate has become a regional economic factor, and changes from one region to another are seen frequently. A boom in California might occur at the same time as a real estate depression in the Deep South. New York prices might flatten out while Seattle's property skyrockets.

For the new home buyer not familiar with an area, intermediate or long-term trends will tell the story about changes in real estate prices. Regional economics might have more impact on real estate prices than anything else. It is, after all, the local economy that draws or repels people, and the number of people needing housing is what ultimately determines price.

Disparity Between Housing Prices and Income

Prices are higher than in the past, and they change more rapidly. But, aside from these realities, the real need for creative mortgage financing results from the growing disparity between housing prices and income.

When salaries *and* housing both kept pace with inflation, it was possible to save money for a down payment and to buy a house within a few years. Today, prices might change so rapidly that the family that cannot afford a house now will never be able to get a house. Not only can they not save enough money, but they also can't qualify for a loan. Even if they could qualify, chances are the payments would be too high.

These problems can be addressed with some form of creative financing. Remember, the real cost of a house is not the price you pay, but the final cost including interest. "Cost" is best defined by the monthly payment you are required to make—or by the percentage of your total income that you have to pay to a lender.

Changes in Interest Rates

Creative financing really came into being in the late 1970s and early 1980s, when interest rates increased rapidly. At one point, rates were above 20 percent, and few people could afford to buy a house through traditional methods.

In those days, price was no object. A home buyer would pay any price, as long as the payments worked out and the deal was affordable. In such a market, the truth about housing prices comes to the surface: the total of payments you actually make determines the real cost, not the price you agree to pay. Making the deal work is what sells houses.

Today, and in the future, interest rates define, to a degree, the strength or weakness of the market. Supply-and-demand tends to vary with interest rates. As rates are lowered, more people can qualify for financing in a broader range. That leads to a higher volume of sales activity. When interest rates rise, people become fearful. They wait to see what will happen. They don't make offers on homes because monthly payments will be too high. They can't qualify for loans according to the lender's rules.

Jump-Start for a Slow Market

Financing can be used as an incentive to sell houses in a slow market. Financing is a sales tool, just as price and discounts are. You see financing at work all the time at car dealerships. The same negotiating takes place in the housing market, but with a few twists. For example, a car dealership will advertise 3 percent financing as a way of providing an incentive to buy a car now, from this dealer.

In the housing market, a builder or developer might offer to provide some or all of the financing for a buyer, at lower than market rates. This is achieved through a number of creative methods, many of which are explained in the next chapter. Lenders also compete in the market when they want more business, by offering low rates as well as lower-than-average financing fees. When lenders want your business, the price—the cost of borrowing—comes down.

Why are there so many different kinds of mortgages?

With home prices higher than in the past, and with the competition among lenders, the market requires flexibility. Some borrowers prefer fixed rates, others want variable rates. Lenders are responding to a changing market demand.

Have higher home prices really affected the types of mortgages on the market?

Yes, and directly. Before the 1970s, housing prices tended to rise slowly, over the long term. But then markets became more regional; prices tended to flatten out or rise dramatically and suddenly in different areas. In some conditions, creative financing more directly influenced closing sales than the actual prices of homes.

How has pricing volatility affected mortgages?

The most dramatic effect has been the growing popularity of the variable-rate mortgage. Lenders who approved long-term loans in the late 1960s, for example, had millions of dollars out, at 6 and 7 percent. However, rates in the early 1980s rose as high as 20 percent. The consequence for lenders was a need for greater flexibility in the terms offered.

Housing prices have risen, but hasn't average household income risen as well?

Yes, it has. But, in many of the hottest regions, increases in personal income have not kept pace or even come close to the inflationary pricing of houses. Regional demand factors often distort housing prices to such an extent that large segments of the local population simply can't afford to buy a new home.

Do prices affect interest rates?

It's actually the other way around. Interest rates change based on the demand and supply of money. As interest rates fall, more people can qualify for a first-time home purchase. Consequently, falling rates mean greater demand for housing; rising rates exclude more would-be buyers. Real demand aside, practical demand for housing declines as interest rates rise.

Does financing actually affect the housing market?

Yes, especially during slow market periods. Incentives offered to new buyers through financing terms and conditions often make a sale happen when it wouldn't otherwise have been possible to close the deal. For example, a seller might offer to carry a large part of a loan, to make it easier for the buyer to qualify with an outside lender.

THE FIXED-RATE MORTGAGE

Homeowners who believe they will keep their houses for many years are naturally drawn to the fixed-rate mortgage. There is a lot of security in the idea that your housing expense will never go up.

You pay for the privilege of getting a fixed rate. Chances are that the interest rate will be higher than the rate charged for an ARM, although the ARM rate can rise too, often far above the level charged for the FRM.

The FRM has the following major benefits:

▶ Your housing costs decline over time. Some people argue, in support of the FRM, that the consistency of payments means your housing costs never rise. In fact, however, your housing costs decline over time, when your payments remain the same.

This occurs for two reasons. First, inflation makes your mortgage payment less significant. When the value of the dollar falls as a consequence of inflation, your mortgage payment becomes literally lower. For example, when the buying power of the dollar is 3 percent lower than it was 2 years ago, the FRM payment is also 3 percent below the real previous spending level.

The second reason your housing costs fall is that income tends to rise over time; the mortgage payments do not.

WEALTH BUILDING PROFILE   *Income Ratios.* When Jack first began paying on his mortgage, his salary was $3,100 per month. Payments are $702, or 22.6 percent of his gross pay. Since payments began, Jack has been given a promotion and two raises. His gross salary is now $3,900 per month. The mortgage is now only 18 percent of his gross pay.

When the ratio between the mortgage and your monthly income falls, you are paying less of your salary to housing costs each month.

▶ You can easily compute what is required to accelerate your payments. You might want to reduce your interest expense and control the payoff date on your mortgage, as part of your long-range planning. This is easily achieved with an FRM. You know what you are required to pay each month, and that amount never varies. You can pay more and quickly figure out the effect.

With an ARM, the plan could be disturbed when interest rates rise. The required monthly payment would then rise as well, which means your long-range plan won't necessarily work.

WEALTH BUILDING PROFILE *Shortening the Term.* Gail is paying on a 30-year mortgage, but would like to retire after 20 years. She checks an interest amortization table and figures out the monthly payment required to accelerate her mortgage. With a fixed-rate contract, this is a simple matter. However, if Gail's contract were on an adjustable-rate basis, any plans she makes today would have to change every time the payment rises.

▶ Your lender may be willing to refinance your loan in future years, especially if interest rates rise. When you have a very high rate on your mortgage loan, the lender will naturally be happy if you continue making payments. People usually want to refinance when interest rates are lower than the rate they are paying.

For a moment, look at this issue from the lender's point of view. If your rate is extremely low, the lender will be motivated to replace that loan with another one.

WEALTH BUILDING PROFILE *Lender Temptations.* Adam and Roberta entered into a fixed-rate mortgage with a 30-year term. The interest rate was set at 8 percent. Today, rates are averaging 10 percent or more. The lender contacts Adam and Roberta and offers them a preapproved home equity loan, with proceeds of more than $30,000. There will be no points, no appraisal fee, and no other fees charged. All they have to do is sign an application form.

Why would a lender waive all fees? To replace a below-market interest rate, and to make the replacement as painless as possible for the borrower. If you really want to take some money out, the smart thing to do is leave the original mortgage intact and apply for a second mortgage secured by the property.

If rates fall below your fixed rate, you have a tremendous advantage. Your low-rate mortgage is an asset in its own right, either in negotiation with the lender or as a planning tool. Because your housing costs will be relatively low in the future, you enjoy the benefits of long-term fixed-rate financing.

These arguments are not as valid if you stay in the house for only a few years. However, even those homeowners who replace one house with another in less than 5 years often believe, at the time of purchase, that they will stay there for several decades. Because a house is a major purchase, it is natural to assume that it will never be necessary to move again. That assumption is likely to change.

If you plan to remain in your house for the full 30 years, it makes sense to get an FRM, but you should be aware of some of the disadvantages. These include the following:

▸ It could be expensive to obtain and to meet payments on a fixed-rate mortgage for two reasons. First, you will start out with a higher interest rate than adjustable-rate mortgagees pay. If interest rates remain the same, or fall, then your fixed-rate mortgage will be expensive to keep.

Second, if rates fall below your fixed-rate level, either you will have to live with paying more than you could elsewhere, or you will need to refinance. You will be paying lender fees all over again, just to get a lower rate.

▸ You might have a problem qualifying for your loan. Some borrowers are forced to take out an ARM for only one reason: they cannot meet the lender's qualifications for a fixed-rate loan. ARMs generally start out with a lower rate and then increase, based on an independent index of interest rates. As insecure as you might feel about having your monthly payments change because of an outside influence, you may not have any choice.

How is qualifying a problem? If the FRM is available at two or three percentage points above the ARM, the monthly payment will also be higher. It could put you over the limit of the income-to-payment ratio the lender applies.

▶ The lender's fees to contract a long-term FRM loan might be significantly higher. Lenders commit themselves to a very long term when they grant a 30-year, fixed-rate mortgage. The future is uncertain, and rates could rise far above the rate they give to you today. With that in mind, the lender will want to be compensated up front, in exchange for the assurances you get by taking out an FRM. That could mean more points and higher lender fees in the beginning.

DOWN PAYMENT STRATEGIES

The problem with an FRM is that many people simply can't qualify for the loan. Their income isn't high enough, according to the lender's rules, so they are forced to take out an ARM, to get the lower initial interest rate.

This makes no sense, even from the lender's point of view. Because the interest rate will probably be far higher in future years than the rate for the fixed-rate loan, the risks are greater, to both the borrower and the lender. If the borrower cannot afford future payments, the bank will have to foreclose. Still, this is the way lenders operate. They set the rules and force all borrowers to follow them.

→ ACTION ITEM ←

Determine the best type of loan to get, based not only on preference, but also on what you can afford. Is it possible to offer a higher down payment?

This situation leads to a dilemma. On the one hand, you like the idea of an FRM, because it provides long-term security. Payments will never vary. On the other hand, the lender says your income is too low, and you can't qualify for an FRM. Instead, you are offered an ARM, which has much more volatility and risk on both sides.

At this point, you may still be able to get the FRM, if you are willing and able to increase your down payment.

WEALTH   *Adjusted Down Payment.* Ned and Sharon bought a
BUILDING   house for $100,000 and offered a $20,000 down pay-
PROFILE   ment. The lender had fixed-rate loans at 9.5 percent.
                 Payments over a 30-year term would be $672.69 for an
$80,000 loan. The lender reviewed Ned and Sharon's application and
rejected the loan, because they didn't meet the qualifications for that
level of payment. The lender required that payments be no more than
28 percent of monthly gross income; Ned and Sharon needed to earn
$2,402 or more per month. They earned only $2,300.

The solution: Ned and Sharon cannot afford more than 28 percent
of their gross income, or $644 per month, in monthly payments. By
referring to amortization tables (see Appendix A), the maximum loan
is easily computed:

Begin with the payment already computed for an $80,000 loan
($672.69).

Subtract the maximum amount possible ($644).

The result is $28.69 per month.

Find the lowest loan amount for which payments exceed $28.69. A
loan of $5,000 requires higher payments than needed, but the
amount for $4,000 would do the trick. (Take the payment for a
$2,000 loan and double it.)

Add the $4,000 to the $20,000 Ned and Sharon originally planned
to put down.

Payments on a loan of $4,000 less, or $76,000, will be $639.06 per
month, and 28 percent of a monthly income of $2,300 is $644. Ned and
Sharon can now qualify for the loan.

Other possible strategies may suit your situation. Consider each of
the following in your planning:

▸ Ask the seller to lower the price or to add in the difference needed.
  You have the right to ask the seller to help out with your financing
  problem. If you don't get your loan, then the seller doesn't have a
  sale. The seller will then have to wait for another buyer to come

along, qualify, and go through escrow. You might find the seller to be exceptionally cooperative if you request a price reduction of a few thousand dollars.

A seller who resists lowering the price might be willing to add a few thousand dollars to your down payment, or to pay for a buy-down—a strategy in which the initial interest rate is lowered, because interest is prepaid. Buy-down is covered in more detail in the next chapter.

————————→ ACTION ITEM ←————————

Negotiate with the seller. Getting a financing concession saves money without having to ask someone to lower the selling price. It is, admittedly, the same thing; but people can be very stubborn about their price, while being willing to negotiate other conditions of the sale.

Some sellers will be willing to put an amount of money toward solving your financing problems, but won't budge on their price. It makes no real difference, because they get the same amount at the end, once the deal closes. But some people are incredibly closed-minded about financial matters, and refuse to be educated. They simply won't see that the difference between sale price reduction and the payment of some of your financing costs is a purely technical distinction. To them, it all translates to a reduction in net proceeds.

▶ Ask your employer for a raise. Here's an idea that some people overlook. Ask your employer to help you qualify for a loan by raising your salary. A raise of $100 per month will often put you over the top with the lender. You must be able to convince your boss that you deserve the raise, of course. You might have to agree to take on more responsibility, go without another raise for two years, or put in longer hours. But if you really want that house, it might be worth it.

You might discover, when you ask, that your boss was going to give you a raise in a few months anyway. If you have a cost-of-living adjustment or a merit increase coming up soon, ask for it earlier. Make a deal to offset the additional early pay.

▶ Seek a convertible ARM loan. This is a type of loan that most people don't even know exists. It has an initial fixed rate. After a few years (usually 3 to 5 years), the rate begins to vary according to an outside index. However, at some point in the future, you have the right to convert the ARM to a fixed-rate loan at the lender's then-current rate.

If this is confusing, think of the convertible ARM as a loan that starts out with a fixed rate for, say, 3 years. After 3 years, the rate can increase as much as 2 percent per year. At any time, from 6 months after the loan begins, you have the right to convert to a fixed-rate mortgage (FRM).

The convertible ARM's rate might be lower than the FRM's rate, which means you could qualify without having to increase the down payment or use another strategy. However, in some instances, this type of loan could be as expensive as the fixed-rate loan, or might even cost more. Your costs will depend on how fearful the lender is about committing to a very long-term rate.

ADJUSTABLE-RATE MORTGAGES

Lenders devised a new type of product in the 1970s, and it has gradually become a standard fixture in the home lending industry. The adjustable-rate mortgage (ARM) is now offered by most lenders along with fixed-rate mortgages (FRMs).

The ARM was first devised as a way for banks and other lenders to protect themselves against large changes in interest rates. Typically, a lender would write an FRM loan at 6 or 7 percent, payable over 30 years. That was fine as long as interest rates remained generally around 6 or 7 percent. In the early 1970s, interest rates began climbing. Rapid changes in the rate market made lenders' risks greater. The idea of being committed to low-rate loans for three decades was a big problem, at least in the lenders' eyes.

The low rates might not have been as much of a disaster as lenders thought. Remember, the typical first-time home buyer stays less than 5 years. The tendency is for a long-term loan to be replaced rather quickly, either through sale and repurchase or at the time of refinancing. In either case, the older rate is replaced by current rates.

In spite of this logic, lenders sought a way to protect themselves against rapidly changing interest rates. The ARM was designed with that in mind. Here's how it works: The initial rate is usually lower than FRM rates, perhaps by as much as two percentage points or more, but the ARM rate increases over a period of years.

The degree of increase is determined by comparison to an independent index of rates. For example, some lenders base their ARM rates on U.S. Treasury Securities rates. A popular index, called the 1 Year Treasury Securities Index, is the weekly average yield on U.S. Treasury Securities. That average rate is adjusted to report what it would be in 1 full year. As that index changes, so does the effective rate on an ARM.

A few rules also protect the borrower:

▶ The contract limits the frequency of rate increases. Most lenders will increase their rate only once per year at the most.

▶ The annual increase is limited. For example, a contract might specify that the lender may not increase the loan rate more than 2 percent per year.

▶ Most important, the ARM contract includes a "lifetime cap," a maximum number of percentage points the loan can be increased overall. For example, a loan might start out at 9 percent, with a provision that it can never rise above 15 percent.

Before the limitations were included, some ARM contracts led to trouble for borrowers. For example, rather than an interest rate maximum, or "cap," some ARM loans included a payment cap. This meant that the amount of monthly payment was limited. However, a problem with a payment cap is that the borrower could owe more in interest than the payment covered.

As an example of the problem, assume that you have an outstanding balance of $80,000 on an ARM loan, and the lender recently increased the interest rate from 9.625 to 11 percent. The loan is due in 15 years, so the amortization payment should be $909.28. Your contract ensures that your payment will never exceed $850 per month.

In this situation, you make the maximum payment and the loan's balance *rises* each month. Your payment is not high enough to pay the interest.

Before safeguards were built into contracts, some lenders attracted ARM business by advertising an extremely low rate. This rate applied only for the first 6 to 12 months, and was then replaced with a much higher rate. The initial rate, which lenders preferred to call the "today rate," was also more accurately referred to as the "teaser" rate. Lenders still offer ARM contracts at lower rates than those for FRMs, but the degree of rate increase is now limited by contract.

ARM loans contain good and bad points. Whether you should use this type of loan depends on your current status, your ability to qualify, and your plans for staying in the house you are buying.

GOOD POINTS ABOUT THE ARM

An ARM offers certain advantages over an FRM. The positive points about an ARM contract are:

▶ Adjustable-rate financing works for you when market rates stay low. There seems to be a constant fear of higher interest rates. Rates *could* soar, and it *could* become prohibitively expensive to obtain financing or to commit yourself to a loan in which the effective rate could increase by 60 percent or more.

But you should consider another possibility: Interest rates could remain low over an extended period of time. If they remain low and you get an ARM at 2 percent below an FRM, then you are far better off with the ARM—if you can live with a little uncertainty about the future cost of your mortgage. If rates do go much higher, you can always refinance. Admittedly, that would be expensive, given the lender's charges and points on the new loan. But if you're willing to risk the advantages of having an ARM, you have to also be willing to suffer the consequences if you're wrong.

▶ The ARM is the best choice when you plan to sell within 5 years. The ARM contract starts out at a much lower interest rate than most comparable FRMs. Think about what this could mean if you plan to move within 5 years. For example, let's say that the ARM contract begins at 8 percent, and the FRM goes for 10 percent. Let's also assume that the lender has the right to increase the rate by as much as 2 percent per year. The worst case would be that, at the end of 3 years, either loan will have averaged the same rate. The ARM would go from 8, to 10, to 12 percent. That's an average of 10 percent per year and matches the FRM.

─────────────────────→ **ACTION ITEM** ←─────────────────────

You are buying your first home and want a fixed-rate, long-term mortgage. The ARM is available at a much lower rate. Take the ARM, and plan to refinance later. You might decide to move within 5 years, so why not save now?

In this worst case, the ARM still costs less. The higher interest rates are applied to lower principal balances, because the loan has been slightly paid down during the first 2 years. By the start of the fourth year, you will have come out ahead with the ARM—and you will probably be thinking of looking for a new house. Chances are very good that an ARM will cost much less in this case. FRMs are for people who plan to be in one house for many decades to come.

▸ The ARM might be necessary to qualify in the first place. The ARM might have been devised originally to protect lenders but, in fact, this type of mortgage is at least as valuable if you are unable to qualify for an FRM. Remember, the lender applies a strict rule in determining whether you will get your loan. Even if your job history and personal life are stable *and* you have excellent credit and references, you won't get your loan if you don't pass the ratio test.

It's not only frustrating, it also makes little sense when the most trustworthy would-be borrower is turned down because his or her income is a few dollars shy of the required amount. Perhaps your mortgage is 1 percent over the allowed ratio, in comparison to income. What makes little sense is that the lender will then work with you to help you quality! It's the lender's rule to begin with. Why will the lender help you to get around it?

This rhetorical question does not require an answer. All you need to know is that the lender will gladly work with you to help you meet the rules. That often means signing up for an ARM at a lower interest rate. This adjustment could help you qualify when you would have no chance to get the higher FRM.

▸ Some ARM contracts include a conversion feature. All ARM contracts limit your risks. If you cannot live with the long-term risk of varying interest rates, remember this point: The lender cannot just keep raising your rate. Lenders are limited in how much your rate can go up per year and over the life of the contract. These points are clearly spelled out in the contract itself. In addition, many ARM loans come with a conversion feature. You then have the right to convert the ARM to an FRM at any time. Some convertible loans, however, limit the conversion period. For example, it might have to be converted within the first 5 years, at which time the conversion period expires.

Conversion is a valuable feature if you end up needing it. For example, what if it looks like interest rates will be going much higher than current levels? Or, what if you originally planned to sell your house within the first 5 years, and then changed your mind? You can stabilize your interest rate by converting to a fixed-rate schedule.

▸ The overall cost could be much lower. The point was made earlier that, on average, the effective interest rate in an ARM contract could be lower than with an FRM. This means the ARM could be cheaper for many, many years. You should remember that higher rates are being applied to your ever lowering principal balances, which reduces your costs as well.

Origination fees and other costs might be substantially lower with ARM contracts than with the fixed-rate variety. Some lenders, in an attempt to encourage borrowers to take out ARMs, will offer market incentives: low points, or even no points; no appraisal fees; or the removal of other fees. All of these sweeteners add to the attractiveness of the ARM, assuming that the comparison is otherwise very close.

▸ Mortgage acceleration is much more effective in the early years of ARM contracts, when the rate is still low. Earlier, the idea of prepaying more principal than is required by your contract was discussed. Accelerating mortgage payments saves a tremendous amount of interest over a long-term loan, and reduces the period needed for full repayment. In addition, acceleration with the ARM contract is most effective in the earlier years, when the interest rates are low.

Consider this example: your ARM contract starts out at 8 percent and can rise by as much as 2 percent per year. The potential maximum during the life of the loan is 14 percent, or 75 percent higher than the rate you are paying now. What does it mean, on a loan of $100,000, if that interest rate does eventually rise by 2 percent? Based on an out-standing balance of $100,000 and a 30-year term:

Interest Rate	Monthly Payment
8%	$ 733.77
10	877.58
12	1,028.62
14	1,184.88

During the life of this ARM, the monthly payment could rise by *$450* above the starting payment level. But now consider a few other points. This increase cannot happen at a faster rate than is allowed by contract, and it cannot continue to increase after it reaches the stated maximum. The actual payment would be lower because the loan will have been paid down at least slightly.

On the other side of this argument, by adding more to principal during the early years—before any interest rate increases are made—you will reduce your principal balance dramatically. As the interest rate rises, you will have a lower ability to accelerate, because more of your payment will have to go to interest.

BAD POINTS ABOUT THE ARM

There are also a few negatives about ARM contracts. You should be aware of the following possibilities:

▶ Interest rates can rise. If they do, the inflation protection associ-ated with real estate is offset by the ARM contract. One of the primary advantages of home ownership is that, traditionally, fixed-rate financing freezes your cost of housing. Compared to rent, which inevitably rises over time, buying a house is supposed to protect you from inflation, at least to a degree. The ARM mortgage offsets this major advantage.

With that in mind, ARM financing should be considered as a short-term alternative to the FRM. The ARM is appropriate until you refinance and replace it with an FRM, or if your plan is to sell within the next 5 years.

▶ ARM provisions can add significantly to the cost of housing. If the lender does, in fact, raise your payments, the difference means a lot more interest. Remember that the interest you pay over the term of your mortgage ultimately decides what you pay for your house. It also determines who makes a profit on the investment, you or the lender. Carrying an ARM for the long term could mean paying a huge premium for your home.

At the onset, many lenders tell borrowers that the ARM contract goes up or down according to an independent index. However, many borrowers have seen interest and payments rise, only to have the payments remain high, even when the independent index declines. Some ARM arrangements turn out to be one-way, and the lenders refer to the carryover of annual ceilings as the explanation. You need to plan ahead and to evaluate the ARM with worst-case planning in mind. Assume that the maximum increase will be put into effect and that, once the rate goes up on an ARM, it will not come back down.

▶ Budgeting for the intermediate and long term is more difficult. You cannot accurately judge your cost of housing over the next decade if you have an outstanding balance on an ARM contract. You have to assume that the lender will hit you with the maximum increase— probably your most accurate assumption. However, you may also need to plan ahead for a target date when you will replace the ARM with permanent, fixed-rate financing, or you will move and find a house where you will want to stay longer than 5 years. In that event, you might also want to replace your ARM with an FRM, or accept the uncertainty of adjustable-rate financing and proceed with a worst-case plan.

→ **ACTION ITEM** ←

Prepare your budget on the assumption that the maximum increase will be put into effect. Save the difference, if the worst-case scenario doesn't come to pass.

▶ Future high interest, coupled with other economic problems, could jeopardize your housing investment. For families on a fixed income, the ARM could present a serious problem in the near future. The rate of increases in monthly payment levels could outpace the increase in monthly family income. An ever growing portion of income must then be paid toward housing costs, thus affecting the family's ability to stay in the house.

This reality also increases risks for the lender. If buyers cannot afford payments on their loans, they will be forced to sell or, even worse, the lender might have to foreclose. Either event cuts off the payment of interest from borrowers to the lender.

▶ Your ability to refinance could be inhibited with an ARM mortgage. If your payments have increased to a very high level, you will, of course, want to refinance. At that point, however, all mortgage rates will be high in the entire market, and you will be forced to seek refinancing at the worst possible time.

You probably won't think about refinancing while rates are low, because there is no problem. However, if you plan to stay in your house for many years, you might want to refinance at the *best* possible time rather than the worst. People have trouble planning when there is no critical need. However, it might be wisest to always look far into the future, to anticipate higher interest rates, and to plan today for that contingency.

The next chapter shows how the two basic forms of mortgage can be creatively modified to suit every lender's needs. Creative financing has made it possible for a large number of homeowners to get loans that wouldn't be available through traditional means.

────────── **POINTS TO REMEMBER** ──────────

▶ Identify the benefits of different types of mortgage contracts. Keep them in mind when shopping for a loan.

▶ Go for fixed-rate contracts, when you plan to stay in your home for many years.

▶ If you take out an adjustable-rate contract, try to get a conversion privilege written into the contract.

▶ Use ARMs when you plan to sell and move on within 5 years.

▶ Be aware of why lenders offer to waive fees to renegotiate loans. It could cost you a lot to give up a relatively low-rate loan.

▶ Be aware of down payment strategies, and be prepared to use them to negotiate the best possible terms for your loan.

▶ Consider alternatives, when you can't get approval. Ask the seller to help.

▶ Be aware of the rules, good and bad, concerning adjustable-rate loans. Negotiate only when you understand all of the provisions in your contract.

▶ If in doubt about any contractual provisions, consult an expert before you sign.

6

Massaging the
Numbers

You might think that, with the combination of fixed-rate and adjustable-rate financing, there are enough choices on the market. Wouldn't those two varieties satisfy just about every borrower's needs and protect against every type of lender risk? The fact is, there are a number of other varieties, designed to meet a broad range of requirements for a number of borrowers.

THE NEED FOR
CREATIVE FINANCING

Lenders and borrowers alike have discovered many ways to finance the purchase of a home. Considering that your financing is what ultimately determines the price of your home, the method you choose is critical.

Keep this rule in mind: the more "creative" the method you select, the more costs will probably be involved. No form of financing is really likely to reduce the interest costs or price of your home. Creative financing exists to help people pay for a house when traditional methods don't do the job. That probably means paying more.

Not everyone seeks special arrangements for the same reasons. The "creative" financing that one borrower wants won't be appropriate for another, because of differences in financial status, investment aims, price, income, credit history, the lender, and any number of other considerations. The following sections describe the most wide-spread reasons for seeking creative methods of financing.

Needing to Qualify

The most common reason given for the existence of creative financ-ing is that, without it, a number of home buyers could not qualify for a loan. The majority of deals that fall through do so because of financ-ing and qualifying problems. Buyers whose income is too low (accord-ing to the lender, at any rate) need to seek other alternatives.

Many people think that a lender's rejection means they should go to another lender. Unfortunately, many borrowers have gone out shop-ping for better mortgage deals when, in fact, there were none to be had among conventional lenders. Instead, these borrowers might find it necessary to go outside of the usual channels, and use a mortgage broker to find a suitable deal. The challenge of qualifying might re-quire that you learn how to finance your purchase in a more creative way. In fact, you can be virtually certain that, if you find an excep-tional deal, it will be because you were willing to do more research than most other people.

Reducing the Purchase's True Cost

Some forms of creative financing actually reduce the cost of a house. The lower cost results from interest being reduced over the financing term, either because of a lower overall or average rate, or because of accelerated principal payments.

This is the exception to the rule, however. The majority of creative financing ideas are designed to reduce initial payments so that a borrower can qualify; to leverage money; or to defer the repayment of the loan. All of these ideas are expensive, and they add to the cost of purchase.

Reducing the Asked Price Without Offending the Seller

Other forms of creative financing are aimed at reducing the initial price. However, sellers often become very stubborn about their "bottom line," and would rather have a sale fall through than give in on their price. Those same people might easily agree to paying some of the buyer's costs, including interest, closing costs, or even some initial loan payments. No matter what you call it, this is a reduction in price. The seller gets less cash at close of escrow, and the buyer is required to put less cash in (or to pay less to the lender). However, as noted before, people see things the way they want, and some forms of creative financing are designed with this reality in mind.

Leveraging Money

Some people prefer leverage over reduced cost. Leverage is nothing more than the maximum use of money. For investors who want leverage, the less put into the house, the better. They would rather use other people's money and control as much property as possible, while investing the least amount themselves.

Some people who use leverage make a fortune in real estate, but they are in the minority and they know what they're doing. Many more people who attempt to leverage their money run into cash flow problems. If you don't have in-depth knowledge of your market before attempting to leverage your money, you shouldn't be taking the risks. Creative financing is often designed to satisfy a lender's need for interest; to turn the seller into a lender; and to defer the payment of principal as long as possible.

➔ ACTION ITEM ◆

Use leverage as an investment technique only if you are convinced that the value of your house will grow at a faster rate than your payment of interest.

Reducing Current Budget by Deferring Some Payments to the Future

One way to qualify according to the lender's rules is to buy a house with very low monthly payments. Given the cost of housing and today's interest rates, that might seem like an impossible task. With creative financing, however, many things are possible. For example, you could qualify for financing that would allow you to buy much more house than you think you can afford.

Some forms of creative financing start out with relatively low payments, achieved by charging lower-than-market interest. The payments gradually increase over the years, according to a predetermined schedule. This arrangement is different from an ARM in two ways:

▶ The changes in payments and rates are scheduled ahead of time;

▶ The lender might be entitled to a portion of profits, if the house is sold before a specified time.

These arrangements depend on the borrower's contract with the lender.

Is creative financing going to cut my interest costs?

The opposite is more likely. "Creative" usually means deferring some of the cost or changing the usual rules. That means higher long-term costs, in exchange for getting the deal done and qualifying for a loan today.

Why would anyone be willing to pay more?

The usual reason is that qualifying for a loan is impossible with traditional methods. A creative form of financing is used instead. For example, interest-only payments might be much lower; you qualify for the loan, but your interest expense is much greater.

Does creative financing ever translate to savings?

Yes. Some forms of creative financing are designed to lower interest costs. Any type of acceleration program will achieve this.

Is creative financing ever used as a negotiating tool?

Quite frequently. One common example is when a seller will not budge on the sale price but will be willing to pay some part of the buyer's up-front financing costs or to carry a mortgage at a relatively low rate of interest.

Does anyone use creative financing to expand an investment base?

Yes. With devices like interest-only payments on loans, investors can leverage their money—they can control more properties.

Is leverage always an advantage?

No. Controlling more properties sounds good from the investor's point of view, but only if the rents cover the much higher interest cost. Leverage also means market and cash flow risk.

How much danger is there in cash flow risk?

This is the greatest risk in real estate investing. If your payments are higher than your rent income (or, if you have no income to cover payments), you probably will lose your properties. You can usually hold on to property long enough to earn a respectable profit—unless you can't make the cash flow.

Does creative financing ever involve deferral of payments? If so, why?

Yes, some loans are negotiated with fairly low initial payments and graduating payments in the future. The reason: The deferral helps buyers to qualify initially, even though their overall expense will be much greater.

TYPES OF CREATIVE FINANCING

Following is a breakdown of many of the varieties of creative financing. Not all of these alternatives are offered by every lender. On the contrary, most lenders offer a relatively limited number of choices. You might have to work with a mortgage broker to find the exact arrangement you want. A mortgage broker actually shops for the appropriate lender in each situation, and can put you in touch with a variety of lenders.

assumable loan   a loan that can be taken over by a new buyer. Many lenders have a long-standing policy of allowing buyers to assume loans. They will want a new buyer to qualify in the same way that everyone must, but will allow the buyer to take over payments.

balloon mortgage   an arrangement in which payments are made for a number of years, but the lion's share of the debt is payable in one big installment at the end. Some balloon mortgages involve interest payments only, with the entire balance due after a specified number of years. Others are set up to amortize loans on a certain schedule, but with an earlier due date. For example, a loan could be amortized over 30 years, but be due in 5 years.

biweekly mortgage   a repayment arrangement, rather than a type of loan. Payments are made every other week instead of once per month. The effect is to make the equivalent of one extra payment per year. Each of the 26 payments is one-half of the monthly amount—the equivalent of 13 payments per year. The extra payment is applied toward the principal, saving money in the long run and reducing the repayment term.

With a biweekly mortgage, a 30-year loan is reduced to between 18 and 20 years for repayment. This type of repayment schedule is offered and marketed by many companies, usually for a fee and with some form of insurance thrown in for "free." Actually, the amount saved is supposed to be used to buy the insurance, which makes the plan more of a gimmick than a money-saving idea. You can arrange to accelerate at a better rate, without a biweekly mortgage, by making an extra payment at the beginning of each year.

buy-down mortgage   an arrangement sometimes offered by a builder or developer as an incentive to buyers to get below-market-rate financing. With a buy-down, a newly built home is offered for sale, with the initial interest rate well below what most lenders are charging. However, the rate will increase to a market level in the near future. To achieve this, the builder has arranged with a lender to provide attractive financing, by agreeing to prepay some of the interest or to buy down the rate. The price of the house is increased to offset this, so that the builder comes out with the same amount of cash.

The buy-down is also used as a way of attracting buyers in a slow market. It may be offered by the seller to a buyer, or by lenders as a way of reducing financing costs. The seller offers to prepay some interest with a lender, or is asked to do so as part of an offer. A 3-2-1 buy-down, for example, involves a reduced rate that grows by 1 percent per year for the first 3 years. The buyer gets reduced initial payments. The seller gets a more attractive deal because of the buy-down offer.

callable feature   a loan that is amortized over a number of years, but *might* be due earlier. The lender has the right to call the loan (demand payment) after a few years, or at regular intervals. If the loan is not called, it continues to be amortized on the schedule established at the time of sale.

convertible mortgage   a mortgage that includes a conversion period of one kind or another. Conversion gives the borrower the flexibility to modify some of the terms. One popular conversion feature allows borrowers with adjustable-rate mortgages to convert to fixed-rate mortgages within a specified deadline. The conversion election should be made if rate trends and levels are favorable to the borrower within the deadline period.

FHA loan   a loan guaranteed by the Federal Housing Administration (FHA). Such loans are available only to owner-occupants and will be given only for residential purchases. The guarantee is granted to the lender for repayment of the loan. Borrowers are required to put down a minimum amount equal to between 3 and 5 percent of the amount of purchase. The maximum purchase amount is set by the FHA. A property is appraised and inspected by the FHA, and must meet minimum standards and condition before the borrower's application is accepted.

graduated payment mortgage   a form of financing in which the lender and borrower agree to a schedule of payments. The interest rate remains the same under most such arrangements, but the payment is increased at regular intervals. This allows the borrower to make fairly low payments for a number of years, and then to accelerate the principal.

Even without this feature written into the agreement, you can convert an FRM or an ARM mortgage into a graduated payment mortgage on your own, by adding to your monthly payment. If you enter a formal contractual arrangement for graduating payments with the lender, there could be a cost involved in refinancing. As payments begin to rise, you will want to replace the loan with another. If the lender has been allowing below-market payments, you will have to make up the difference to get out of the deal.

growing equity mortgage   another term for mortgage acceleration. The minimum payment is fixed, but payments are increased on a predetermined schedule, with the entire amount of additional payment going into the principal. A payoff is achieved much more rapidly than with the traditional amortization schedule.

The disadvantage of accelerating under contract is that you don't have as much control. If you accelerate by choice, you can always suspend the plan when money is tight, and start it up again later. If you have to accelerate by contract, then you cannot vary payments even when you might like to do so.

purchase money mortgage   a mortgage for the entire amount to be financed, or the purchase price minus the down payment. When the seller provides a purchase money mortgage, no outside lender is required. For many buyers and investors, this is the most attractive arrangement, because the seller might be more motivated to enter into a financing agreement than a lender would be. In addition, when the seller is also acting as the lender, a buyer does not need to go through the review a lending institution will impose.

rollover mortgage   a type of mortgage in which the lender and borrower agree to a term for repayment, often 15 or 30 years. However, the mortgage rate is rolled over, or renegotiated, every few years. For the lender, this allows for periodic changes to then-current interest rates, and avoids the problem of being stuck with very long-term commitments well below the market. For the borrower, the uncertainty can be offset by refinancing at a later date, if necessary.

second mortgage   a home mortgage that has a lower priority than another mortgage, in the event of default. Upon default, the first mortgagee has the first right to repayment of an outstanding balance. Once the first mortgage is satisfied, the second mortgage (and then any other liens) is repaid. Because the risks are greater when the mortgage is not in first position, second mortgages often call for much higher interest, to offset the risk to the lender.

seller financing   an arrangement in which the seller provides some of the financing. The buyer asks the seller to "carry a second": instead of getting all of the equity in cash at the time of closing, the seller gets some cash and some paper. The paper is a note, which is usually secured by a second deed of trust.

shared appreciation mortgage   a loan provided by the lender at a rate well below the market rate. This arrangement reduces the payment, but the lender is also entitled to a share of the profits when the home is sold, or at some specified date in the future. The shared profit might be payable only when the owner sells or after a certain number of years. In the latter instance, the amount due will be based on an appraisal, and the owner might need to take out additional financing to pay off the original lender.

shared equity mortgage   an agreement between an investor and the resident homeowner. Both contribute money to the down payment, or to monthly payments, or to both. Each side owns a share of the house. The investor is paid off, either by refinancing later or upon sale. For the homeowner, this arrangement might be the only way to afford a first home purchase. For the investor, it means tax benefits and future profits with minimal investment. (The next chapter explains equity sharing plans in more detail.)

VA loan   a loan whose repayment is guaranteed by the Veterans Administration (VA). An owner-occupant can apply for such a loan if he or she is a veteran or the spouse of a veteran. The loan is granted with little or no down payment and minimal closing costs, and may be repaid over a period as long as 30 years.

wraparound mortgage   an arrangement whereby the buyer assumes a loan that already exists, or takes over responsibility for paying the debt. Part of the remainder of the purchase price is financed with an additional mortgage, usually one on which the interest rate is higher. In combination, the rate of the two loans is lower than the current market rate. The total of payments is combined, or "wrapped."

By some definitions, a wraparound involves an original loan plus seller financing. The seller continues making payments on the original loan, even though the house has been sold; the buyer's direct payment to the seller consists of (a) the payment for the original loan and (b) a payment for a second mortgage owned by the seller.

THE IMPORTANCE OF CREATIVE FINANCING

Virtually all forms of creative financing, by nature, must involve some delay of interest expense or a higher level of interest payments. The house you buy with a creative form of financing will cost more than one bought with a more traditional method. In some versions, however, the buyer reduces his or her costs by shifting some of the burden to the seller. (A buy-down is an example.) Creative financing changes the way the purchase deal is put together, but it is still possible to shift some or all of that burden to the seller.

Creative financing might be appropriate for buyers, even when it means a higher cost of purchase. There are many instances in which you would be unable to buy a house, without some modification away from traditional financing. In fact, many people with a good understanding of real estate already know that a deal usually rests more on the financing terms than on the price. If you have the goals or circumstances described in the following sections, creative financing might be right for you.

Get Around Qualification Rules

From the borrower's point of view, the reason for even considering creative financing is the lender's qualification rules. If you can figure out some way to reduce monthly payments, even if only on a temporary basis, then the deal can be done. Failing that, everyone loses out. For many people, just getting in is the highest priority. A contract can always be refinanced later.

→ **ACTION ITEM** ←

Be persistent. Even if one lender turns down your application, try again with another. Not all lenders have the same qualification rules.

You might need to go as low as interest-only with your payments for a few years, and plan to refinance when a balloon payment comes due. Or, you may have to accept a shared-equity loan or a graduated payment loan, just so that the initial payment doesn't represent too high a percentage of your income.

Arrive at Affordable Payments Schedule

Some people look for creative alternatives because, although they can qualify, the monthly payments are too high. In this instance, creative financing might just delay the inevitable: they might not be able to buy a house costing as much as they want. Or, if the market is favorable, values could be built up during the period the property is held. In that case, the creative financing risk pays off. Remember, if you can't afford to keep a house (or any other investment), you always have the option to sell.

Implement Possible Growth of Market Value Above Financing Costs

People usually want to buy real estate because they recognize its basic value. For many, this is frustrating because they don't believe they can afford to get into the market. With creative financing methods, they could possibly get around the barriers that prevent many people from making a wise investment.

How can you know when housing values will outpace the cost of financing? The key factors are the cost of financing and the strength of the market in your area. There is no way to know the future. Real estate investments *overall* have proven to be valuable, but you may have to hold on to a property for many years. Your timing is critical. If you can afford to keep your real estate long enough, it will become profitable; you just can't know how long is "long enough." Your property might yield a fast profit, but you should not place yourself at risk, assuming that you will double your money in a few months.

Find Money for a Down Payment

Generally speaking, if you can't afford a down payment, you're probably not ready to go into real estate. However, as soon as that is said, exceptions begin to come to mind. For example, FHA and VA loans involve little or nothing down. If you can find a house that the owner is willing to finance, it might be possible to get in with no down payment. In some creative financing methods, you might be able to get around the down payment requirement altogether.

Finding no-down-payment deals is not easy; it demands a lot of research and acquisition of knowledge. With the right information in hand, you will understand how to make the real estate deals suited to your own financial situation. The financing is the key, not the asked price. For the home buyer who cannot meet the conventional rules and requirements, creative financing is a necessity.

The next chapter explains equity-sharing plans. These are not only creative; they are often practical ways for homeowners and investors to work together to buy a first house.

————— POINTS TO REMEMBER —————

▶ Study the different types of creative lending vehicles available. Use those that are beneficial to you.

▶ Remember that virtually all creative financing methods are likely to cost you more in the long run. Be sure you get a convenient arrangement as well as a financially sound one.

▶ You might need creative financing methods just to qualify. Be willing to spend more in this case, but also plan to refinance later, when your income is higher or your property is worth more.

▶ Use leverage if it makes sense and if you really know what you're doing. Otherwise, recognize that leverage is very expensive and should be avoided.

▶ Use creative financing to reduce payments to an affordable level, but be aware that to do so inevitably means higher interest costs.

▶ Use creative financing methods when you believe that your home's value will grow at a faster pace than the cost of borrowing.

7

The Shared Experience

*C*reative financing might not be the answer for everyone. Some borrowers cannot qualify for a loan, because they simply don't earn enough money. Or, even if they can qualify, the monthly payments are too high, their credit history is poor, or housing costs are too high in their region.

For these people, the choices are to do nothing or to look for the ultimate in creative financing: a partner who is willing to share equity while helping to buy that first home.

THE BASIC RULES

Like all good ideas, equity sharing only works if all of the parties involved are able to benefit. If a plan is beneficial to a lender and to an investor but not to the home buyer, then it won't work. All sides need to win, in order for any deal to make sense. The buyer needs to get the home at a reasonable price. The lender wants to get back the money it places at risk. An investor must be rewarded for helping the home buyer get the home. As long as the arrangement is fair, it can work well and satisfy everyone's needs.

In equity sharing, two people are involved in the purchase: the home buyer, who will live in the house, and the investor, who helps the buyer in one of several ways. The investor might supply the down payment, contribute part of the monthly payments, or co-sign a loan to satisfy the borrower's needs.

If the investor co-signs as a backup for the borrower, what does that mean? The investor is providing the lender with a guarantee of payments. The lender's risks are reduced because the investor is willing to ensure that payments will be made, even if the buyer defaults. Co-signing is more difficult to arrange today than in the past. Instead of just accepting a co-signer and approving the application, many lenders today demand that the borrower must still qualify for the loan without the co-signer's help.

Whether the arrangement is for partial payment of the monthly payments or the down payment, or is just a backup co-signing, the equity-sharing rules work in the same way. Let's look at an example involving a backup co-signing arrangement. The home buyer puts all of the down payment money into the deal *and* makes all of the payments. Let's assume that the buyer and the investor have agreed to share on a 50/50 basis. Here's how the co-signing works:

▸ The investor places no money into the deal. All the investor provides is the payment guarantee. By co-signing on the loan, the investor promises the lender that the mortgage will be paid.

The advantage to the investor is that, with no actual cash money in the deal, future equity will be earned. The risk is that, in the event of default, the investor's credit will be affected.

→ **ACTION ITEM** ←

Before seeking an equity share, find out what rules lenders will impose. Some will not lend on the standard arrangement, but will require that you put some money into the deal.

For the home buyer, this might be the only way to get a loan approved. The approval is worth giving up some future equity; the only other choice is to pass up a real estate opportunity altogether.

▸ The home buyer makes the full mortgage payment to the lender each month, just as he or she would if there were no equity partner. Half of the monthly payment is treated as a mortgage payment, and the other half is treated as rent. The buyer pays rent to the investor for half of the house because, in effect, the investor is renting half of the investment to the buyer. Accordingly, the investor can claim depreciation, and part of the maintenance costs of owning the home, as tax deductions. The investor must also report rental income for tax purposes.

▸ After a specified period of time, the home buyer has the right to buy out the investor. The purpose of equity sharing is to enable the buyer to get a first home while allowing the investor to earn a profit. By mutual agreement, the home buyer can buy out the investor's interest in the property after a certain period of time has passed. The exact details, limitations, minimum or maximum payments, and other contractual rules have to be worked out according to current law and the exact circumstances. The amount of future equity is determined by an appraisal or is based on the actual sale price.

Let's assume that the buyer put up the entire down payment, and the house was purchased for $100,000. By agreement, the two sides agree to share future profits on a 50/50 basis. However, the contract also states that the investor's share is to be valued at no less than $5,000. The buyer can buy out the investor at any time, but must pay off the investor upon sale or within 10 years, whichever comes first.

⟶ **ACTION ITEM** ⟵

Be extremely specific on the buy-out clause and put it in writing. Have the entire deal reviewed by your attorney *before* finalizing it.

Let's also assume that, after 3 years, property values are rising quickly. The home buyer decides it's time to buy out the investor, and wants to refinance in order to do so. The house is appraised at $120,000. The investor is entitled to 50 percent of the increase in equity, or $10,000:

Current appraised value	$120,000
Less: Purchase price	−100,000
Increased equity	$ 20,000
50 percent of increased equity	$ 10,000

This would not be an untypical example of equity sharing. However, some would-be buyers might think it unfair that the investor should earn half of the increased equity without having invested anything. They forget that, by pledging for the buyer, the investor enables the borrower to qualify for a loan. The investor risks his or her credit for the period of time the co-signature is on the title.

THE TAX STRATEGY

The income tax issues for real estate equity sharing can be quite complex, unless the arrangement is entered with a clear understanding. Only 100 percent of a deductible expense may be claimed. If both the home buyer and the investor think they are entitled to a deduction, the entire deal could be headed for trouble.

In addition, both sides should decide in advance how the payments will be handled. Should the homeowner pay the entire mortgage balance directly? Who will pay property taxes? Should payments be managed through a trust account? What expenses or payments, if any, will be handled by the investor? How will each side be able to monitor the other? An accountant with expertise in real estate and a lawyer familiar with equity sharing should be consulted, to get the deal going and keep both sides protected.

Here are the basic tax rules for equity sharing (all of the tax discussions are based on a 50/50 split):

▶ The home buyer owns only half of the house and can therefore claim only half of the normal itemized deductions. Each side owns only half of the property when the equity sharing is a 50/50 deal. If it is a 60/40, for example, then the percentages have to be changed accordingly.

The home buyer is entitled to an itemized deduction equal to half of the mortgage interest paid and half of the property taxes. The other half is a rental payment to the investor.

▶ The investor is allowed to deduct half of the usual expenses allowed to investors; these include items that homeowners cannot claim. Real estate investors can deduct not only the mortgage interest and property taxes, but a number of other items as well: fire insurance, maintenance expenses, and incidentals—mileage to check out the property, the cost of repairs and maintenance, and office supplies needed to keep books on the investment.

→ **ACTION ITEM** ←

You might be able to take 100 percent of the deductions the homeowner can't claim, but you will probably have to make the full payment. Check with a tax expert.

The equity-sharing rules work for both sides. If the arrangement is 50/50, then the investor is entitled to only half of the normal investment expenses. In addition, half of the mortgage payment made by the home buyer is to be treated as rental income. If the arrangement is other than on the basis of 50/50, the allowable portion has to be adjusted accordingly.

▶ The investor can deduct only half of the allowable depreciation, because he or she owns only half of the house. Real estate investors are allowed to write off residential investments over 27.5 years. Only the building and improvements can be claimed; land cannot be depreciated. In the case of equity sharing, only the investor's portion can be depreciated. For example, in a 50/50 arrangement for a $100,000 home, only half of the value of the building can be depreciated. If the land is valued at $25,000, the building is worth $75,000. The investor can depreciate half that value, or $37,500, over 27.5 years—an annual deduction of $1,364.

▶ Any money placed into the deal by the investor must be treated as equity, and not as a loan. Otherwise, the tax deductions could be lost. The advantages of equity sharing could be unintentionally lost because the investor's share is treated as a loan. Any money placed into the investment is an equity position, and not a loan. If it is written up as a note from the home buyer to the investor, then equity-sharing tax benefits will not be allowed.

▶ The entire equity-sharing arrangement must be entered into with a written contract. Without the contract, the tax benefits will not be allowed. You need a written contract in order to claim a legitimate equity-sharing deal. The tax write-offs will not be allowed by the Internal Revenue Service (IRS) without such a contract. In addition, the deal will be complicated enough that both sides should insist on putting the arrangement in writing. To not do so is asking for trouble later on.

COMMON-SENSE RULES

In addition to the rules set down for tax purposes, you should set some common-sense rules for yourself, whether you are the home buyer or the investor. These rules should include the following:

▶ Select property intelligently, whether an equity share is involved or not. Many investment plans go sour because the participants lose sight of their real purpose. They make selections based on the structure of the deal, rather than following their own instincts. For example, you probably have a fairly good idea of what attributes make a house a good investment. Whether you are the home buyer or the investor, those qualities remain the same. Whether you are the only investor involved or are going in with someone else, the features that make the house a worthwhile investment still apply.

—————————→ **ACTION ITEM** ←—————————
Enter equity-sharing deals only on properties you have selected. If you really want control of them, don't let the homeowner call all of the shots.

───────────────────────────

▶ Make sure the equity share works out profitably for both sides. Both the home buyer and the investor have to win. Both sides have to believe that the deal is profitable and worthwhile. Bad feelings will destroy the equity share—or any other joint venture. Fairness should govern the deal at the beginning as well as later, when one side buys out the interests of the other.

▶ Don't make any moves just to reduce taxes. It is easy to lose sight of your own investment goals; it is also far too easy to forget that you want to make a profit. Too many ill-advised moves have been made in the name of tax reduction. Keeping a mortgage in effect when you can afford to pay it off, for example, makes no economic sense. Doing anything because you think you need the tax write-off won't make sense, either. Before accepting that senseless notion, look at the numbers. Consider both the pretax and the after-tax profit or loss. Make your decision based on how the bottom line really works out.

▸ Set goals and establish target dates for establishing the equity-share arrangement, for one side's buy-out of the other, and for all other financial decisions. For example, the home buyer should be able to buy out the investor's interest at any time, with a guaranteed minimum, or should be allowed to sell or refinance after a specified period of time. These matters should always be put in writing.

▸ Honor your contract. Make sure it spells out the terms of the deal precisely, covering all bases and leaving no doubts open to interpretation. The contract should be extremely clear and easy to understand. You will need an attorney to phrase the contract correctly, and you should be willing to pay for good preventive legal advice on this arrangement. Once you have structured the deal and put it in writing, honor the contract—both the written one and the one you know you entered with your investment partner.

▸ Work with people you trust and like. A lot of people seem to think that it's the deal itself that counts—the money, the property, or the terms. Your deal will be pleasant or unpleasant based on how you and your partner get along with each other. You should trust and like the people with whom you go into business, whether full-time or in a temporary deal like an equity share. If you don't, the advantages you will get from the terms of the deal will not be worth the aggravation and conflict you will have to endure.

What portion of itemized deductions can each side claim in an equity-sharing arrangement?

Only the portion equal to its own share of the total ownership. For example, if you control 55 percent of the property, you are entitled to 55 percent of deductions.

Can the investor deduct more than the homeowner?

Yes. For an investor, operating expenses are all deductible. These include insurance, maintenance, and incidentals. However, the investor will probably be limited to deducting only the portion equal to the percentage of ownership, unless he or she pays more for those expenses.

Can the investor claim depreciation?

Yes, but again, subject to the ownership ratio. For example, if you control 45 percent of the property, you are entitled to 45 percent of the allowable depreciation.

What if I enter an equity-sharing arrangement by loaning money to the homeowner?

Then it's not a bona fide equity share. You will not be entitled to a deduction of any of the expenses associated with the property unless you actually have an equity position.

If I enter an equity share with a close friend or a relative, can it be done informally?

No. You always need a written contract for a real estate deal, even with a trusted friend or family member. If for no other reason, the written contract protects your tax position.

Will equity sharing work even with marginal houses?

The rules for selecting properties should apply, no matter what sharing arrangements you have. A well-chosen investment is better than one entered for the wrong reasons.

What if the deal is structured so that I make all of the profit? Isn't that a better idea for me?

No. Equity sharing works best when both sides benefit. A one-sided deal leads to trouble or abandonment later on.

Does equity sharing make sense as a tax dodge?

Under today's rules, you should not make any investment decisions primarily as a way to reduce taxes. Sound economic motives should rule your investment decisions, with tax benefits a secondary consideration.

Should the equity-sharing arrangement be open-ended?

It's a much better idea to set goals and target dates. For example, you and the occupant might want to select a tentative date for a buy-out.

What intangible considerations are involved in equity sharing?

Because you as an investor will have to work with an occupant-homeowner, the whole arrangement makes more sense if you trust and like the other person. If your instincts tell you not to enter a long-term contract with someone, you should listen to yourself very carefully.

THE SALE–LEASEBACK

Another plan of creative financing, the sale–leaseback, is very similar to the equity share but has some notable distinctions. It most often occurs between family members.

Imagine this situation: An elderly woman needs more income than is currently being earned through social security and a modest retirement plan. Her home is owned free and clear and has a lot of equity. Her son would like to purchase a home but does not have enough money for a down payment. Because he is earning a high salary, he would also like to have the tax benefits associated with owning a home.

Both the mother and the son would achieve their immediate goals through a sale–leaseback. The mother sells her home to her son, who then leases it back to his mother. Because the mother also finances the purchase, her monthly income from rent should adequately cover the rent payment and still provide additional income. The son then has interest expenses and property taxes to write off. Because the house is a rental, the son can write off maintenance expenses, homeowner's insurance, and other expenses of owning the investment property.

→ ACTION ITEM ←

Check with your attorney before trying to put together a sale–leaseback contract. Be sure tax considerations are included in the structure of the contract.

For a sale-leaseback to be acceptable to the IRS, the following rules should be observed:

▶ The lease must be written. If you enter a sale-leaseback agreement with your parents, be sure to put the terms of the lease in writing. If you don't, it could be considered as something other than a lease, such as a plan to reduce taxes by shifting benefits from a parent to a child. In addition, you need to specify in the lease that the parent is being given a life estate in the property (if that's the plan). Otherwise, you have to allow for the contingency of where the parent (or parents) will live after you sell the house. For example, you might want to not grant a life estate, in the fear that the day may come when your parents have to be moved to a rest home.

▶ The lease payments should be comparable to market levels in your area. It is essential that the lease arrangement you enter into is a legitimate lease, not a sham for tax purposes. The rent you charge your parents has to approximate the level of rents charged for comparable homes in the same area.

▶ You should exchange checks each month. In a sale-leaseback, interest and rent are offset. The buyer (child) owes interest—and possibly principal—on a loan. The seller/renter (parent) owes rent. For practical reasons, think about paying the net difference between these amounts. For example, if rent is $600 and the mortgage payment is $750, give mom and dad a check for $150.

You're safer if each payment is made separately each month. The parent should write out a check for $600 and the child should make the full mortgage payment of $750. This system helps establish the legitimate nature of the lease and keeps things clean for IRS inspection.

▶ The arrangement works only if both sides get what they need and want. The sale-leaseback is only practical if both sides benefit from it. The parent would be interested only if he or she needed more income per month. If all of the mortgage payment is used to pay rent, the parent doesn't achieve his or her goal. The child wants tax benefits and investment value, but might not be able to afford negative cash flow. If the mortgage payment is substantially higher than the rent, the whole idea could fail.

The child should be able to pay substantially more than the parent is paying in rent because, without the sale-leaseback, the child would be paying rent somewhere else. Any objection that an extreme difference in the monthly exchange of funds is a hardship has to be mitigated by this fact.

The sale–leaseback idea has been practiced more widely on the commercial side of real estate than on the residential side. For example, a company builds a multiple-story building for its headquarters. After the construction phase is complete, the company decides to sell the building and lease from the new owner some (or all) of the space it needs.

Why would a company prefer leasing to owning, and why would it give up potential growth in market value? In some circumstances and in some types of businesses, it could be possible to earn a higher rate of return by converting real estate investment to working capital. If the rate of return from the operation of a business is greater than the return from investing in real estate, then the sale–leaseback makes sense.

Either an equity-sharing plan or a sale–leaseback should be used as a creative alternative only in the following circumstances:

▶ Both sides will win. Any joint venture involves a risk beyond what the numbers show. For a variety of reasons, the partners might not get along well, see eye-to-eye, or even concur as to what the agreement really is. One side might get scared and want to reverse the terms. These possibilities can turn a seemingly logical and sensible idea into a difficult situation.

Be certain that you and the other people involved are completely happy with the terms, and that both sides can see how they will profit from entering the agreement.

▶ You need to work with someone else. Creative financing enables you to do things you would not otherwise be able to do, but it should only be used when you have no other way. For example, you (or the other side) can't get financing; or you have invested broadly and lenders won't allow you to commit yourself further, but they will let you co-sign for someone else; or you and a relative both have financial and tax needs that can be satisfied creatively. All of these situations point to the possibility that an equity share or sale–leaseback will help.

Avoid entering into a deal merely because you like the arrangement and would like to experience it, or because it seems like an attractive deal to someone else. You need to understand it *and* to need it.

▶ You thoroughly understand how the deal works. Any contract should be understood completely, before you sign. Never enter a contract in which you have not exhaustively researched your questions and received answers that satisfied your concerns.

▶ You are aware of all the tax benefits or consequences of the deal. Never enter into a contract solely for tax reasons. Many poor decisions have been made because of a tax motive, only to be regretted later. When you are motivated by taxes, you will often make poor decisions.

Know how your taxes will be affected, and know the rules for qualifying for all deductions you plan to claim. Especially in situations such as equity sharing, you must take great care to structure the deal so that it meets all of the rules. Otherwise, you could lose valuable tax benefits.

▶ The contract defines how and when the deal will be canceled or closed out. Every deal has to be finite; it needs a beginning and an end. You could conceivably enter into a real estate contract that could go on indefinitely and satisfy all parties. But the contract should also give you and your partners a way out, if a situation develops where that would be desirable. If that option is missing, it's a bad contract. You don't have to *take* the way out, but it should be there, as a way to escape if you really want to end the contract.

The next chapter explains how mortgage amortization is calculated, and how the various interest tables work. Any deal you enter will involve calculations of interest. You should never automatically trust someone else to calculate interest for you; you should know how to perform the calculations yourself.

—————— POINTS TO REMEMBER ——————

▶ Learn the basic rules for equity sharing, and be sure the buyer understands them, too.

▶ Make sure you can find a lender that will work with you as an investor in an equity share.

▶ Arrange the deal so that you maximize your tax benefits, but only after consulting with a tax expert to make sure you follow the rules.

▶ Identify the buy-out term specifically, to avoid any trouble in the future.

▶ Always pick properties for sound investment reasons, and never only to accommodate an equity-share deal.

▶ Be sure to work with people you like and trust. The equity share is a partnership, and you will be involved with the buyer for several years to come.

▶ Check with a professional tax adviser before signing a contract for a sale–leaseback.

▶ Put the entire deal in writing.

8

Unraveling the Mystery

*T*he process of buying a house through a long-term mortgage is unavoidably connected to the calculation of compound interest. Many people would prefer to let the lender figure out how much interest to charge,
and waive the need to know how to make the calculations on their own.

Their attitude is understandable, but lenders can and do make mistakes, even when their calculations are done by computer. You might
save a lot of money by policing the lender. You're more in control when
you can track the lender's calculations and compare them to your own.
If you're off by a few pennies, that's probably a consequence of rounding. But if there is a large difference, you should contact the lender and
ask for an explanation.

In Chapter 1, the precise method of calculating mortgage interest was
explained. Let's briefly review this procedure before going on to how to
apply the mortgage amortization formula, set up your own record, and
use interest tables. None of the subject matter here is so complex that
you cannot master it with a few minutes of study. Once you know how
it's done, you'll have more control over your financial future, if only
because you understand what calculations the lender uses.

CALCULATING PRINCIPAL
AND INTEREST

To quickly review how interest works, remember that mortgages are
usually calculated with monthly compounding. You make a payment

once per month; part of it goes toward interest and part to principal. The interest is an expense, and the principal payments reduce the debt balance. Only the interest can be deducted as an itemized deduction on your tax return. Because interest payments are very high during the earlier years of the mortgage term, your deduction is also higher. It reduces gradually, over the years you have the mortgage.

The higher your debt balance, the higher the amount of your payment that goes toward interest. If you make an additional payment, even a modest one, toward principal in the earlier mortgage years, that will save interest for the remainder of your loan term. This method reduces your tax benefit somewhat, but the savings—even on an after-tax basis—in overall housing costs are significant.

The basic interest formula involves principal, an interest rate, a compounding method, and time. The principal, in the case of a mortgage, is the outstanding debt. The interest rate is expressed on an annual basis. The compounding method is usually monthly for mortgages: the effective monthly rate is $1/12$ of the annual rate. The time involved determines how much of a total payment (principal plus interest) is required to repay the loan by the due date. For example, a higher payment is needed to pay off a loan in 15 years, because more has to go toward principal each month; a lower payment is required for a 30-year loan.

Let's take an example of 10 percent per year, compounded monthly. To calculate the monthly interest, divide the annual rate by 12 (months):

$$\frac{10.00\%}{12} = .833\%$$

To make it possible to figure the interest using a calculator, let's express this monthly interest rate in decimal form. You were taught in school that, to convert a percentage to its decimal form, you need to move the decimal point two places to the left. Your .833 percent becomes .00833 in decimal form.

Next, let's assume you're starting out with a mortgage balance of $80,000. By referring to the amortization table (Appendix A), you see that a 10 percent mortgage amortized over 30 years requires a monthly payment of $702.06. (The tables are discussed later.) How does the payment of $702.06 break down?

The monthly interest rate is applied against the outstanding loan balance, so you need only to multiply that loan balance by the decimal form of the monthly rate:

$$\$80,000 \times .00833 = \$666.67$$

If you try this math using only the few digits expressed above, you will find that, due to rounding, the interest payment comes out somewhat lower. For example, using the exact numbers above, the payment would be $666.40. Because .00833 has a $1/3$ digit at the end, the closest rounded interest level is $666.67.

Next, subtract the interest from the total payment to arrive at the principal amount:

Total payment	$702.06
Less: Interest	−666.67
Principal payment	$ 35.39

The principal payment for the first month of this loan is only $35.39. The loan's balance forward, reduced by this amount, goes from $80,000 to $79,964.61. The second month's payment will be slightly more to principal and slightly less to interest (about 30 cents).

The shift from interest to principal seems painfully slow, with a 30-year amortization. From the first to the second month, only 30 cents more goes to principal! This loan will be only half paid off in its 24th year. Eventually, as the balance outstanding declines, more and more finally goes into principal.

TRACKING YOUR DEBT

Keep close tabs on your debt by tracking it monthly. Do a calculation of your own, keep a record of it, and compare it to your lender's reports. Some lenders report the balance each month; others give you details only at the end of the year. If your lender doesn't give you frequent breakdowns and reports on the outstanding balance, check with the lender quarterly. Find out what is stated as the outstanding balance. Investigate any discrepancies, before a full year goes by.

Keep a running record like the one shown in Figure 8-1. Each month, write down the date and amount of your payment. You have the

Mortgage Record

Lender _____

Address _____

City_____

Telephone _____

Contact Person _____

Loan Number _____ Interest Rate _____

DATE	PAYMENT	INTEREST	PRINCIPAL	BALANCE

Figure 8-1
Sample format of mortgage record.

right to pay a little extra whenever you want and have it applied against the principal balance. In that way, you can reduce the total interest— and the cost of your home. You can also cut down the number of months required to pay off your debt.

Following are some advantages you have by keeping track of your mortgage balance from one month to another:

▶ You might catch a lender's error. Lenders often have powerful internal systems and automated processes of the highest caliber. Still, they are managed and input by humans, and a slip of someone's fingers can mean a big difference in the way your loan is amortized. Knowing how the process is done will help you to act as a watchdog in your own behalf.

Lender errors might be rare, but would you want to be the home buyer whose account had an expensive undetected error in it? Take charge of your financial future by applying some diligence in your own behalf. You could save yourself thousands of dollars.

▶ You'll have help in tracking your mortgage acceleration and making sure that your extra payment is applied correctly. Many people accelerate mortgages in a modest way, perhaps adding $10 to $20 per month to the principal payment. What would you do if you found out the lender was applying that payment incorrectly? For example, what if the lender added it to impound balances, allowing it to grow to a large sum? In that case, you would get no interest and no acceleration. Worst of all, you wouldn't *know*, unless you were figuring out the acceleration for yourself. By knowing what the balance should be, you can easily compare your records to those of the lender.

→ ACTION ITEM ←

Check the lender's figures every month. Never assume the lender doesn't make mistakes.

▶ Your running record will help you with tax planning. As you approach the end of the year, you will probably want to estimate your tax liability, to know either what you will owe or what you will be getting back in the form of a refund. If your lender reports to you only at the end of the year, you have to wait for the report before you can accurately estimate your interest expense and itemized deductions. The more information you have on hand, the more accurately you can plan ahead. Your running record is one more way in which you can take charge of your financial future.

▶ Knowing how the calculation works puts you in control of your finances. You won't be at the mercy of the lender's computer. You have probably seen, time and again, an attitude that, if "the computer says" something is so, that's the end of the discussion. How often have you thought it would be nice to know how it works? You should be able to check on the computer because, alarmingly, computers are as full of errors as are other systems. They are programmed by people, and all of the information that goes into and comes out of computers is generated by flawed humans, like you and me.

Why is interest higher in the early years of the mortgage, and lower in the later years?

Interest is computed based on the current outstanding loan balance. The higher the balance, the higher the amount of your payment that goes to interest.

How is each month's interest figured?

The monthly interest is $1/12$ of the annual interest rate. If your mortgage is 10 percent, each month's interest is .833 percent.

Why do I need to know my monthly interest?

Because that's how you figure your interest each month. Multiply the monthly interest by the balance of the loan, to calculate this month's interest expense.

How do you figure principal?

Deduct interest from the total payment. The answer is principal, which reduces your loan balance.

Why should I figure the breakdown each month, when the lender does it for me?

For several reasons. You could catch a rare error. It's important to know how your mortgage payments are being applied. Do it as part of your financial control.

Can I pay more to principal?

Millions of homeowners send in a little extra to pay down their loan more quickly. By tracking the loan each month, you can make sure the lender applies your extra payment correctly.

Will keeping this record help with my taxes?

It is certainly useful to be able to plan your taxes at least 1 year in advance. Once you know how to track interest and set up your record, you have much more information than you do without it.

Why can't I just trust the lender's computer?

You probably can, although occasional errors do occur. The major reason, though, is to give yourself control and not have to depend on what the lender reports to you.

THE AMORTIZATION TABLE

Calculating the amount of interest and principal to be applied each month is not difficult. You would not want to calculate each and every month for 30 years. A lot of time and 360 calculations would be involved. But you might wonder, how is the right amount arrived at? In other words, how do you use the interest amortization table?

If you refer to Appendix A, you will find a series of interest amortization tables. The various tables report monthly compounding at stated rates of interest. Each table includes a number of different loan amounts up to $100,000.

The amortization tables have a number of easy-to-use features. They include the following:

▶ Each interest amortization table identifies the compounding method used. In Appendix A, "monthly" is always indicated in the headings. Be aware, however, that, in other sources, such as interest amortization books, other compounding methods might be in use. Always be sure you're using the right method.

▶ A wide array of tables is available. We are dealing strictly with payments required to amortize a loan. That is one of six types of interest tables. If you own a book of tables, you will find up to five other types within the book. As confusing as it might seem, each of the different tables serves a distinct purpose. For mortgage management, you only need to know about one table.

▸ Each table is clearly marked for an interest rate. By studying and comparing one rate to another, you can see how significantly a slight change affects the total cost of a home over the long haul. For example, a 10 percent loan for $80,000 requires payments of $702.06 per month. If the same loan were available at 10.5 percent, the payments would be $731.80 per month. That payment difference of $29.74 per month adds up over 30 years to a total of more than $10,000.

▸ The amount of required payment varies, based on the loan amount. That might seem obvious; in one respect, it is. But to those unfamiliar with the time value of money, it's a point worth making. The more you borrow, the more you need to pay, in order to retire your loan.

▸ The loan's number of years affects the payments required per month; they vary according to the repayment schedule. If you want to repay a loan in 5 years, you would be required to make substantially higher payments than for a 30-year schedule. The tables specify the repayment term in years.

—————————————→ **ACTION ITEM** ←—————————————

Look at the amortization tables in Appendix A. Identify each of the features listed above for the table that most closely represents the mortgage you have on your house.

TWO TYPES OF TABLES

The tables shown in Appendix A list the actual amount of monthly payment. The major advantage of this presentation is that, at a glance, you can easily see how payments change over time—not only because of the interest rate and amount, but because of the number of years involved. In that respect, the amount tables are convenient.

Their major inconvenience is that, when the amount of a loan is not listed, you have to add two or more different amounts together.

WEALTH   *Amount-Listed Table.* Paul and Nancy are seeking a
BUILDING   mortgage loan in the amount of $42,550, to be repaid
PROFILE   in 30 years. Referring to a book of amount-listed tables for interest amortization, Paul and Nancy need to
add together several different amounts:

Amount	Monthly Payment
$40,000	$351.03
2,000	17.56
500	4.39
50	.44
$42,550	$373.42

Several steps may be required to get the amount of monthly payment for a loan with an odd amount. The convenience of the amount-
listed tables becomes somewhat offset by the awkward problem
involved in this situation. Because not every amount can be listed, the
tables can be difficult to use.

A second type of table solves this problem. Some books of tables
offer factors rather than amounts. A factor is multiplied by the loan
amount, and the result is the monthly payment. This type of table is
easy to use in the situation above, but the table reveals less information for scanning and comparing.

Factor tables are not as easy to use for comparing rates and payment levels from one interest rate to another, nor from one loan
amount or repayment term to another. The factors are too remote to
relate to dollars and cents.

The factors in the tables look like this, for a 10 percent rate of
interest, compounded monthly:

Years	Factors	Years	Factors
21	0.0095078	22	0.0093825
23	0.0092718	24	0.0091739
25	0.0090870	26	0.0090098
27	0.0089410	28	0.0088796
29	0.0088248	30	0.0087757

To see how this table works, refer to the earlier Wealth Building Profile. Paul and Nancy's loan amount was $42,550. Multiply this by the factor in the row for 30 years:

$$\$42,550 \times 0.0087757 = \$373.41$$

The total is within one penny of the previously figured monthly payment, because of rounding. In this instance, having a list of factors is more convenient than having only the amounts for selected levels of mortgage loans.

———————————→ **ACTION ITEM** ←———————————

Calculate your mortgage payment using both methods explained above. Compare your calculations to what your lender charges. Remember, if you are off a few pennies, it's because of rounding.

For the purpose of studying the tables to see the differences in rates, repayment terms, and amounts borrowed, the amount-listed tables have definite advantages. For fast calculations of odd amounts, select the factor-listed tables.

INTERPOLATING THE PAYMENT

Books of amortization tables generally include information for every ¼ percent, at the most. You can find out the monthly payment at 10, 10.25, 10.5, and 11.0 percent, but not for the percentages in between. In comparison, lenders may quote rates at ⅛ percent intervals. They may write your loan at 10.125, 10.375, 10.625, or 10.875 percent. In these cases, how do you figure out the monthly payment?

You can get a very accurate idea by learning how to interpolate, or estimate, the payment. This can be done using either a payment-listed or factor-listed table. The examples here are based on payments, because complete tables of this type are shown in Appendix A.

WEALTH   *Estimating Payments.* Keith and Lorraine have
BUILDING   been offered financing at 10.125 percent. Their book
PROFILE   of monthly payments shows only 10.0 and 10.25 percent payments. To figure out the required payment
for an $80,000 loan for 30 years, they must follow these steps:

1. Find the monthly payment for the interest rate above and below
    their target rate. The 10.0 percent payment would be $702.06;
    the 10.25 percent payment would be $716.89.

2. Find the average of the two payments identified in step 1. Add
    them together, and then divide by 2:

$$\frac{\$702.06 + \$716.89}{2} = \$709.48$$

The approximate monthly payment required for an $80,000 loan, to
be repaid over 30 years at 10.125 percent interest, is $709.48.

Interpolating when you don't have the ¼ percent tables requires
more steps.

WEALTH   *A Step Further.* What if Keith and Lorraine had a
BUILDING   book that showed only ½ percent payments? An extra
PROFILE   step would be needed, as follows:

1. Find the monthly payment for the interest rate above and below
    their target rate. The 10.0 percent payment would be $702.06;
    and the 10.5 percent payment would be $731.80.

2. Find the average of the two payments identified in step 1. Add
    them together and then divide by 2:

$$\frac{\$702.06 + \$731.80}{2} = \$716.93$$

3. Step 2 is the interpolated payment for the midpoint between
    10.0 and 10.5, or for 10.25 percent. Next, interpolate the

required payment by averaging this payment and the already known payment for 10.0 percent:

$$\frac{\$702.06 + \$716.93}{2} = \$709.50$$

Using this method, the outcome is only 2 cents higher than in the previous example. For most applications, this is close enough. You do not need each and every table that is available, as long as you can interpolate when you need to.

REMAINING BALANCE TABLES

One final type of table, the remaining balance table, is useful in controlling your mortgage. This table shows the percentage of a loan that remains outstanding at the end of each year.

Remaining balance tables are useful in several ways:

▸ They demonstrate exactly how mortgages are paid off over the term. The remaining balance table shows with extreme clarity what it takes to pay off a mortgage. (See Appendix B.) Under the 10 percent remaining balance table, you can see that only half of a 30-year loan is paid off at about the 24th year. Compare the repayment schedule for shorter repayment terms, and you'll have a very clear idea about what your house really costs.

▸ They help you to plan ahead and to target repayment ideas, or to determine how and when to accelerate payments. Good planning requires information. With the remaining balance tables, you can decide how and when to repay your loan, and even devise a plan for your own refinancing. Used in combination with the amortization table, the remaining balance table can help you to pick the best possible plan for your circumstances.

▸ They help you identify the likely equity available for refinancing in the future. Let's say you plan to refinance your home in 3 years. You assume some rate of market growth, based on the past. In addition, you are building equity through your monthly payments. The remaining balance tables give you an idea of how much equity you can expect to have in the future. The unknown in this case is the current market value of your home.

The amortization table and remaining balance table are very useful tools, when you decide to take control of your financial future. The next chapter explores the details of mortgage acceleration. The tables will come in handy, once you begin examining the advantages of eliminating your mortgage debt more rapidly than your lender requires.

―――――――― **POINTS TO REMEMBER** ――――――――

▸ Study the methods for calculating principal and interest on your loan. Get to a point where you know how to do it quickly and easily.

▸ Check your lender's calculations every month.

▸ Track your debt, especially when you're accelerating your mortgage. Make sure the lender is applying extra payments correctly.

▸ Learn how to read amortization tables, so that you can plan and manage your finances directly.

▸ Become familiar with both types of amortization tables. Use the one that is most comfortable for you.

▸ Learn how to estimate your payment through the use of interpolation.

▸ The remaining balance table is a useful financial tool. Learn how to read it as an aid in making decisions about your mortgage.

9

Speeding Up the Debt

When it comes to buying a house, the question might well be: "Do you want to spend $100,000, or do you want to spend $270,000?"

We would all answer $100,000. But if you settle for that 30-year mortgage and don't accelerate, then, in fact, you are paying the higher amount. These figures are based on a purchase of a $100,000 home with $20,000 down and a 30-year, fixed-rate mortgage at 10 percent.

Mortgage acceleration has been previously mentioned several times in this book. This chapter shows in more detail when and why the idea makes sense and saves money—and how you can take control of your finances and determine the cost of your home more effectively.

It isn't just saving money that matters so much; it's the bottom line, the true cost of your home. Deciding to accelerate your mortgage can save $100,000 or more over the repayment term, and can cut the repayment term in half. When you consider how such time and money savings affect your financial plan, the need for taking control over your mortgage becomes obvious.

Some facts about mortgages and interest (based on mortgages with rates of 10 percent, to be repaid on a 30-year term) are worth noting:

▶ If you make one additional payment (equal to the monthly payment) at the beginning of the 30-year term, your repayment period is reduced by 1 full year.

▶ Paying an extra $25 per month will reduce a 30-year mortgage by about 5 years, because principal is reduced more rapidly.

130

▶ Paying an extra $100 every month will reduce the repayment term by about 12 years. Because interest is assessed on the outstanding balance each month, the more acceleration, the faster the loan is repaid.

▶ The money you put into accelerating your mortgage can be thought of as an investment. That money "earns" a compounded rate of return equal to what you are paying on your mortgage. In other words, when you cut your interest costs over time, you are, in effect, putting money in the bank and earning interest on your savings.

A SENSIBLE IDEA

Mortgage acceleration makes sense—much of the time. That statement is qualified because there are cases when acceleration is not smart. For example, if you can earn a higher return elsewhere with a comparable level of risk, then it wouldn't make sense to pay off your mortgage rapidly. You could have a very long-term, low-interest mortgage costing you far below what you can earn in other safe investments.

→ ACTION ITEM ←

Using the amortization tables in Appendix A, calculate the savings you would achieve by taking 5 years off your repayment term. How much will you save? How much will it change your monthly payment?

You need to understand that mortgage acceleration is an illiquid investment decision. You cannot get your money back once it is spent, except in one of two ways: refinancing, or selling the house. Either of those alternatives could be unacceptable, unless you have carefully planned ahead.

With these qualifications in mind, consider why it usually makes sense to accelerate your mortgage and to think of your acceleration as an investment:

▶ The rate of return is higher than the rate you can earn in most other places. This is the point that critics stubbornly ignore, time and again. If you are spending money on a high-rate mortgage, you are *losing* that rate of return each month. It's the exact opposite of earning an equally high rate of return on a good investment. If you accelerate a 12 percent mortgage, you are *earning* 12 percent on your money—as you would by placing the same amount in an investment.

The true profit from mortgage acceleration is equal to the percentage you are paying on your mortgage. If your mortgage charges 12 percent, that's what you earn with each dollar added to your principal payment.

▸ Acceleration is an extremely safe investment. A different investment that matches or exceeds the rate you're paying on your mortgage is *not* necessarily a comparable investment. You must consider not only the rate of return, but the risk level as well. For example, your home is insured through homeowner's insurance. You are there every day, maintaining the investment and protecting it. Based on historical information, you have every reason to believe your home will grow steadily in value over the years.

However, a mutual fund that has historically yielded as much as your home is not insured, nor can you depend on its steady growth. Furthermore, you have no control over the value of shares. The same rate of return, or even a higher rate, does not mean the two investment choices are comparable.

▸ You can cut the cost of your home by as much as $100,000 or more. The real cost of your house depends on the amount of interest you will pay over the term of your mortgage. A $100,000 house, with 20 percent paid down, $80,000 financed, and a 30-year, fixed-rate mortgage of 10 percent, costs $272,742. If that mortgage can be accelerated so that it's paid off in 14 years, the total cost is $168,944, or $103,798 less. This is accomplished by increasing payments by $184.51 per month. The numbers can be examined any number of ways, and the savings will still be significant—not only in money, but in time. Your mortgage will be eliminated completely in 15 years rather than in 30 years.

▸ You can reduce the repayment term by half. With a relatively small amount of extra payment per month, the repayment term can be cut significantly. Examine the amortization tables in Appendix A, to see how rapidly the repayment term falls when you contribute a few extra dollars each month. Using the 10 percent tables as an illustration, 5 years are cut from an $80,000 mortgage by adding only $25 per month; about 12 years come off by adding $100 per month. The additional payments are *not* money spent and gone. The investment of additional payments reduces interest costs significantly.

▶ It becomes possible, through mortgage acceleration, to plan and control your financial future. All of the points that can be made in favor of mortgage acceleration point to one basic fact: the concept makes sense for homeowners. It cuts costs and repayment term, builds equity faster than the contractual plan, and, most of all, it puts *you* in charge of your future.

   If you know how amortization works (you have the easy formula in hand) and you are tracking the mortgage from month to month, then you can plan and schedule your repayment. You are in control of your housing costs, because you know when the debt will be repaid. For investors, it could make more sense to take the highly leveraged approach, allowing tenants to pay the mortgage while controlling as many properties as possible. For homeowners, the desire should be to build equity quickly, to determine the date the mortgage will be repaid, and to take control.

▶ You can start, stop, increase, or decrease the degree of acceleration whenever you want. You might have to agree to a 30-year mortgage, just to qualify for the lender's rules, but it might still be desirable to repay the mortgage more rapidly. With this informal approach, you can easily start and stop the acceleration plan whenever you want. The flexibility to alter your investment is an important benefit. For example, an emergency might occur, putting a strain on your budget. You may want to suspend acceleration for a few months. Of, if you receive a promotion and a raise that increases your take-home pay by $200 per month, you might decide to put half of the new income into accelerated mortgage payments.

▶ Acceleration increases equity, even if you move before the repayment of the mortgage. You might think mortgage acceleration makes sense only if you plan to stay in your home for the full 30 years. It also makes sense if you are planning to move sooner or if you just don't know yet how long you'll stay. The more you accelerate today, the more rapidly you build equity within a few years.

   You can see the effects of accelerating by checking the remaining balance tables, in Appendix B. Using 10 percent as an example, let's see what happens to mortgages of different terms. Let's base our assumptions on the belief that you will sell and move after being in your house about 5 years (the length of time the average first-time home buyer stays).

With a 30-year mortgage of $80,000, you will have a remaining balance of 96.6 percent after 5 years. That means you will have paid off 3.4 percent, or $2,720. Remember, though, that over the same 60 months, your payments totaled $42,124. Of that, $39,404 went to interest!

→ **ACTION ITEM** ←

Calculate how much your mortgage will be paid down after 5 years. What difference would it make if you added $25 per month?

If you had accelerated the same mortgage over a 15-year schedule, the outcome would have been quite different. Your payments, at $859.69 per month, would have totaled $51,581 over 60 months. After 5 years, the remaining balance would have been 81.3 percent, so the mortgage would have been 18.7 percent paid off. You would have built equity by $14,640, or $11,920 more than with the 30-year schedule. Yet, your payments would have been only $9,457 higher. By accelerating your mortgage over the 5 years you owned the house, you profited by $5,183 (the difference between increased equity and higher monthly payments). To summarize the comparison:

	30-Year Term	*15-Year Term*	*Difference*
5-year remaining balance	96.6%	81.3%	−15.3%
Total payments	$42,124	$51,581	$ 9,457
Interest	$39,404	$36,941	$ 2,463
Principal	$ 2,720	$14,640	$11,920

Why should I accelerate my mortgage payments?

Acceleration is the most direct way for you to control what your house costs. By prepaying your principal, you can reduce your housing costs by $100,000 or more.

That seems like an exaggeration. How could I possibly save six figures?

It's not an exaggeration at all. Multiply your payments by the number of months you will make payments on your mortgage. Then imagine cutting $100,000 from that cost. It's not that hard to do.

I can only afford about $25 more per month. That's hardly worth the trouble, isn't it?

If you're paying 10 percent on a 30-year mortgage, that additional $25 per month will cut 5 years from your repayment term.

But I'd rather invest the money. Isn't acceleration a poor idea?

Acceleration is an investment. The return is equal to the compounded rate you're paying on your mortgage. You're unlikely to find an investment that can equal that return each and every year with as little risk.

Then why don't more people accelerate?

Because the advantages are not widely understood. People hesitate to save, especially when the method is so illiquid.

Why is acceleration considered an illiquid investment?

Because the only ways to get the money back out are to either sell the house or take out another loan.

Aren't illiquid investments bad?

Not always. But before you accelerate, you should be sure you have an adequate liquid cash reserve.

What is the most important advantage in accelerating?

It places you in direct control of the cost of your house and allows you to determine your financial future.

But what if I change my mind later? How do I get out of the acceleration plan?

As long as you decide when and how much to accelerate, you can start, stop, increase, decrease, or suspend payments at your own choosing.

Why does acceleration have the greatest effect in the early years?

Because most of your payment is going to interest in the first few years. For example, when your 30-year mortgage of 10 percent has been paid for 5 years, only 3.4 percent of your principal balance has been paid off. After 24 years, only about half of the debt has been repaid.

TYPES OF PLANS

There are a number of methods you can use to speed up the repayment of your mortgage debt. The method you choose should be the most convenient and suitable for your own budget, priorities, and current financial status. The nice feature of self-designed acceleration plans is that they can be changed whenever you want.

The most difficult part of such a plan is discipline. Because you will do best if you stick to the plan you select, you need a way to make it part of a routine. Choosing a specific amount and paying that amount each month helps to make the plan consistent; the payments become a part of your budget. You won't miss the money because it is built into the payment itself, each and every month.

A successful plan should suit your budget and your personal financial goals. It must also be practical, given the limitations of income and other expenses you have to meet. Select your plan from among the following:

▶ Add the same amount each month. Perhaps the most successful techniques for acceleration are designed in recognition of a problem: we do not easily follow our own plans, in order to reach our goals. Thus, putting aside the same amount each month is often critical if we are to achieve our goals, whether the money is put into a savings account or applied against a mortgage debt. Add the same amount to your principal and interest payment each month, and you will be able to calculate the precise repayment date. Use the amortization tables in Appendix A to estimate the number of years it will take. By comparing the payments in one column to those in another, you will be able to coordinate the desired repayment term with your personal budget.

▸ Put a portion of your pay raises into acceleration. Another problem with acceleration is that your budget might not allow the necessary flexibility. By committing a portion of your pay raises to the plan, you will be able to exert financial control and repay your mortgage sooner, without affecting your family budget. You might put half of your newly added take-home pay into the plan, for example, and use the other half to help with the budget.

▸ Base the monthly payment on the desired pay-off date. Calculate when you want to repay your mortgage, and then devise the payment amount that will reach that goal. If you cannot afford the payment required to meet the goal, pay what you can. Financial conditions will change in the future, and you might well reach your goal by changing your plan again in a few years. The amount of acceleration should be determined by your financial goals, even if you cannot ensure reaching them in one step, right now.

▸ Accelerate with income tax refunds. Some families, already strained from one month to another, don't have the immediate resources for mortgage acceleration. Some disciplined budgeting and careful planning might help, but adding extra payments to the family budget, at least right away, could prove too much of a burden. One alternative is to use annual income tax refunds to accelerate the mortgage. A $300 refund is the equivalent of paying $25 per month toward a faster repayment and, if kept up from year to year, takes 5 years off the 30-year repayment term.

▸ Use the biweekly method, but devise your own plan. If you are paid every 2 weeks instead of twice per month, you have 26 pay periods per year. At times, the timing of payday can create a budgeting problem—or an opportunity. In practice, you try to budget half of the paycheck every other week, to cover the mortgage, which comes up 12 times per year. But if you budget half of *every* paycheck, you could save for 13 payments. That extra payment each year can be applied toward principal.

Some companies offer biweekly plans designed, as their ads say, to help you repay your mortgage quickly. But there is no magic to these plans. You can repay on your own. Most of the companies offering such plans are selling insurance, which is paid for partially with the extra payment. You don't need to buy extra insurance, but you can put your 13th payment into principal payments each month.

Try this method. When you receive the year's first paycheck, deposit half of the monthly mortgage amount into your savings account. Continue doing this each time you are paid; at the end of each month, transfer the mortgage amount to your checking account and pay it. You will notice that, after a few months, there is an extra amount accumulating in your savings—part of that 13th payment. Once it's there, transfer it over and apply it toward principal.

▶ Refinance to reduce interest costs. One of the least painful methods of mortgage acceleration is refinancing. You can reduce your interest cost by exchanging a relatively high interest rate for a relatively low one. It's even possible that you could do so *and* take out some equity. You need to check the numbers to see if this is possible in your own case.

Remember, refinancing is worthwhile *if* you will own your home long enough to cover the costs involved. Divide the costs of refinancing by the monthly savings in your payment. The answer is the number of months it will take you to break even. If you plan to remain in your house longer than that, then refinancing makes a lot of sense. It also cuts interest expense and reduces the real cost of buying your house.

ADJUSTABLE-RATE MORTGAGE PLANS

Acceleration might involve a bit more strategy when your mortgage includes an adjustable rate. With a fixed-rate mortgage, the future is completely predictable, because you know what your minimum payments will be. In other words, with a simple multiplication, you can determine the cost of buying your house. When the interest rate can be changed each year, your house could end up costing you a lot more than you had estimated.

A different strategy is required for adjustable-rate mortgages. Consider some of these ideas:

▶ Pay at higher rate levels. A respectable degree of acceleration is achieved when you pay more than you are required, based on the interest rate. For example, a contract that starts out at 9 percent per year may provide for an increase of no more than 1 percent at the end of each future year. Acceleration is achieved by starting out with the payment amount that would be required at 10 percent. If the rate is raised at the end of the year to 10 percent, increase your payment to the 11 percent level.

On an $80,000 loan, the 1 percent jump makes a different of about $60 per month. Acceleration at a constantly higher rate than is required fixes you on a budget, and the higher payment becomes a nearly painless, routine expense.

→ ACTION ITEM ←

You have just signed a mortgage contract on an adjustable-rate basis. Plan to accelerate during the first year or two, and you will achieve maximum cost reduction.

▶ Accelerate more in lower-interest years. Generally speaking, you should expect the earlier years of an adjustable-rate mortgage to be lower-rate years. Because the tendency will be for the interest rate and the payment to climb over time, you will achieve a lot by accelerating in the earlier years. The effects of acceleration are more significant when the balance is higher. In addition, because you are accelerating above a relatively low required payment, you can probably afford more acceleration.

Finally, consider the benefit when the rate does go up. Because the balance is much lower as a result of early years' acceleration, the future required payment at a higher rate will be lower, too. The new monthly payment will be based on both the interest rate and the balance, so any acceleration in the early years helps hold down the payment burden when rates go up later, and reduces the total interest expenses for the life of the mortgage.

▶ Accelerate more in higher-interest years. An opposite strategy might also be applied. If you accelerate as rates go up, you will still cut interest costs while accepting a higher monthly payment. For example, you might begin making payments at 9 percent; the rate may then rise to 10 percent after 1 year. If the required monthly payment increases by $60, you could accelerate your payments by $100 or more.

At the end of the second year, the same technique is applied. Each time the interest rate is increased, increase your payment above and beyond what is required. The effect is an ever growing rate of acceleration.

▸ Identify the point where refinancing makes sense as an acceleration technique. At some point in the life of the long-term adjustable-rate mortgage, it will make sense to refinance. This assumes a couple of facts: that rates will rise, and that fixed rates will be passed by, at some point. Another basic assumption is that, as that point arrives, you will still own the house and plan to stay there for a while.

It makes sense to refinance when those conditions prevail. You need to remain in the house long enough to justify the costs of refinancing. The total costs are divided by the amount of monthly savings, and the answer is the number of months required to break even. If you will stay in the house longer than that number of months, it makes sense to refinance. With an adjustable-rate mortgage, this is an appropriate strategy for acceleration.

Do I have to add the same amount each month?

No, although that does allow you to budget the extra payment, a method for ensuring that you won't "miss" the amount given over to acceleration.

What should I do when I get a pay raise?

One idea is to add part of the pay raise to the amount of acceleration. In this way, your budget doesn't have to be changed, but some degree of improved living allowance is introduced.

How do I know how much to accelerate?

The best method is to base the amount on the desired pay-off date. For example, if you want to be debt-free in 19 years, pick a payment level that will accelerate your payoff date to 19 years from now.

Do I have to accelerate each and every month?

No. For example, you can pay extra when you get a windfall. Some families use income tax refunds or annual bonuses to reduce their principal.

Is the biweekly method worthwhile?

It is one of many acceleration techniques. You put aside half of the monthly payment every 2 weeks. Because there are 52 weeks in the year, the sum will cover 13 payments. That extra payment is put toward acceleration.

Is refinancing a method worth considering?

Absolutely. If current rates are lower than the rate you're paying, consider refinancing your mortgage. In some cases, you might be able to reduce your payment *and* the repayment term.

What about the costs involved in refinancing?

It's worth the costs if your breakeven point justifies it. How many months will it take to absorb the costs, based on the savings in your monthly payment? If you plan to remain in your home longer than the breakeven term, then refinancing is worthwhile.

Can I accelerate with an adjustable-rate mortgage?

Yes. In fact, it makes sense to accelerate this year if you expect the rate to go up next year. Why? Because next year's recomputed monthly payment will be based on the outstanding principal balance. The lower you get it now, the lower your future payments.

Can't I also accelerate more when my income rises?

Yes. Just because you have an adjustable-rate mortgage doesn't mean you have to stop accelerating later. It is still beneficial to reduce overall interest costs.

RETURN AND RISK

As you can see, there are a number of different ways to accelerate your mortgage. You might come up with an idea that is suitable in your own case and hasn't been listed here. The key is to fit the plan to your budget, not the other way around.

We have mentioned the rate of return from mortgage acceleration, comparing it to other investments. It is a simple calculation. The compound rate of return you earn from acceleration is equal to the rate you pay on your mortgage. Every dollar you put into additional payments of principal will yield that interest rate to you for the remainder of your mortgage term.

Keeping this calculation in mind makes it easier to compare acceleration to other choices. If you have $100 available each month, does it make sense to put it into faster mortgage payments? Or can you find some other investment that will yield more?

The question is complicated by several factors—liquidity, safety, and other risks. You will probably not be able to find an investment as safe as your own home, which is lived in and insured and sure to grow in value over time. But you will enjoy much higher liquidity with a number of other investments. Making a valid comparison requires a complete awareness of the risks—both those of the outside investment and those of accelerating your mortgage.

The risks of mortgage acceleration are discussed in the following sections.

Illiquidity

Mortgage acceleration is an extremely illiquid investment: you can't get your money back easily, because it's not readily available. You can only remove the money by borrowing again or by selling the house. In comparison, a savings account or mutual fund is highly liquid; you can take out money whenever you want.

Reduced Tax Deductions

The more you accelerate, the lower your itemized deductions. In addition, because the mortgage will be paid off sooner, you will lose the interest deduction sooner, too. Some people see this as a compelling reason to avoid acceleration. However, the amount you save is substantially higher than the lost deduction, which makes the "problem" of a lost tax deduction not really a problem at all. Acceleration still makes sense, although its financial value has to be discounted with the tax situation in mind.

For example, if you pay taxes at the rate of 28 percent per year, you need to discount the advantages of acceleration by that degree. If you save $1,000 through acceleration, the after-tax savings are $280 less, or $720—still a decent amount of savings.

Missed Opportunities in Other Investments

Another risk of mortgage acceleration is that you will not have that money available when other, better opportunities come along—at least, this is a popular argument against the idea. To satisfy your concern, ask yourself two questions:

▶ Are you likely to find an investment that will be as profitable as acceleration? Probably not.

▶ Based on the past, will you be able to save your money while you wait for that unusual opportunity? Many of us cannot.

The illiquidity of mortgage acceleration works well for people who have trouble holding on to their money in a passbook savings account or a mutual fund.

Inflexibility in Family Planning

Another possible risk is the lack of flexibility in the family budget. Many people are already paying up to the hilt and have nothing left over for occasional dinners out or modest vacations. Acceleration would only worsen their money problem.

The best financial plan will only work if the money is there. The budget has to be practical, as a first requirement. If you cannot afford acceleration now, you have to wait until you can. To do so prematurely would be a serious mistake.

THE EMERGENCY RESERVE

Acceleration is worth some risks, assuming that your budget is adequate and you can survive without liquidity. Having money available is of critical importance to most families. With this in mind, it makes sense to first establish a liquid fund, in case any emergencies arise.

Emergencies may include the sudden loss of a job; any unexpected expenses, like car repairs, hospital bills, or home maintenance; or payment of property taxes or insurance, which are not due every month. Your budget will be hit when such expenses arise. If you have not set aside some money in an emergency reserve, you could regret tying up all your money in an illiquid investment—including mortgage acceleration.

As urgent as it might be to start a plan of acceleration as soon as possible, establishment of an emergency reserve should take precedence. This is not to say that you can't begin acceleration, but it should be undertaken modestly, until you have an adequate reserve. For example, you might want to put $100 per month into acceleration. Start by putting $75 into the emergency reserve, and only $25 into acceleration. After your reserve is established, all of the extra money can be put into the acceleration plan.

How much is "adequate"? That depends on a number of factors. You may want to save a certain number of months' take-home income, probably 3 months' or more. How long do you think it would take to find a new job, if you left your current employment? If you think it might take up to 6 months, then you might need to save that much as an emergency reserve fund.

Your reserve amount also depends on your sources of income. If you and your spouse both work, then your fund probably can be much smaller. Chances are good that you would not both lose your jobs at the same time, unless you both have the same employer and the company fails.

Job security is only one of the risks to guard against with your emergency reserve. Review your budget and expenses for the past 12 months. Where did you spend above your budget? How can you anticipate and plan for the same pattern in the next 12 months? Such a review will indicate the type and amount of reserve that you need to set up now.

After your reserve is secure, you will be able to proceed with the less liquid acceleration plan with confidence. You will have overcome the greatest risk in the plan.

As an alternative to establishing a reserve fund, you might be able to refinance your mortgage as a line of credit or to set up an equity line of credit as a second mortgage. This is generally not advisable for many people, but it would make sense if you have a strong sense of discipline over your financial affairs.

Remember, however, that using an equity line of credit as a contingent reserve fund is not the same as saving money first. A cash emergency reserve is your equity. The money earns interest while it is sitting in an account. However, if you use an equity line of credit, you will have to repay it as a form of borrowed money.

Considering the circumstances under which you would need the reserve fund, going into debt might not be the best move at the time. You probably will not have income coming in, and yet your budget will have to continue from month to month. Incurring new debt could put you far under where you meant to be. As part of a wise financial plan, you are better off with cash in the bank for emergencies. If an equity line of credit is ever to be appropriate, it should come well after you have established adequate cash reserves for all of your needs.

WHEN YOU HAVE A CHOICE

The emergency reserve is a feature of financial life that you may need in many circumstances, regardless of earning levels and personal security. It's always nice to have a ready reserve for those unexpected times when you need more money than you thought you would. Look well beyond the monthly payments you have now. Imagine having the choice of not even having to make payments on a mortgage.

For a variety of reasons, the day may come when you no longer have to have a mortgage. If you wait long enough and keep up your payments, you will eventually pay off the entire debt. Or, you might inherit money. Or, through mortgage acceleration, your debt can be eliminated much sooner than you expected.

When you have an opportunity to get rid of your mortgage, you will face the decision with taxes in mind. Others may advise you to keep the mortgage for its tax write-off. As discussed earlier, this argument does not make sense.

It is unlikely that you would be able to find a situation in which keeping a mortgage (when you can pay it off) makes financial sense. There is one exception: when an outside investment can earn a better yield than the compound rate you're paying on the mortgage, *and* where the risks are truly comparable. For example, if your mortgage is 8 percent and you believe you can earn 11 percent elsewhere, you would earn more than you're paying on the mortgage.

WEALTH   *The Tax Myth Applied.* Joel and Carla have a mort-
BUILDING   gage with a current balance of $80,000, and they are
PROFILE   paying over 30 years. Unexpectedly, a relative passed
                away and left them an inheritance of $130,000. Their
first thought was to pay off their mortgage, which was costing them
10 percent. They doubted whether they could invest the money elsewhere and earn as much. Friends told them not to give up the tax
deduction the mortgage gave them.

Joel and Carla's marginal federal tax bracket was 28 percent; in
addition, they paid 9 percent in state income tax. They paid about
$8,000 last year in interest, which saved $2,960 in taxes (they itemize
their deductions). However, if they paid off the entire mortgage, they
would save $8,000 in interest, versus losing a write-off of $2,960. Joel
and Carla paid off the mortgage and saved the difference between the
two amounts, or about $5,040 per year.

Remember to compare risk levels, not just yields. Chances are strong
that the 11 percent yield on another investment will involve substantially more risk, and the margin between 8 percent and 11 percent is not
enough to justify risking your capital. You will probably be better off,
when you have the opportunity, using your money to eliminate debt
rather than putting it into investments that might go down in value.

Another argument against paying off the mortgage is that the
money can be used in a "growth" investment: the asset you purchase
can increase in value. An example is common stock. The income is the
dividend, and the growth is an increase in market value of the shares.

Acceleration is sometimes criticized as an "income-only" use of
money, but your house has a growth feature that is similar to that of
common stock. Market value increases over time, with demand. Investing cash to reduce your debt is similar to putting money into a growth
investment.

DISPELLING THE MYTHS

There are many arguments against mortgage acceleration. Most of
them are myths, and their flaws are easily explained and exposed.
The myths include these familiar arguments:

▶ "You need the tax deductions." As demonstrated earlier, you don't "need" the tax deduction. You're better off doing away with the interest expense altogether. The way it really works is this: the tax deduction, an attractive feature in the law, reduces the interest burden by reducing taxable income. However, that reduction does not do away with the fact that you still pay more than the purchase price for your house. For example, if you pay substantially less in interest, because of acceleration, you lose some deductions, but your overall after-tax savings are *much* greater.

Spending money for tax purposes is poor planning. You do not earn more or spend less by paying more in interest or in any other deduction. Remember, if the maximum tax percentage is 35 percent, any elimination of interest is still a 65 percent savings. Cutting $100 from your expense budget saves $65 after taxes. That's better than spending $100 in interest just to save $35.

▶ "You can earn more money somewhere else." This *might* be true, if you look only at the percentage yielded. This argument is often used in conjunction with the previous one: you can make more money *and* you need the tax benefits. This is flawed advice.

You could exceed the percentage paid on your mortgage, but it is critical to also compare the risks. You are probably not going to find a comparable investment, in terms of yield and risk. Your home is most likely to be the safest investment available. An exception is when your interest rate is unusually low. A long-term fixed-rate mortgage below 8 percent might qualify in this case. If you're paying more than 8 percent, you should remember to compare both yield and risk.

▶ "The purchase price is what you have paid for your home." The purchase price is only a starting point. It's amazing that people will lose out on a purchase contract for the "perfect" house, including a reasonable price, because of a few thousand dollars' difference between the two sides. The sellers won't budge, and the buyers won't either. This is especially ironic when you consider how little the purchase price matters in the long run.

You really earn or lose money on the decisions you make later on. The timing of refinancing, selling, or replacing the home; adding improvements; accelerating the mortgage—all these actions have much more effect on what your house costs than the price you agreed on at the time of purchase.

You can apply a very fast test, to prove the big difference that interest expense makes. Choose any percentage rate and, assuming a mortgage of $80,000, compare the monthly payments for 15-year and 30-year terms. The shorter-term payment is higher, but, over the entire period of repayment, the total cost is substantially higher with a 30-year mortgage. Even discounted for the benefits of itemized deductions, you're still paying the purchase price several times over, unless you begin an acceleration plan to reduce interest expense.

▶ "Fixed-rate mortgages protect you from inflation, so acceleration is unnecessary." A fixed-rate mortgage does provide you with protection against inflation. Because income tends to rise along with prices, a fixed-payment mortgage represents an ever diminishing percentage of income over time. You benefit greatly by keeping that mortgage in effect (assuming the interest rate is low, compared to other rates).

Having an FRM does not mean you don't need to accelerate. If you want to control the cost of your house, you need to plan a payoff date (which might not coincide with the contractual date). You also need to consider whether you should refinance at some future point. A lot of decisions that are within your power to make will affect the true cost of your house. The inflationary benefits of fixed-rate financing don't replace the need for careful and thoughtful planning.

▶ "Equity is built up primarily from increases in market value." At certain points in the past, market values rose so quickly that any housing purchase was probably going to be profitable. Values in the 1970s in certain markets were growing so quickly that mortgage acceleration was not necessary. In hindsight, it was possible to buy on a highly leveraged basis, get all the property available for as little money as possible, and then wait for market values to grow.

This might happen again in some markets in the future, but no one can predict when or where. It might not happen again within the time you are buying your house, so you can't depend on market values to grow, at least not quickly enough to justify what you're paying in interest. For that reason, you need to take control and manage your mortgage: come up with a plan to reduce the cost of the house to pay off the debt when *you* want, not when the lender wants.

In the context of risk, it was mentioned earlier that your house is a safe investment because it is insured. The next chapter explains the various types of homeowners/mortgage insurance available, and how to pick the best coverage.

───────── POINTS TO REMEMBER ─────────

▸ Mortgage acceleration is not just about saving money. It also enables you to control the period of time you remain in debt.

▸ Mortgage acceleration is an extremely illiquid investment, and should not be the only thing you do with your money. You can only get the money back by selling your home or getting a new mortgage.

▸ Acceleration is an extremely safe investment: your home is insured and you're there every day, keeping it maintained.

▸ Acceleration can save you $100,000 or more, without even taking drastic action or being especially lucky. It requires only simple math, and it really works.

▸ Acceleration puts *you* in command of your mortgage and, largely, of your own financial future.

▸ There are countless methods of acceleration. You can devise or select one suited to you.

▸ A program can be started or stopped, increased or decreased, whenever you want.

▸ You do not need to hire anyone to help you with an acceleration plan. You can do it all by yourself.

▸ Refinancing to reduce interest is one of the easiest and most sensible ways to practice mortgage acceleration.

▸ Plans for ARM mortgages should be approached differently from those for fixed-rate mortgages.

▸ Be aware of the risks as well as the rewards involved with mortgage acceleration.

▸ Always establish a liquid emergency reserve fund before investing cash in acceleration.

▸ Be aware of the myths about acceleration, and why they are myths.

10

Convenient Dangers

*M*ortgages come in many shapes and sizes. Most of us think of mortgages as having a specific interest rate, repayment terms, and an agreement concerning monthly payments. However, there are many ways to borrow money, including home equity loans and equity lines of credit.

Both of these are wonderful conveniences, if used for the right purposes. Both may spell financial disaster and might serve as money traps, if used for the wrong reasons or in the wrong ways.

THE MYTH OF IDLE EQUITY

You have probably read lenders' ads in your local paper and heard them on the radio: "Don't let your equity sit idle in your home. Put it to work!"

What does that really mean? There is only one way to "put your equity to work," and that is to borrow money by placing that equity at risk. The question you need to ask when considering a response to the lender's ad is this: Why do you need the money, and should you borrow it? Or, if you want the longer point of view, perhaps the question should be: Do you want to risk your equity by pledging it as security?

Equity is never idle as long as it is in your home. It will be there for you to transfer when you sell and trade up, or to borrow when you want to refinance. Generally speaking, you won't ever take out equity in the real sense, because it will constantly be reinvested in another home. The day might come, however, when you really will take out your equity, without putting it somewhere else.

———————————→ **ACTION ITEM** ←———————————
Never make a decision because you are being pressured by someone. "Idle" equity is the best kind, so know your facts before you give in to what someone else says is best.

WEALTH   *A Smaller Home.* Brian and Betty recently retired
BUILDING   and they now want to sell their home. When their
PROFILE   children were growing up, having four bedrooms and
2,500 square feet was an advantage. Now, it's a lot of space to heat and cool and to maintain. They need a much smaller place. In this situation, they will probably take out equity and reinvest only a portion of their profit.

With proper financial planning and foresight, a nice retirement scenario can be made to happen for a number of people. Upon retirement, their house is sold and they move to a smaller place. They come of the deal with cash in hand, which improves their retirement security. If they are over 55 at the time, they will be able to avoid taxes on as much as $125,000 in profits.

Lenders like to appeal to the anxiety of homeowners, because the loans secured by home equity are virtually risk-free, from the lender's side. The security is in the equity. For you, however, putting your "idle" equity to work means taking a big risk. If you lose your job and can't continue making higher payments, you could lose the house, too.

Advice on what you should do with *your* equity should be taken with as much care and concern as possible. Many people overlook the reality: the equity in your home, once "taken out," is a loan. The proceeds become cash. This point is made for a reason: you might not think of that equity as cash. In the lender's ads, you have probably noticed an absence of certain words, such as "borrow."

Many of us do not equate taking out equity with borrowing money,
but that's exactly what it is. You need to think about whether you
would, indeed, use borrowed money for the intended purpose of an
equity loan.

In some cases, the question of whether it is appropriate to use
"idle" equity for other purposes is not clear. The reason is that people
don't set distinct policies for themselves, so they aren't sure whether
it's a good idea.

The solution for you is that you should clearly define your own
investment standards and rules. Is it appropriate to borrow money
through an equity loan? If so, for what purposes will that money be
used? What purposes would violate your risk standards?

In setting your standards, remember the important points covered
in the following sections.

Higher Costs from Borrowing

Your house will cost more if you borrow, because borrowing money
means paying interest. Amortizing a loan over many years means a lot
of interest and a higher overall cost for your house. This point is not

emphasized in lenders' ads: lenders don't want you thinking about the facts. For example, would you respond to an ad that told the whole truth? "Pay for your house three times over!! We can show you how." Those realities have to be revealed when you prepare to sign papers, but, when the ad runs, the lender wants you to picture yourself enjoying a vacation on some faraway beach.

Longer Debt Term

It will take you longer to pay off your overall mortgage debt. The timing of your debt is critical. You will want to retire at a specific age, or you will hope to gain a higher level of financial freedom. To do either, your mortgage should be paid off or under control. All too often, the retirement and financial freedom people work so hard to achieve are lost because of poor planning and poor use of "idle" equity.

Continued Debt Service

Your debt service continues, regardless of what happens to the money you borrow. Some salespeople like to point out what you can do with borrowed money right now; they forget to tell you about the future. Remember, just as the lender is motivated to put your "idle" equity to work earning interest for the lender, most salespeople make their money on commissions. The more of your idle equity they can turn over in investment sales, the more they earn.

You might be told, for example, that your 10 percent equity loan can be invested in a guaranteed bond fund now paying 12 percent. Sounds good, but think about the realities. First, you will need to get money out each month to pay your mortgage, and the 12 percent is probably a compounded return. That means you won't be able to make 12 percent unless you come up with your mortgage payment somewhere else. Second, that "guaranteed" rate is only the current rate. What happens next year, if rates go down? You might be on the hook for your mortgage payment for 30 years. Will the income guarantee last that long? The answer is no. You need to examine the long-term implications of the decision, not just what will happen in the current year.

Higher Personal Risk

Your risk is much higher than the bank's. Keep in mind this question: Who really cares whether your equity is idle? If you borrow money and use it unwisely, your risk is substantially higher than the bank's. You stand to lose your house if, for any reason, you cannot continue making those payments.

The bank's interest in putting your money to work earning money for them is much greater than your interest in getting supposedly idle equity out.

As a standard for financial control, you should only borrow money when you are certain that the use of the borrowed funds will surpass the interest payment. You also have to be concerned about cash flow. You need to ensure that your use of the borrowed funds will yield enough each and every month—for the remainder of your mortgage term—to make the extra payment. That is a tough order to fill.

Is it a mistake to leave my equity idle?

Usually, it is not. Idle equity is the only kind that grows. If you can find a way to increase net worth, it's not a mistake to use your equity to do so. But those opportunities are rare.

Then why are lenders always encouraging me to put my idle equity to work?

Because banks only make money if you borrow it. The best kind of loan, from the bank's point of view, is one that's secured by real estate. That's what "idle equity" really means.

Isn't using equity a smart investment strategy?

No, when you consider that, to put equity to work, you have to borrow money. Remember, a mortgage is nothing less than a loan secured with your equity.

Why is borrowing a poor idea?

It's a poor idea if you use the proceeds unwisely. If you spend the money on a vacation, a new car, and debt consolidation, you do nothing to increase your equity. You only spend it. The result is a conversion of your equity to the lender's profits.

In the long run, what difference does it make?

Borrowing now means your house costs more. The purpose of financial planning concerning your home is to control and reduce the real cost of housing.

Won't it still be paid off by the end of the mortgage term?

Yes, if that original term is left intact. Many people "take out" equity and, at the same time, extend their payoff date. That means higher expense *and* more years in debt.

Doesn't it make sense, though, to borrow the money and invest it, say, in a high-yielding mutual fund?

That might seem wise today, but what if the fund's performance drops in later years? Remember, you are on the hook for those mortgage payments each and every month, even if your investment turns sour a few years from now.

Is there really any risk in borrowing? If the lender is willing to loan the money, why is it risky for me?

The loan is secured by your home. So if you suffer reverses, the lender can foreclose and get its money back. The lender's equity is never idle, especially when it's yielding high interest from you!

HOME EQUITY LOANS

Your home equity is worth preserving and protecting. Too many homeowners misuse their equity, and current federal tax laws encourage misuse. You are allowed to claim home mortgage interest as an itemized deduction, but not any other type of interest. As a consequence, many people borrow money through home equity loans, to pay off credit card and other consumer debt, and to replace nondeductible interest with deductible interest.

Aside from the unfortunate feature in the law, some homeowners sign up for home equity loans to consolidate their debts. The theory sounds great, but this is often a serious mistake.

Here's how the idea is supposed to work: You have a number of payments on credit cards, an auto loan, and periodic payments to an orthodontist. All of these payments add up to about $500 per month. If you borrow $9,000, you can pay off all of these debts and your payment will be about $200 per month. Your new debt would be paid off in 5 years.

It does sound like a good idea. Your payments are lowered from $500 to $200, and your interest will be deductible if the new loan is secured by your home. Some people even resolve to save the difference of $300 each month, but that never quite seems to work out. Others decide to just stick with the program under their revised budget, at least for the 5 years it will take to pay off the new loan. Unfortunately, that doesn't always work out either.

What goes wrong? Chances are, you will need a new car—and a new car loan—before the 5 years is up. Whether we like it or not, it's difficult to stop using credit cards, especially when they're all paid off. You would probably owe money on the cards again within 3 to 6 months. Other unexpected expenses—doctor bills, car repairs, insurance, a leaking roof—always seem to be there month after month.

Most people who borrow money to consolidate other bills through a home equity loan end up further in debt. They then owe not only the home equity funds they borrowed, but the same debts they thought they were replacing.

⟶ ACTION ITEM ⟵

Don't review only half of the issue. Most people look ahead 1 year or less, even when payments will continue for 3 decades.

You can avoid these problems and take charge of your equity with some sound financial planning. Make it a rule that you will spend income, but you will save and preserve your assets. Home equity is not the source for easy and fast money. It is a valuable asset that should not be spent or thrown away. If you consolidate your existing debts, it might be necessary to throw away your credit cards, place yourself on a strict budget, and set limits on your vacation spending.

There are appropriate reasons for borrowing money with equity pledged as collateral. Try to follow this basic rule: borrow only when you're certain that you will earn more money by borrowing than you will spend on interest.

An example is the addition of a room to your house. If you borrow money through a home improvement loan and use it to hire contractors to increase living space, that adds to your house's value.

Another example is the purchase of a different asset that either retains its value or enables you to earn more money. For example, a self-employed person might need to purchase a computer, a truck, or other capital assets. Having the assets increases sales and profits to a level that will cover the payment *and* provide the immediate cash flow to make the idea work. Given all of those qualifiers, it would make sense to borrow.

The whole question of borrowing, controlling equity, and planning well into the future should be coordinated into your financial plan. Too much borrowing occurs on the spur of the moment, without consideration for the long-term consequences of a borrowing decision. For example, if you want to borrow money today to take an expensive vacation, what does that mean? You have the instant gratification of the vacation. Then you come back home and the mortgage payment is due. That bill will arrive every month, for many months to come. Your house will now cost a lot more, and it will take years more to repay the loan.

Considering that the loan might cost three times more than the amount you borrow (due to compound interest), what is the real cost of your vacation? It probably isn't worth the expense. You might investigate other alternatives, such as planning a less expensive vacation, saving the money first, or shopping for a cheaper package deal.

The overall goal of establishing policies concerning your mortgage is to control the process and the outcome. You want to control:

▸ The overall cost of housing
▸ The repayment date
▸ The family budget.

These three elements are not always easy to manage at the same time. Conflicting priorities arise, and you have to decide which is more important. When you devise a plan today, you are not expected to stick with it for the next 30 years. Financial planning is a process of constant revision and replacement of goals. However, as long as today's goals continue to be valid, you need policies and limits placed on yourself, if the plan is to work. Those who meet their goals have done so by following that single rule.

LINES OF CREDIT

Equity lines of credit have gained in popularity in recent years, probably because of the tax benefits they provide. Like equity loans, interest paid on lines of credit is deductible. In comparison, other types of
interest cannot be claimed as deductions.

A lender providing the line of credit appraises your house and establishes the line of credit. The amount is normally 80 percent of the
value of the house, less any other outstanding mortgage balances.
Some lenders may allow you to carry lines of credit above the 80
percent level.

Suppose, for example, that you have an existing mortgage balance
of $60,000. Your house is appraised at $125,000, and you want a line of
credit. The maximum amount allowed by the 80 percent rule is
$40,000:

Appraised value	$125,000
80 percent	100,000
Less: Current mortgage	−60,000
Balance	$ 40,000

If you accept the total available line of credit, the lender will be
granted a lien up to that amount. You would then be allowed to draw
up to $40,000, and you would be assessed interest only on the amount
actually outstanding.

In comparing lines of credit to traditional mortgages, these key
features should be kept in mind:

▸ Interest is charged only on what you use. With the traditional mortgage, the entire amount you borrow is subject to interest from the
first day. When you don't plan to use all of the money right away, a
mortgage is very expensive.

For example, you might be planning to use proceeds to do a major
home improvement over the next 6 months. Quite a lot of the expense will occur later on. If you take out a mortgage, interest must
be paid from the day you start. With a line of credit, you will be
assessed only as you withdraw funds from the line.

▸ Most lines of credit are demand notes. Mortgages include a contractual date on which the balance is due. The lender cannot demand
the money before that date, unless you violate the contract or sell
the property. A line of credit, however, is probably going to be set up

as a demand note. That means the lender can force you to pay the entire balance at any time.

This provision protects the lender and will be enforced only in extreme circumstances, but it *can* be enforced whenever the lender wants. This adds an extra element of risk to the equation.

▸ Required payments on lines of credit are usually for interest only. This is a dangerous point. A line of credit can edge up over time as you withdraw relatively small amounts. If you make only the required payment, you will never reduce the outstanding balance. Most lenders demand only that you pay the outstanding interest on the line of credit. Many unfortunate homeowners have suddenly found themselves deeply in debt and unable to remember where all the money went. A consolidation of other debts, a vacation, a few car repairs—it all adds up over time.

▸ Interest will probably be assessed at a variable rate. Lines of credit are usually arranged with a variable rate, not a fixed rate. This could mean, in the future, less control over your monthly payments for interest.

For example, your line-of-credit balance could become progressively higher over the next few years and not be identified as a problem because interest rates are fairly low. However, by the time your balance has grown substantially, interest rates could be quite high again. In a variable-rate situation, a large balance could lead to big trouble. Not only is the rate higher; your outstanding balance is higher as well.

▸ Money is withdrawn by writing checks, usually provided in advance by the lender. The lender usually gives you a booklet of blank checks, to use as you wish, with your line of credit. The checks are convenient but extremely tempting. For example, if you have an available line of credit of $40,000, you can certainly afford a few luxuries now. But remember, you're using your equity, and the more you spend, the less you will have. The loan has to be repaid later, usually at a high compound rate of interest.

For many of us, the easy availability of equity—the very feature the lenders promote to bring in business—is the very reason to *not* take out a line of credit. If you think there's a possibility you will misuse your equity in that situation, don't take out a line of credit. It could be too expensive.

If used properly, the line of credit is a wonderful convenience, but can you assume that you have the discipline to really use it in an appropriate way? Most people do not have that much control, even when their own financial future is at stake.

Appropriate use of your line of credit allows sound investments, or temporary borrowings from the line.

In comparison, an inappropriate use would be spending the money. Preserve your assets and spend your income; that rule is worth following.

Consider the effects of two sets of circumstances:

▸ You are an experienced stock market investor who occasionally wants to make an additional purchase in the market. At times, however, all of your available cash is already committed and you need funds for about 2 weeks. At those times, using a line of credit is appropriate—assuming that you will be able to repay the borrowed funds shortly.

▸ You are self-employed and earn enough money to live well. However, your income is irregular, and you never know when revenues will be received. You use your line of credit to equalize your draw for personal expenses. When income comes in, you pay down the line of credit. In this case, the line of credit is a convenient utility used to offset the problems of irregular income.

THE LENDER'S PERSPECTIVE

It's sometimes easy to forget an essential fact about lenders: they are in the business of lending money and making a profit on their loans. They are not public agencies that owe us anything; when a loan defaults, the lender stands to lose rather than earn money.

If you remember that the lender has a business to run, you will understand more easily how and why they operate as they do—and why some loan applications are turned down. If a borrower presents too great a likelihood of default, the lender will not want to risk its capital.

You will be more likely to succeed in borrowing the money you need if you view the lender as a business. Both sides—you and the lender—have risks or concerns. You don't want to lose your investment and your family's shelter. The lender doesn't want to lose its capital. A mortgage might be secured by real property, but the lender doesn't want to have to foreclose to get its money back. Foreclosure is expensive and time-consuming, and is often not the best way to proceed. The lender would prefer that you make all of your payments on time.

Lenders are often cast in the role of heartless, greedy mortgage holders. Capitalism does have a heartless and greedy side, but it is certainly not difficult to appreciate the priorities of a business. You can succeed as a borrower by respecting that fact and giving the lender its due. The lender is entitled to a profit, just as you are entitled to the enjoyment of your house.

 **ACTION ITEM**

Talk to your lender with a clear understanding that lenders are in business to make a profit. Don't kid yourself into believing the lender is there to do you a favor.

Because lenders are in business, they like to put together loan packages that are beneficial to them. Beneficial deals, like all business deals, come in many types. If both sides are happy, then the deal is sound and worthwhile. If the lender is happy and you are not (or the other way around), then the deal is not so good and can only lead to problems. When you find yourself in a bad deal, figure out a way to get out of it. Refinance with a different lender whose loan alternatives make more sense and cost less. You will probably lose some money along the way, but learn from the experience and remember to do your research next time, before signing the papers.

Avoid borrowing under pressure. Mortgages and lines of credit are long-term debt commitments, and you could save or spend thousands of dollars with a few days' research and comparison. If you are under pressure and have to resolve problems now, consider getting a delay from your creditors, rather than taking the first loan you can get.

You will have a wide variety of programs to choose from when you make your comparisons, whether you stay with one lender or apply to several. Begin your process by comparing each deal. You need to know the up-front costs, as well as the terms of the deal. Initial and overall costs of the loan are important considerations. Pay close attention to call features, conversion rights, and fixed or variable rules of each loan.

Determining the best deal is not an easy process. You might need the help of an experienced financial professional, to sort out the different loans available to you. However, before agreeing to pay someone for advice, be sure that person knows how to figure out the best deal for you. Find a planner or other professional who specializes in real estate.

Always remember that your mortgage is a debt. If you want to "take money out," you will face going further into debt, paying more interest and, probably, accepting a longer term of repayment on your house. The next chapter summarizes the book's key points and offers some financial planning ideas.

POINTS TO REMEMBER

▸ Your equity is never idle as long as it's being left alone. It's an investment fund, and should be preserved and protected.

▸ Lenders make money by generating loans. They are motivated to appeal to you and to make you feel as though you *should* borrow money secured by equity.

▸ The more you borrow, the higher your house will cost you in the long run.

▸ You will be required to make payments every month on borrowed money, for the whole term of the loan—even if you spend all the money you borrow.

▸ Your risks when borrowing money secured by home equity are much higher than the bank's risks. If you don't make your payments, you will lose your house.

▸ You should borrow only when you will increase your net worth as a result of the use of funds. If you plan to borrow to spend the money, then you are giving up equity.

▸ Debt consolidation might seem like a smart idea today, but unless you solve the underlying problem, consolidation will only increase your debt level.

▸ Equity lines of credit are convenient, but extremely dangerous. They make it easy to misuse equity. Take out a line of credit only if you are very well-disciplined and have a specific plan.

11

Becoming a Happy Homeowner

*C*hoices. Everyone wants them, but few people allow themselves to attain them. You might believe that your income limits your ability to have choices; or you might recognize that, with proper planning, you can have all of the financial freedom you want.

This book has demonstrated that possibility, in discussions of mortgage planning and management. *You* decide how much your house will cost, when it will be paid off, and whether you should refinance. You have an opportunity, through mortgage planning, to make a real difference for your own future. Either you will slowly accumulate a little equity, while your lender converts a lot of your equity to its profits; or you will examine the numbers with great care, and devise a plan to control the price of your house. Those are your choices.

THE ASSETS-AND-INCOME DISTINCTION

A big mistake is made by many people when they fail to make the distinction mentioned many times throughout the book: spend your income but preserve your assets. To many people, "cash" is all the same, whether it comes from earnings or from a lender. For those people, everything is very immediate. They ignore the most important distinction: borrowed money has to be paid back. Whenever you borrow with your home as collateral, you reduce your main asset's value until the mortgage loan is paid back.

When people don't make this critical distinction in their financial lives, they invite future trouble. By not seeing the importance of not borrowing money pledged with equity, they may be denying their most basic goal.

WEALTH   *A Basic Mistake.* Al and Sonya are struggling with
BUILDING   monthly bills and need to make some changes. Their
PROFILE   payments are unmanageably high. The first solution
                that occurs to them is to consolidate their debts and
reduce their overall payments by spreading them over a longer period. They take out a second mortgage.

This solution only makes the problem worse, in the majority of cases. Yet, it's the most common way that people solve an excessive debt problem: they add more debt and ensure that they will stay in debt longer! Unfortunately, they have not solved any of their problems.

Other possible solutions can be recommended, as follows.

Increase Monthly Income

Telling someone to go out and earn more money might seem like unsound advice. How do you actually increase income? Easily. Take a night or weekend job until your debts are under control. If the entire paycheck from a second job is put into the payment of old debts, they will disappear more quickly than if you try to budget partial payments each month from your present income.

Get Rid of Credit Cards

Even though you are concerned with the problem in front of you today, look to the future as well. If you have problems controlling your spending habits, remove the temptation. Cut up all or most of your credit cards. You probably only need one or two cards, anyway. Change your habits, and limit the amount of easy credit available to you. Just do it! It has long-term rewards.

─────────────→ ACTION ITEM ←─────────────
Pay off your entire credit card debt each month. If you can't afford to, then you're using the card too much.

Negotiate a New Repayment Plan

Talk to your creditors. Negotiate a new, easier plan you can live with. You might even persuade a creditor to suspend interest for a while, so that all of your payments go directly into reducing the balance. Even if that isn't possible, you might be able to lower your monthly payments by negotiating a new schedule.

The point here is that there are obvious solutions, short of spending equity that you would rather preserve. You will need to protect so-called "idle" equity by leaving it alone and allowing it to grow. One exception occurs when you identify a way to increase your net worth above and beyond the interest expense involved with mortgage borrowing. Those opportunities are rare but, when you find them, the risk might be worthwhile.

AN EASIER DECISION

Once you set your rule for spending income but preserving assets, every financial decision becomes easier. You have a clear policy. You know what you want and where you are going. More to the point, you also know where you are *not* going.

Why is this so important? You will probably be paying on your mortgage for many years to come. Even if you accelerate and pay off your mortgage in 15 years instead of 30, it is still a long-term financial obligation. If you move four or five times in the next two decades, you will no doubt have a mortgage for most of that time.

What you want to make sure of is this: At the end of the 15-to-20-year period, you will have built up some equity. Otherwise, all of your payments will have gone to the bank, which made a profit, and none of the market value increases will be yours! That is what happens to too many people.

WEALTH   *Lost Equity.* Larry and Sarah purchased their home
BUILDING   15 years ago, when prices were around $80,000. To-
PROFILE   day, after a tremendous period of market growth,
their home is worth $150,000. However, they refi-
nanced several years ago to consolidate their debt payments. Last
year, they took out an equity line of credit to solve another generation
of debt problems. Today, they are still in debt, and they have no equity.

Over the same period of time when a house grows in value, lenders
make it too easy for you to borrow against that value. You can borrow
money as soon as the equity is there to be pledged. You never really
build any net worth; essentially, you hand it over in the form of
higher interest payments, spent equity, and longer-term mortgage
commitments.

With a financial policy, your decision-making process is clarified.
For example, if your policy is to never borrow money with your home
pledged as security, then you have a clear definition of what you
want. That doesn't mean you will be able to keep the policy in force or
never renege on it. It does mean that, for the present, you have a clear
idea of what you want and don't want. When a lender comes along
with an attractive offer for an equity line of credit, you won't be
tempted to go with it; it violates your own rules.

A financial policy is an important rule for living. With the policy in
effect, you never need to wonder whether a new idea is valid. If it
violates your personal rule, you can end the debate before it really
gets started. Here are some examples:

▸ Your policy is to never buy anything in response to a telephone
solicitation. When a call comes through, you end the discussion
before the sales pitch gets off the ground.

▸ Your policy is to preserve your housing asset. When a salesperson
advises borrowing money to buy other investments, you turn down
the idea without any hesitation. Your rule limits such activity to
dire emergencies.

▸ Your policy is to avoid refinancing. On your current schedule, your
house will be paid off in about 18 years. When your debts rise and
you're tempted to consolidate them with a refinancing loan, you
seek other alternatives, rather than break your rule.

?

What is the importance of the distinction between my assets and my income?

Assets (things you own) should be preserved and made to grow. Income, though, may be spent, to an affordable level. As long as you keep this distinction in mind, financial decisions are clearer and easier.

How can I improve my debt situation when I have a fixed income?

Unless you are retired or disabled, you are *not* limited to the income you earn on your primary job. If you are having debt problems, take a part-time or temporary job, and use your second income to eliminate or reduce your debts.

I seem to have a problem overusing credit cards. What's the solution?

Discipline yourself to *not* use your credit cards excessively. If you can't afford to pay off the whole balance each month (except for emergencies), you are overusing your card. If you can't control your spending habits, cut up the card and throw it away.

My creditor payments are too high. What can I do, short of a consolidation loan?

Try to get creditors to extend the time and monthly payment amount, to ease your budget problems. Ask whether they will forgive a portion of the interest.

What is the best way to preserve the equity in my home, and not give in to the temptation to borrow against it?

First, never take out a loan for spending. Only borrow to take advantage of lower rates, add on to your home, or otherwise increase your net worth. Second, resist lender promotions offering you easy approval and fast service. These offers only make it easier to keep yourself in debt.

How do I keep myself clear about my goals?

You need a financial plan. Only with a plan can you formulate and enforce personal policies. By being in control rather than just reacting, you will escape the cycle of debt and the usual trend that victimizes most homeowners.

FOCUSING YOUR POINT OF VIEW

One of the most widespread reasons that people fail with their finances is that they don't establish any policies. They don't *know* where they want to go. They are not reaching toward specific goals; they have no clear long-term direction. The idea of controlling the cost of housing and selecting a payoff date is downright revolutionary to most homeowners.

You can and should be in control. Your point of view should be focused keenly on what you and your family want and need. With this basic step, you can make a huge difference in the way your future cash flow and wealth are divided. How much will you keep? How much will go to one lender or another?

You can improve your focus by gaining basic information about financial matters. Few people know how lenders calculate interest and break down their monthly payments. They think a computer is required to make that calculation, but it is not. Once you know how to use amortization tables, how to break down monthly interest and principal, and how to plan for the long-term without having to depend on someone else, you're well on your way to having the control you want.

This information level is critical. When you ask questions of other people, the answers might not be right or might not be in your best interests.

You need to plan for yourself and then decide how to use outside help. Otherwise, you will have no objectivity guiding your decisions. Most professional advisers welcome knowledgeable clients who know what they want; they make the adviser's job easier. Instead of having to educate these clients, the adviser can quickly and easily find out what they want, and then concentrate on showing them how to get it.

WEALTH   *The Commission Problem.* Alice wants to acceler-
BUILDING   ate her 30-year mortgage so that it will be paid off in
PROFILE   18 years. She met with a financial adviser to ask how
                    she could do this. Instead of answering, the adviser
told her that there were numerous better ways to put her money to
work. Translation: There is no commission available to the adviser
from mortgage acceleration.

Too much time between salespeople and clients is wasted in a strug-
gle to define terms and answers. However, the questions are often not
agreed on in advance. The client might want to accelerate mortgage
payments, with a clear financial goal in mind; the salesperson might
be selling mutual funds that day. The results of meetings often demonstrate whose goals win out: the client's or the salesperson's.

You can avoid the problem of arguing with the very people who are
supposed to be helping you. Lay down the following ground rules at
the very beginning:

▶ You set up the meeting. Most meetings with salespeople don't occur
by design. In one way or another, the salespeople arrange to meet
with you. Perhaps you "win" a free consultation or respond to a telephone solicitation. Whatever the contact point, you will rarely get
what you need or want by working with someone in this way. *You*
should set up the meeting, for your convenience, and select the person with whom you will work.

▶ You set the agenda. Most of us don't get what we want financially
because we let other people tell us what we want and need. If you
don't take control, your best interests will never get served. *Your*
agenda should rule the meeting. If the adviser or salesperson tries
to change your agenda, stop the meeting and find someone else to
work with.

▶ You decide your goals by the time the meeting begins. You will only
be able to remain in control if you know exactly what you want, not
only in the distant future, but during the meeting as well. For example, you might have decided to invest money in two ways: mortgage
acceleration, and some other, more liquid method. You call the
meeting to discuss alternatives for your second investment alternative. That is your agenda, and you should cut off any argument from

a salesperson about the wisdom of mortgage acceleration. That de-cision has already been made, and you know what you want. Insist on staying in control.

▶ You will not allow anyone to try and change your goals. Salespeople sometimes think their job is to tell you what you want. In the major-ity of cases, the client doesn't know the answer, so the salespeople have a pretty easy task. The client, the sellers' argument goes, wants whatever the salesperson happens to be selling, and a good sales-person will be able to prove this adage to be true. However, you are the exceptional client. You already know what you want. And you will get it; if not from this salesperson, then from another one.

▶ Any suggestions given must clearly be designed to reach the ex-pressed goals. One of the rules you need to set right at the beginning of your meeting is that any advice given must be directed at reach-ing your goals. If the salesperson is not able to keep discussion pointed in that way—or is not willing to abide by this rule—then your meeting can and should be a very brief one.

SETTING LONG-TERM GOALS

Mortgage planning is difficult because it involves the far distant fu-ture. You found it tough to qualify for your loan, and making today's monthly payments is already a strain on your budget. When you're concentrating on your financial survival, thinking about where you'll be in 20 or 30 years becomes a very low priority.

Changing your way of thinking, however, can help you to set and reach your long-term goals. Switch some concentration to control and to deciding what *should* be a priority. Don't allow yourself to shrug and say that the lender sets the rules and "there's nothing we can do about it."

Give thought to some long-term goals that you can set and do some-thing about right now. Put one or more of the following actions into motion for your future.

Pick Your Mortgage Repayment Date

This is a straightforward and easy goal to set; reaching it might be another matter. Remember that setting a goal is the first step, and that you don't have to take immediate action, especially if you can't afford to.

Sometimes, knowing what you need to do to reach a goal leads to solutions, but that route can only be traveled if you already have the goal. You might be scheduled to pay on your mortgage for the next 30 years, but you'd rather pay it off in 20. What can you do today? First, find out how much more you need to pay each month to reach your goal. Can you afford it? Can you afford part of it? If you get a pay raise, can you put some of the new net take-home pay toward accelerating your mortgage? Be willing to review your goal in a couple of years and to revise the steps you can take to make the goal a reality.

Decide When (or Whether) to Refinance

Refinancing is a benefit of owning a home, even when your payment schedule isn't building equity for you at a fast clip. Market value by itself might add market value *and* equity. Treat it as a benefit; don't make it a disadvantage by the way you use (or protect) the equity. You can set a firm policy for preserving or using the equity in your home; by restricting the available reasons, the decision to refinance becomes easier. For example, your list of good reasons to refinance might include getting a lower interest rate, adding to your living space, or in some other way increasing asset value. Then, don't refinance for any reasons not on your list. Never refinance in response to a lender's advertisement, or because a novel approach sounds like a good deal. Shut off any developing sense of guilt about leaving equity "idle" in your home. Staying idle is the best thing your equity can do for you.

Set a Rule Not to Misuse Your Home Equity

This is more a policy than a goal. Protection of your equity is the ultimate goal. Not misusing your home equity is of critical importance, if you hope to keep it and make it grow. The hardest rules to follow and the hardest goals to reach involve keeping and increasing your equity. Lenders make it incredibly easy for you to misuse your equity. Borrowing money secured by real estate is easy, because the lender's risks are minimal.

Decide the Total Cost of Your House

This is what this book is all about. You can and should control and decide the cost of your housing, which is the total of your payments, not the purchase price. To be completely correct and accurate, the real cost is the total of your payments minus the reduction in taxes you achieve by claiming itemized deductions related to your house.

Each time you refinance or apply for a second mortgage, you incur additional costs. These costs add to your housing cost, over time. By allowing a 30-year repayment schedule to stay in effect, you add greatly to your costs. By accelerating even modestly, you can drastically reduce your overall cost.

TAKING CHARGE OF YOUR MORTGAGE

All of us want financial control. Even a small amount of it is most rewarding, especially if we've had none in the past. You are not at the mercy of lenders, who have specialized knowledge, computers, and an inside track. You will discover, as you improve your own financial knowledge, that the people working for the lender know very little beyond their narrowly focused job emphasis. You have just as much capability for understanding financial matters, at least as they affect you and your housing costs.

You should be in charge of your mortgage. If you defer to the lender, you must realize that the lender's best interests will be served, not yours. By letting anyone else—a lender, a salesperson or adviser, or a friend—dictate your financial future, you give up one of the most important attributes you can gain.

By remaining in charge of your mortgage and other financial matters, you set your own course and ensure your own financial success. No one will be more concerned with your financial freedom and control than you will. No one else can be expected to care, to the same degree, about how well you succeed. No one else knows your long-term goals as well as you do, or shares your interest in seeing you reach them.

Good professional advice is a valuable commodity that should be taken whenever it is available. However, you need to control the agenda, set your own goals, and stay on course.

Each of us, individually, must take care of our financial affairs, in order to reach our goals. By resolving to become financially free, you can make an amazing difference in your own future. Freedom comes from setting goals, gaining knowledge and confidence about financial matters, and setting rules and limits for yourself. Then, with everything in place, you will be ready to decide not only what your house costs, but how comfortably you will live both during your work years and your retirement.

POINTS TO REMEMBER

▶ The decision about how much your house costs is primarily up to you and results from the choices you make concerning the amount of interest and the span of years for your mortgage repayment.

▶ Most people fail to make distinctions between assets (which should be preserved) and income (which may be spent). Keeping that distinction in mind is the key to financial control and success.

▶ There are a number of ways to escape the destructive cycle of debt. You will benefit from learning and applying them.

▶ Setting a personal financial policy is the first step in taking control of your financial future. It is essential, if your financial plan is to work.

▶ Professionals can be invaluable in helping you to implement your plan, but only if they understand that you are in control.

▶ Long-term planning is difficult because the future is so uncertain. However, you know well in advance how your mortgage repayment will proceed. It's within your power to control that schedule.

Appendix A
Mortgage
Amortization

See page 123 for a discussion of Mortgage Amortization Tables.

8.00% Amount	5 Years	10 Years	15 Years	20 Years	25 Years	30 Years
50	1.02	.61	.48	.42	.39	.37
100	2.03	1.22	.96	.84	.78	.74
500	10.14	6.07	4.78	4.19	3.86	3.67
1000	20.28	12.14	9.56	8.37	7.72	7.34
2000	40.56	24.27	19.12	16.73	15.44	14.68
5000	101.39	60.67	47.79	41.83	38.60	36.69
10000	202.77	121.33	95.57	83.65	77.19	73.38
15000	304.15	182.00	143.35	125.47	115.78	110.07
20000	405.53	242.66	191.14	167.29	154.37	146.76
25000	506.91	303.32	238.92	209.12	192.96	183.45
30000	608.30	363.99	286.70	250.94	231.55	220.13
35000	709.68	424.65	334.48	292.76	270.14	256.82
40000	811.06	485.32	382.27	334.58	308.73	293.51
45000	912.44	545.98	430.05	376.40	347.32	330.20
50000	1013.82	606.64	477.83	418.23	385.91	366.89
55000	1115.21	667.31	525.61	460.05	424.50	403.58
60000	1216.59	727.97	573.40	501.87	463.09	440.26
65000	1317.97	788.63	621.18	543.69	501.69	476.95
70000	1419.35	849.30	668.96	585.51	540.28	513.64
75000	1520.73	909.96	716.74	627.34	578.87	550.33
80000	1622.12	970.63	764.53	669.16	617.46	587.02
85000	1723.50	1031.29	812.31	710.98	656.05	623.70
90000	1824.88	1091.95	860.09	752.80	694.64	660.39
95000	1926.26	1152.62	907.87	794.62	733.23	697.08
100000	2027.64	1213.28	955.66	836.45	771.82	733.77

8.25% Amount	5 Years	10 Years	15 Years	20 Years	25 Years	30 Years
50	1.02	.62	.49	.43	.40	.38
100	2.04	1.23	.98	.86	.79	.76
500	10.20	6.14	4.86	4.27	3.95	3.76
1000	20.40	12.27	9.71	8.53	7.89	7.52
2000	40.80	24.54	19.41	17.05	15.77	15.03
5000	101.99	61.33	48.51	42.61	39.43	37.57
10000	203.97	122.66	97.02	85.21	78.85	75.13
15000	305.95	183.98	145.53	127.81	118.27	112.69
20000	407.93	245.31	194.03	170.42	157.70	150.26
25000	509.91	306.64	242.54	213.02	197.12	187.82
30000	611.89	367.96	291.05	255.62	236.54	225.38
35000	713.87	429.29	339.55	298.23	275.96	262.95
40000	815.86	490.62	388.06	340.83	315.39	300.51
45000	917.84	551.94	436.57	383.43	354.81	338.07
50000	1019.82	613.27	485.08	426.04	394.23	375.64
55000	1121.80	674.59	533.58	468.64	433.65	413.20
60000	1223.78	735.92	582.09	511.24	473.08	450.76
65000	1325.76	797.25	630.60	553.85	512.50	488.33
70000	1427.74	858.57	679.10	596.45	551.92	525.89
75000	1529.72	919.90	727.61	639.05	591.34	563.45
80000	1631.71	981.23	776.12	681.66	630.77	601.02
85000	1733.69	1042.55	824.62	724.26	670.19	638.58
90000	1835.67	1103.88	873.13	766.86	709.61	676.14
95000	1937.65	1165.20	921.64	809.47	749.03	713.71
100000	2039.63	1226.53	970.15	852.07	788.46	751.27

8.50%	Amount	5 Years	10 Years	15 Years	20 Years	25 Years	30 Years
	50	1.03	.62	.50	.44	.41	.39
	100	2.06	1.24	.99	.87	.81	.77
	500	10.26	6.20	4.93	4.34	4.03	3.85
	1000	20.52	12.40	9.85	8.68	8.06	7.69
	2000	41.04	24.80	19.70	17.36	16.11	15.38
	5000	102.59	62.00	49.24	43.40	40.27	38.45
	10000	205.17	123.99	98.48	86.79	80.53	76.90
	15000	307.75	185.98	147.72	130.18	120.79	115.34
	20000	410.34	247.98	196.95	173.57	161.05	153.79
	25000	512.92	309.97	246.19	216.96	201.31	192.23
	30000	615.50	371.96	295.43	260.35	241.57	230.68
	35000	718.08	433.95	344.66	303.74	281.83	269.12
	40000	820.67	495.95	393.90	347.13	322.10	307.57
	45000	923.25	557.94	443.14	390.53	362.36	346.02
	50000	1025.83	619.93	492.37	433.92	402.62	384.46
	55000	1128.41	681.93	541.61	477.31	442.88	422.91
	60000	1231.00	743.92	590.85	520.70	483.14	461.35
	65000	1333.58	805.91	640.09	564.09	523.40	499.80
	70000	1436.16	867.90	689.32	607.48	563.66	538.24
	75000	1538.74	929.90	738.56	650.87	603.93	576.69
	80000	1641.33	991.89	787.80	694.26	644.19	615.14
	85000	1743.91	1053.88	837.03	737.65	684.45	653.58
	90000	1846.49	1115.88	886.27	781.05	724.71	692.03
	95000	1949.08	1177.87	935.51	824.44	764.97	730.47
	100000	2051.66	1239.86	984.74	867.83	805.23	768.92

8.75%	Amount	5 Years	10 Years	15 Years	20 Years	25 Years	30 Years
	50	1.04	.63	.50	.45	.42	.40
	100	2.07	1.26	1.00	.89	.83	.79
	500	10.32	6.27	5.00	4.42	4.12	3.94
	1000	20.64	12.54	10.00	8.84	8.23	7.87
	2000	41.28	25.07	19.99	17.68	16.45	15.74
	5000	103.19	62.67	49.98	44.19	41.11	39.34
	10000	206.38	125.33	99.95	88.38	82.22	78.68
	15000	309.56	188.00	149.92	132.56	123.33	118.01
	20000	412.75	250.66	199.89	176.75	164.43	157.35
	25000	515.94	313.32	249.87	220.93	205.54	196.68
	30000	619.12	375.99	299.84	265.12	246.65	236.02
	35000	722.31	438.65	349.81	309.30	287.76	275.35
	40000	825.49	501.31	399.78	353.49	328.86	314.69
	45000	928.68	563.98	449.76	397.67	369.97	354.02
	50000	1031.87	626.64	499.73	441.86	411.08	393.36
	55000	1135.05	689.30	549.70	486.05	452.18	432.69
	60000	1238.24	751.97	599.67	530.23	493.29	472.03
	65000	1341.43	814.63	649.65	574.42	534.40	511.36
	70000	1444.61	877.29	699.62	618.60	575.51	550.70
	75000	1547.80	939.96	749.59	662.79	616.61	590.03
	80000	1650.98	1002.62	799.56	706.97	657.72	629.37
	85000	1754.17	1065.28	849.54	751.16	698.83	668.70
	90000	1857.36	1127.95	899.51	795.34	739.93	708.04
	95000	1960.54	1190.61	949.48	839.53	781.04	747.37
	100000	2063.73	1253.27	999.45	883.72	822.15	786.71

9.00%

Amount	5 Years	10 Years	15 Years	20 Years	25 Years	·30 Years
50	1.04	.64	.51	.45	.42	.41
100	2.08	1.27	1.02	.90	.84	.81
500	10.38	6.34	5.08	4.50	4.20	4.03
1000	20.76	12.67	10.15	9.00	8.40	8.05
2000	41.52	25.34	20.29	18.00	16.79	16.10
5000	103.80	63.34	50.72	44.99	41.96	40.24
10000	207.59	126.68	101.43	89.98	83.92	80.47
15000	311.38	190.02	152.14	134.96	125.88	120.70
20000	415.17	253.36	202.86	179.95	167.84	160.93
25000	518.96	316.69	253.57	224.94	209.80	201.16
30000	622.76	380.03	304.28	269.92	251.76	241.39
35000	726.55	443.37	355.00	314.91	293.72	281.62
40000	830.34	506.71	405.71	359.90	335.68	321.85
45000	934.13	570.05	456.42	404.88	377.64	362.09
50000	1037.92	633.38	507.14	449.87	419.60	402.32
55000	1141.71	696.72	557.85	494.85	461.56	442.55
60000	1245.51	760.06	608.56	539.84	503.52	482.78
65000	1349.30	823.40	659.28	584.83	545.48	523.01
70000	1453.09	886.74	709.99	629.81	587.44	563.24
75000	1556.88	950.07	760.70	674.80	629.40	603.47
80000	1660.67	1013.41	811.42	719.79	671.36	643.70
85000	1764.47	1076.75	862.13	764.77	713.32	683.93
90000	1868.26	1140.09	912.84	809.76	755.28	724.17
95000	1972.05	1203.42	963.56	854.74	797.24	764.40
100000	2075.84	1266.76	1014.27	899.73	839.20	804.63

9.25%

Amount	5 Years	10 Years	15 Years	20 Years	25 Years	30 Years
50	1.05	.65	.52	.46	.43	.42
100	2.09	1.29	1.03	.92	.86	.83
500	10.44	6.41	5.15	4.58	4.29	4.12
1000	20.88	12.81	10.30	9.16	8.57	8.23
2000	41.76	25.61	20.59	18.32	17.13	16.46
5000	104.40	64.02	51.46	45.80	42.82	41.14
10000	208.80	128.04	102.92	91.59	85.64	82.27
15000	313.20	192.05	154.38	137.39	128.46	123.41
20000	417.60	256.07	205.84	183.18	171.28	164.54
25000	522.00	320.09	257.30	228.97	214.10	205.67
30000	626.40	384.10	308.76	274.77	256.92	246.81
35000	730.80	448.12	360.22	320.56	299.74	287.94
40000	835.20	512.14	411.68	366.35	342.56	329.08
45000	939.60	576.15	463.14	412.15	385.38	370.21
50000	1044.00	640.17	514.60	457.94	428.20	411.34
55000	1148.40	704.18	566.06	503.73	471.02	452.48
60000	1252.80	768.20	617.52	549.53	513.83	493.61
65000	1357.20	832.22	668.98	595.32	556.65	534.74
70000	1461.60	896.23	720.44	641.11	599.47	575.88
75000	1566.00	960.25	771.90	686.91	642.29	617.01
80000	1670.40	1024.27	823.36	732.70	685.11	658.15
85000	1774.80	1088.28	874.82	778.49	727.93	699.28
90000	1879.20	1152.30	926.28	824.29	770.75	740.41
95000	1983.60	1216.32	977.74	870.08	813.57	781.55
100000	2087.99	1280.33	1029.20	915.87	856.39	822.68

9.50%	Amount	5 Years	10 Years	15 Years	20 Years	25 Years	30 Years
	50	1.06	.65	.53	.47	.44	.43
	100	2.11	1.30	1.05	.94	.88	.85
	500	10.51	6.47	5.23	4.67	4.37	4.21
	1000	21.01	12.94	10.45	9.33	8.74	8.41
	2000	42.01	25.88	20.89	18.65	17.48	16.82
	5000	105.01	64.70	52.22	46.61	43.69	42.05
	10000	210.02	129.40	104.43	93.22	87.37	84.09
	15000	315.03	194.10	156.64	139.82	131.06	126.13
	20000	420.04	258.80	208.85	186.43	174.74	168.18
	25000	525.05	323.50	261.06	233.04	218.43	210.22
	30000	630.06	388.20	313.27	279.64	262.11	252.26
	35000	735.07	452.90	365.48	326.25	305.80	294.30
	40000	840.08	517.60	417.69	372.86	349.48	336.35
	45000	945.09	582.29	469.91	419.46	393.17	378.39
	50000	1050.10	646.99	522.12	466.07	436.85	420.43
	55000	1155.11	711.69	574.33	512.68	480.54	462.47
	60000	1260.12	776.39	626.54	559.28	524.22	504.52
	65000	1365.13	841.09	678.75	605.89	567.91	546.56
	70000	1470.14	905.79	730.96	652.50	611.59	588.60
	75000	1575.14	970.49	783.17	699.10	655.28	630.65
	80000	1680.15	1035.19	835.38	745.71	698.96	672.69
	85000	1785.16	1099.88	887.60	792.32	742.65	714.73
	90000	1890.17	1164.58	939.81	838.92	786.33	756.77
	95000	1995.18	1229.28	992.02	885.53	830.02	798.82
	100000	2100.19	1293.98	1044.23	932.14	873.70	840.86

9.75%	Amount	5 Years	10 Years	15 Years	20 Years	25 Years	30 Years
	50	1.06	.66	.53	.48	.45	.43
	100	2.12	1.31	1.06	.95	.90	.86
	500	10.57	6.54	5.30	4.75	4.46	4.30
	1000	21.13	13.08	10.60	9.49	8.92	8.60
	2000	42.25	26.16	21.19	18.98	17.83	17.19
	5000	105.63	65.39	52.97	47.43	44.56	42.96
	10000	211.25	130.78	105.94	94.86	89.12	85.92
	15000	316.87	196.16	158.91	142.28	133.68	128.88
	20000	422.49	261.55	211.88	189.71	178.23	171.84
	25000	528.11	326.93	264.85	237.13	222.79	214.79
	30000	633.73	392.32	317.81	284.56	267.35	257.75
	35000	739.35	457.70	370.78	331.99	311.90	300.71
	40000	844.97	523.09	423.75	379.41	356.46	343.67
	45000	950.60	588.47	476.72	426.84	401.02	386.62
	50000	1056.22	653.86	529.69	474.26	445.57	429.58
	55000	1161.84	719.24	582.65	521.69	490.13	472.54
	60000	1267.46	784.63	635.62	569.12	534.69	515.50
	65000	1373.08	850.01	688.59	616.54	579.24	558.46
	70000	1478.70	915.40	741.56	663.97	623.80	601.41
	75000	1584.32	980.78	794.53	711.39	668.36	644.37
	80000	1689.94	1046.17	847.50	758.82	712.91	687.33
	85000	1795.57	1111.55	900.46	806.24	757.47	730.29
	90000	1901.19	1176.94	953.43	853.67	802.03	773.24
	95000	2006.81	1242.32	1006.40	901.10	846.59	816.20
	100000	2112.43	1307.71	1059.37	948.52	891.14	859.16

10.00% Amount	5 Years	10 Years	15 Years	20 Years	25 Years	30 Years
50	1.07	.67	.54	.49	.46	.44
100	2.13	1.33	1.08	.97	.91	.88
500	10.63	6.61	5.38	4.83	4.55	4.39
1000	21.25	13.22	10.75	9.66	9.09	8.78
2000	42.50	26.44	21.50	19.31	18.18	17.56
5000	106.24	66.08	53.74	48.26	45.44	43.88
10000	212.48	132.16	107.47	96.51	90.88	87.76
15000	318.71	198.23	161.20	144.76	136.31	131.64
20000	424.95	264.31	214.93	193.01	181.75	175.52
25000	531.18	330.38	268.66	241.26	227.18	219.40
30000	637.42	396.46	322.39	289.51	272.62	263.28
35000	743.65	462.53	376.12	337.76	318.05	307.16
40000	849.89	528.61	429.85	386.01	363.49	351.03
45000	956.12	594.68	483.58	434.26	408.92	394.91
50000	1062.36	660.76	537.31	482.52	454.36	438.79
55000	1168.59	726.83	591.04	530.77	499.79	482.67
60000	1274.83	792.91	644.77	579.02	545.23	526.55
65000	1381.06	858.98	698.50	627.27	590.66	570.43
70000	1487.30	925.06	752.23	675.52	636.10	614.31
75000	1593.53	991.14	805.96	723.77	681.53	658.18
80000	1699.77	1057.21	859.69	772.02	726.97	702.06
85000	1806.00	1123.29	913.42	820.27	772.40	745.94
90000	1912.24	1189.36	967.15	868.52	817.84	789.82
95000	2018.47	1255.44	1020.88	916.78	863.27	833.70
100000	2124.71	1321.51	1074.61	965.03	908.71	877.58

10.25% Amount	5 Years	10 Years	15 Years	20 Years	25 Years	30 Years
50	1.07	.67	.55	.50	.47	.45
100	2.14	1.34	1.09	.99	.93	.90
500	10.69	6.68	5.45	4.91	4.64	4.49
1000	21.38	13.36	10.90	9.82	9.27	8.97
2000	42.75	26.71	21.80	19.64	18.53	17.93
5000	106.86	66.77	54.50	49.09	46.32	44.81
10000	213.71	133.54	109.00	98.17	92.64	89.62
15000	320.56	200.31	163.50	147.25	138.96	134.42
20000	427.41	267.08	218.00	196.33	185.28	179.23
25000	534.26	333.85	272.49	245.42	231.60	224.03
30000	641.11	400.62	326.99	294.50	277.92	268.84
35000	747.96	467.39	381.49	343.58	324.24	313.64
40000	854.82	534.16	435.99	392.66	370.56	358.45
45000	961.67	600.93	490.48	441.74	416.88	403.25
50000	1068.52	667.70	544.98	490.83	463.20	448.06
55000	1175.37	734.47	599.48	539.91	509.52	492.86
60000	1282.22	801.24	653.98	588.99	555.83	537.67
65000	1389.07	868.01	708.47	638.07	602.15	582.47
70000	1495.92	934.78	762.97	687.16	648.47	627.28
75000	1602.77	1001.55	817.47	736.24	694.79	672.08
80000	1709.63	1068.32	871.97	785.32	741.11	716.89
85000	1816.48	1135.09	926.46	834.40	787.43	761.69
90000	1923.33	1201.86	980.96	883.48	833.75	806.50
95000	2030.18	1268.63	1035.46	932.57	880.07	851.30
100000	2137.03	1335.40	1089.96	981.65	926.39	896.11

10.50% Amount	5 Years	10 Years	15 Years	20 Years	25 Years	30 Years
50	1.08	.68	.56	.50	.48	.46
100	2.15	1.35	1.11	1.00	.95	.92
500	10.75	6.75	5.53	5.00	4.73	4.58
1000	21.50	13.50	11.06	9.99	9.45	9.15
2000	42.99	26.99	22.11	19.97	18.89	18.30
5000	107.47	67.47	55.27	49.92	47.21	45.74
10000	214.94	134.94	110.54	99.84	94.42	91.48
15000	322.41	202.41	165.81	149.76	141.63	137.22
20000	429.88	269.87	221.08	199.68	188.84	182.95
25000	537.35	337.34	276.35	249.60	236.05	228.69
30000	644.82	404.81	331.62	299.52	283.26	274.43
35000	752.29	472.28	386.89	349.44	330.47	320.16
40000	859.76	539.74	442.16	399.36	377.68	365.90
45000	967.23	607.21	497.43	449.28	424.89	411.64
50000	1074.70	674.68	552.70	499.19	472.10	457.37
55000	1182.17	742.15	607.97	549.11	519.30	503.11
60000	1289.64	809.61	663.24	599.03	566.51	548.85
65000	1397.11	977.08	718.51	648.95	613.72	594.59
70000	1504.58	944.55	773.78	698.87	660.93	640.32
75000	1612.05	1012.02	829.05	748.79	708.14	686.06
80000	1719.52	1079.49	884.32	798.71	755.35	731.80
85000	1826.99	1146.95	939.59	848.63	802.56	777.53
90000	1934.46	1214.42	994.86	898.55	849.77	823.27
95000	2041.93	1281.89	1050.13	948.47	896.98	869.01
100000	2149.40	1349.36	1105.40	998.38	944.19	914.74

10.75% Amount	5 Years	10 Years	15 Years	20 Years	25 Years	30 Years
50	1.09	.69	.57	.51	.49	.47
100	2.17	1.37	1.13	1.02	.97	.94
500	10.81	6.82	5.61	5.08	4.82	4.67
1000	21.62	13.64	11.21	10.16	9.63	9.34
2000	43.24	27.27	22.42	20.31	19.25	18.67
5000	108.09	68.17	56.05	50.77	48.11	46.68
10000	216.18	136.34	112.10	101.53	96.21	93.35
15000	324.27	204.51	168.15	152.29	144.32	140.03
20000	432.36	272.68	224.19	203.05	192.42	186.70
25000	540.45	340.85	280.24	253.81	240.53	233.38
30000	648.54	409.02	336.29	304.57	288.63	280.05
35000	756.63	477.19	392.34	355.34	336.74	326.72
40000	864.72	545.36	448.38	406.10	384.84	373.40
45000	972.81	613.53	504.43	456.86	432.95	420.07
50000	1080.90	681.70	560.48	507.62	481.05	466.75
55000	1188.99	749.87	616.53	558.38	529.16	513.42
60000	1297.08	818.04	672.57	609.14	577.26	560.09
65000	1405.17	886.21	728.62	659.90	625.37	606.77
70000	1513.26	954.38	784.67	710.67	673.47	653.44
75000	1621.35	1022.55	840.72	761.43	721.57	700.12
80000	1729.44	1090.71	896.76	812.19	769.68	746.79
85000	1837.53	1158.88	952.81	862.95	817.78	793.46
90000	1945.62	1227.05	1008.86	913.71	865.89	840.14
95000	2053.71	1295.22	1064.91	964.47	913.99	886.81
100000	2161.80	1363.39	1120.95	1015.23	962.10	933.49

11.00% Amount	5 Years	10 Years	15 Years	20 Years	25 Years	30 Years
50	1.09	.69	.57	.52	.50	.48
100	2.18	1.38	1.14	1.04	.99	.96
500	10.88	6.89	5.69	5.17	4.91	4.77
1000	21.75	13.78	11.37	10.33	9.81	9.53
2000	43.49	27.56	22.74	20.65	19.61	19.05
5000	108.72	68.88	56.83	51.61	49.01	47.62
10000	217.43	137.76	113.66	103.22	98.02	95.24
15000	326.14	206.63	170.49	154.83	147.02	142.85
20000	434.85	275.51	227.32	206.44	196.03	190.47
25000	543.57	344.38	284.15	258.05	245.03	238.09
30000	652.28	413.26	340.98	309.66	294.04	285.70
35000	760.99	482.13	397.81	361.27	343.04	333.32
40000	869.70	551.01	454.64	412.88	392.05	380.93
45000	978.41	619.88	511.47	464.49	441.06	428.55
50000	1087.13	688.76	568.30	516.10	490.06	476.17
55000	1195.84	757.63	625.13	567.71	539.07	523.78
60000	1304.55	826.51	681.96	619.32	588.07	571.40
65000	1413.26	895.38	738.79	670.93	637.08	619.02
70000	1521.97	964.26	795.62	722.54	686.08	666.63
75000	1630.69	1033.13	852.45	774.15	735.09	714.25
80000	1739.40	1102.01	909.28	825.76	784.10	761.86
85000	1848.11	1170.88	966.11	877.37	833.10	809.48
90000	1956.82	1239.76	1022.94	928.97	882.11	857.10
95000	2065.54	1308.63	1079.77	980.58	931.11	904.71
100000	2174.25	1377.51	1136.60	1032.19	980.12	952.33

11.25% Amount	5 Years	10 Years	15 Years	20 Years	25 Years	30 Years
50	1.10	.70	.58	.53	.50	.49
100	2.19	1.40	1.16	1.05	1.00	.98
500	10.94	6.96	5.77	5.25	5.00	4.86
1000	21.87	13.92	11.53	10.50	9.99	9.72
2000	43.74	27.84	23.05	20.99	19.97	19.43
5000	109.34	69.59	57.62	52.47	49.92	48.57
10000	218.68	139.17	115.24	104.93	99.83	97.13
15000	328.01	208.76	172.86	157.39	149.74	145.69
20000	437.35	278.34	230.47	209.86	199.65	194.26
25000	546.69	347.93	288.09	262.32	249.56	242.82
30000	656.02	417.51	345.71	314.78	299.48	291.38
35000	765.36	487.10	403.33	367.24	349.39	339.95
40000	874.70	556.68	460.94	419.71	399.30	388.51
45000	984.03	626.27	518.56	472.17	449.21	437.07
50000	1093.37	695.85	576.18	524.63	499.12	485.64
55000	1202.71	765.43	633.79	577.10	549.04	534.20
60000	1312.04	835.02	691.41	629.56	598.95	582.76
65000	1421.38	904.60	749.03	682.02	648.86	631.32
70000	1530.72	974.19	806.65	734.48	698.77	679.89
75000	1640.05	1043.77	864.26	786.95	748.68	728.45
80000	1749.39	1113.36	921.88	839.41	798.60	777.01
85000	1858.73	1182.94	979.50	891.87	848.51	825.58
90000	1968.06	1252.53	1037.12	944.34	898.42	874.14
95000	2077.40	1322.11	1094.73	996.80	948.33	922.70
100000	2186.74	1391.69	1152.35	1049.26	998.24	971.27

11.50% Amount	5 Years	10 Years	15 Years	20 Years	25 Years	30 Years
50	1.10	.71	.59	.54	.51	.50
100	2.20	1.41	1.17	1.07	1.02	1.00
500	11.00	7.03	5.85	5.34	5.09	4.96
1000	22.00	14.06	11.69	10.67	10.17	9.91
2000	43.99	28.12	23.37	21.33	20.33	19.81
5000	109.97	70.30	58.41	53.33	50.83	49.52
10000	219.93	140.60	116.82	106.65	101.65	99.03
15000	329.89	210.90	175.23	159.97	152.48	148.55
20000	439.86	281.20	233.64	213.29	203.30	198.06
25000	549.82	351.49	292.05	266.61	254.12	247.58
30000	659.78	421.79	350.46	319.93	304.95	297.09
35000	769.75	492.09	408.87	373.26	355.77	346.61
40000	879.71	562.39	467.28	426.58	406.59	396.12
45000	989.67	632.68	525.69	479.90	457.42	445.64
50000	1099.64	702.98	584.10	533.22	508.24	495.15
55000	1209.60	773.28	642.51	586.54	559.06	544.67
60000	1319.56	843.58	700.92	639.86	609.89	594.18
65000	1429.52	913.88	759.33	693.18	660.71	643.69
70000	1539.49	984.17	817.74	746.51	711.53	693.21
75000	1649.45	1054.47	876.15	799.83	762.36	742.72
80000	1759.41	1124.77	934.56	853.15	813.18	792.24
85000	1869.38	1195.07	992.97	906.47	864.00	841.75
90000	1979.34	1265.36	1051.38	959.79	914.83	891.27
95000	2089.30	1335.66	1109.79	1013.11	965.65	940.78
100000	2199.27	1405.96	1168.19	1066.43	1016.47	990.30

11.75% Amount	5 Years	10 Years	15 Years	20 Years	25 Years	30 Years
50	1.11	.72	.60	.55	.52	.51
100	2.22	1.43	1.19	1.09	1.04	1.01
500	11.06	7.11	5.93	5.42	5.18	5.05
1000	22.12	14.21	11.85	10.84	10.35	10.10
2000	44.24	28.41	23.69	21.68	20.70	20.19
5000	110.60	71.02	59.21	54.19	51.74	50.48
10000	221.19	142.03	118.42	108.38	103.48	100.95
15000	331.78	213.05	177.62	162.56	155.22	151.42
20000	442.37	284.06	236.83	216.75	206.96	201.89
25000	552.96	355.08	296.04	270.93	258.70	252.36
30000	663.55	426.09	355.24	325.12	310.44	302.83
35000	774.15	497.11	414.45	379.30	362.18	353.30
40000	884.74	568.12	473.66	433.49	413.92	403.77
45000	995.33	639.14	532.86	487.67	465.66	454.24
50000	1105.92	710.15	592.07	541.86	517.40	504.71
55000	1216.51	781.17	651.28	596.04	569.14	555.18
60000	1327.10	852.18	710.48	650.23	620.88	605.65
65000	1437.70	923.20	769.69	704.41	672.62	656.12
70000	1548.29	994.21	828.90	758.60	724.36	706.59
75000	1658.88	1065.23	888.10	812.79	776.10	757.06
80000	1769.47	1136.24	947.31	866.97	827.84	807.53
85000	1880.06	1207.26	1006.52	921.16	879.58	858.00
90000	1990.65	1278.27	1065.72	975.34	931.32	908.47
95000	2101.25	1349.28	1124.93	1029.53	983.06	958.94
100000	2211.84	1420.30	1184.14	1083.71	1034.80	1009.41

12.00% Amount	5 Years	10 Years	15 Years	20 Years	25 Years	30 Years
50	1.12	.72	.61	.56	.53	.52
100	2.23	1.44	1.21	1.11	1.06	1.03
500	11.13	7.18	6.01	5.51	5.27	5.15
1000	22.25	14.35	12.01	11.02	10.54	10.29
2000	44.49	28.70	24.01	22.03	21.07	20.58
5000	111.23	71.74	60.01	55.06	52.67	51.44
10000	222.45	143.48	120.02	110.11	105.33	102.87
15000	333.67	215.21	180.03	165.17	157.99	154.30
20000	444.89	286.95	240.04	220.22	210.65	205.73
25000	556.12	358.68	300.05	275.28	263.31	257.16
30000	667.34	430.42	360.06	330.33	315.97	308.59
35000	778.56	502.15	420.06	385.39	368.63	360.02
40000	889.78	573.89	480.07	440.44	421.29	411.45
45000	1001.01	645.62	540.08	495.49	473.96	462.88
50000	1112.23	717.36	600.09	550.55	526.62	514.31
55000	1223.45	789.10	660.10	605.60	579.28	565.74
60000	1334.67	860.83	720.11	660.66	631.94	617.17
65000	1445.89	932.57	780.11	715.71	684.60	668.60
70000	1557.12	1004.30	840.12	770.77	737.26	720.03
75000	1668.34	1076.04	900.13	825.82	789.92	771.46
80000	1779.56	1147.77	960.14	880.87	842.58	822.90
85000	1890.78	1219.51	1020.15	935.93	895.25	874.33
90000	2002.01	1291.24	1080.16	990.98	947.91	925.76
95000	2113.23	1362.98	1140.16	1046.04	1000.57	977.19
100000	2224.45	1434.71	1200.17	1101.09	1053.23	1028.62

12.25% Amount	5 Years	10 Years	15 Years	20 Years	25 Years	30 Years
50	1.12	.73	.61	.56	.54	.53
100	2.24	1.45	1.22	1.12	1.08	1.05
500	11.19	7.25	6.09	5.60	5.36	5.24
1000	22.38	14.50	12.17	11.19	10.72	10.48
2000	44.75	28.99	24.33	22.38	21.44	20.96
5000	111.86	72.46	60.82	55.93	53.59	52.40
10000	223.71	144.92	121.63	111.86	107.18	104.79
15000	335.57	217.38	182.45	167.79	160.77	157.19
20000	447.42	289.84	243.26	223.72	214.35	209.58
25000	559.28	362.30	304.08	279.65	267.94	261.98
30000	671.13	434.76	364.89	335.57	321.53	314.37
35000	782.99	507.22	425.71	391.50	375.12	366.77
40000	894.84	579.68	486.52	447.43	428.70	419.16
45000	1006.70	652.14	547.34	503.36	482.29	471.56
50000	1118.55	724.60	608.15	559.29	535.88	523.95
55000	1230.41	797.06	668.97	615.22	589.46	576.35
60000	1342.26	869.52	729.78	671.14	643.05	628.74
65000	1454.12	941.98	790.60	727.07	696.64	681.14
70000	1565.97	1014.44	851.41	783.00	750.23	733.53
75000	1677.83	1086.90	912.23	838.93	803.81	785.93
80000	1789.68	1159.36	973.04	894.86	857.40	838.32
85000	1901.54	1231.82	1033.86	950.78	910.99	890.72
90000	2013.39	1304.28	1094.67	1006.71	964.57	943.11
95000	2125.25	1376.74	1155.49	1062.64	1018.16	995.51
100000	2237.10	1449.20	1216.30	1118.57	1071.75	1047.90

12.50% Amount	5 Years	10 Years	15 Years	20 Years	25 Years	30 Years
50	1.13	.74	.62	.57	.55	.54
100	2.25	1.47	1.24	1.14	1.10	1.07
500	11.25	7.32	6.17	5.69	5.46	5.34
1000	22.50	14.64	12.33	11.37	10.91	10.68
2000	45.00	29.28	24.66	22.73	21.81	21.35
5000	112.49	73.19	61.63	56.81	54.52	53.37
10000	224.98	146.38	123.26	113.62	109.04	106.73
15000	337.47	219.57	184.88	170.43	163.56	160.09
20000	449.96	292.76	246.51	227.23	218.08	213.46
25000	562.45	365.95	308.14	284.04	272.59	266.82
30000	674.94	439.13	369.76	340.85	327.11	320.18
35000	787.43	512.32	431.39	397.65	381.63	373.55
40000	899.92	585.51	493.01	454.46	436.15	426.91
45000	1012.41	658.70	554.64	511.27	490.66	480.27
50000	1124.90	731.89	616.27	568.08	545.18	533.63
55000	1237.39	805.07	677.89	624.88	599.70	587.00
60000	1349.88	878.26	739.52	681.69	654.22	640.36
65000	1462.37	951.45	801.14	738.50	708.74	693.72
70000	1574.86	1024.64	862.77	795.30	763.25	747.09
75000	1687.35	1097.83	924.40	852.11	817.77	800.45
80000	1799.84	1171.01	986.02	908.92	872.29	853.81
85000	1912.33	1244.20	1047.65	965.72	926.81	907.17
90000	2024.82	1317.39	1109.27	1022.53	981.32	960.54
95000	2137.31	1390.58	1170.90	1079.34	1035.84	1013.90
100000	2249.80	1463.77	1232.53	1136.15	1090.36	1067.26

12.75% Amount	5 Years	10 Years	15 Years	20 Years	25 Years	30 Years
50	1.14	.74	.63	.58	.56	.55
100	2.27	1.48	1.25	1.16	1.11	1.09
500	11.32	7.40	6.25	5.77	5.55	5.44
1000	22.63	14.79	12.49	11.54	11.10	10.87
2000	45.26	29.57	24.98	23.08	22.19	21.74
5000	113.13	73.92	62.45	57.70	55.46	54.34
10000	226.26	147.84	124.89	115.39	110.91	108.67
15000	339.38	221.76	187.33	173.08	166.36	163.01
20000	452.51	295.68	249.77	230.77	221.82	217.34
25000	565.64	369.60	312.21	288.46	277.27	271.68
30000	678.76	443.52	374.66	346.15	332.72	326.01
35000	791.89	517.44	437.10	403.84	388.17	380.35
40000	905.02	591.36	499.54	461.53	443.63	434.68
45000	1018.14	665.28	561.98	519.22	499.08	489.02
50000	1131.27	739.20	624.42	576.91	554.53	543.35
55000	1244.40	813.12	686.87	634.60	609.98	597.69
60000	1357.52	887.04	749.31	692.29	665.44	652.02
65000	1470.65	960.96	811.75	749.98	720.89	706.36
70000	1583.78	1034.88	874.19	807.67	776.34	760.69
75000	1696.90	1108.80	936.63	865.36	831.79	815.02
80000	1810.03	1182.72	999.07	923.05	887.25	869.36
85000	1923.16	1256.64	1061.52	980.74	942.70	923.69
90000	2036.28	1330.56	1123.96	1038.44	998.15	978.03
95000	2149.41	1404.48	1186.40	1096.13	1053.60	1032.36
100000	2262.54	1478.40	1248.84	1153.82	1109.06	1086.70

13.00% Amount	5 Years	10 Years	15 Years	20 Years	25 Years	30 Years
50	1.14	.75	.64	.59	.57	.56
100	2.28	1.50	1.27	1.18	1.13	1.11
500	11.38	7.47	6.33	5.86	5.64	5.54
1000	22.76	14.94	12.66	11.72	11.28	11.07
2000	45.51	29.87	25.31	23.44	22.56	22.13
5000	113.77	74.66	63.27	58.58	56.40	55.31
10000	227.54	149.32	126.53	117.16	112.79	110.62
15000	341.30	223.97	189.79	175.74	169.18	165.93
20000	455.07	298.63	253.05	234.32	225.57	221.24
25000	568.83	373.28	316.32	292.90	281.96	276.55
30000	682.60	447.94	379.58	351.48	338.36	331.86
35000	796.36	522.59	442.84	410.06	394.75	387.17
40000	910.13	597.25	506.10	468.64	451.14	442.48
45000	1023.89	671.90	569.36	527.21	507.53	497.79
50000	1137.66	746.56	632.63	585.79	563.92	553.10
55000	1251.42	821.21	695.89	644.37	620.31	608.41
60000	1365.19	895.87	759.15	702.95	676.71	663.72
65000	1478.95	970.52	822.41	761.53	733.10	719.03
70000	1592.72	1045.18	885.67	820.11	789.49	774.34
75000	1706.49	1119.84	948.94	878.69	845.88	829.65
80000	1820.25	1194.49	1012.20	937.27	902.27	884.96
85000	1934.02	1269.15	1175.46	995.84	958.67	940.27
90000	2047.78	1343.80	1138.72	1054.42	1015.06	995.58
95000	2161.55	1418.46	1201.99	1113.00	1071.45	1050.89
100000	2275.31	1493.11	1265.25	1171.58	1127.84	1106.20

13.25% Amount	5 Years	10 Years	15 Years	20 Years	25 Years	30 Years
50	1.15	.76	.65	.60	.58	.57
100	2.29	1.51	1.29	1.19	1.15	1.13
500	11.45	7.54	6.41	5.95	5.74	5.63
1000	22.89	15.08	12.82	11.90	11.47	11.26
2000	45.77	30.16	25.64	23.79	22.94	22.52
5000	114.41	75.40	64.09	59.48	57.34	56.29
10000	228.82	150.79	128.18	118.95	114.68	112.58
15000	343.22	226.19	192.27	178.42	172.01	168.87
20000	457.63	301.58	256.35	237.89	229.35	225.16
25000	572.04	376.98	320.44	297.36	286.68	281.45
30000	686.44	452.37	384.53	356.83	344.02	337.74
35000	800.85	527.77	448.61	416.31	401.35	394.03
40000	915.26	603.16	512.70	475.78	458.69	450.31
45000	1029.66	678.56	576.79	535.25	516.02	506.60
50000	1144.07	753.95	640.87	594.72	573.36	562.89
55000	1258.47	829.34	704.96	654.19	630.69	619.18
60000	1372.88	904.74	769.05	713.66	688.03	675.47
65000	1487.29	980.13	833.13	773.13	745.36	731.76
70000	1601.69	1055.53	897.22	832.61	802.70	788.05
75000	1716.10	1130.92	961.31	892.08	860.03	844.34
80000	1830.51	1206.32	1025.39	951.55	917.37	900.62
85000	1944.91	1281.71	1089.48	1011.02	974.70	956.91
90000	2059.32	1357.11	1153.57	1070.49	1032.04	1013.20
95000	2173.72	1432.50	1217.65	1129.96	1089.37	1069.49
100000	2288.12	1507.89	1281.74	1189.44	1146.71	1125.78

13.50% Amount	5 Years	10 Years	15 Years	20 Years	25 Years	30 Years
50	1.16	.77	.65	.61	.59	.58
100	2.31	1.53	1.30	1.21	1.17	1.15
500	11.51	7.62	6.50	6.04	5.83	5.73
1000	23.01	15.23	12.99	12.08	11.66	11.46
2000	46.02	30.46	25.97	24.15	23.32	22.91
5000	115.05	76.14	64.92	60.37	58.29	57.28
10000	230.10	152.28	129.84	120.74	116.57	114.55
15000	345.15	228.42	194.75	181.11	174.85	171.82
20000	460.20	304.55	259.67	241.48	233.13	229.09
25000	575.25	380.69	324.58	301.85	291.42	286.36
30000	690.30	456.83	389.50	362.22	349.70	343.63
35000	805.35	532.97	454.42	422.59	407.98	400.90
40000	920.40	609.10	519.33	482.95	466.26	458.17
45000	1035.45	685.24	584.25	543.32	524.55	515.44
50000	1150.50	761.38	649.16	603.69	582.83	572.71
55000	1265.55	837.51	714.08	664.06	641.11	629.98
60000	1380.60	913.65	779.00	724.43	699.39	687.25
65000	1495.65	989.79	843.91	784.80	757.67	744.52
70000	1610.69	1065.93	908.83	845.17	815.96	801.79
75000	1725.74	1142.06	973.74	905.54	874.24	859.06
80000	1840.79	1218.20	1038.66	965.90	932.52	916.33
85000	1955.84	1294.34	1103.58	1026.27	990.80	973.61
90000	2070.89	1370.47	1168.49	1086.64	1049.09	1030.88
95000	2185.94	1446.61	1233.41	1147.01	1107.37	1088.15
100000	2300.99	1522.75	1298.32	1207.38	1165.65	1145.42

13.75% Amount	5 Years	10 Years	15 Years	20 Years	25 Years	30 Years
50	1.16	.77	.66	.62	.60	.59
100	2.32	1.54	1.32	1.23	1.19	1.17
500	11.57	7.69	6.58	6.13	5.93	5.83
1000	23.14	15.38	13.15	12.26	11.85	11.66
2000	46.28	30.76	26.30	24.51	23.70	23.31
5000	115.70	76.89	65.75	61.28	59.24	58.26
10000	231.39	153.77	131.50	122.55	118.47	116.52
15000	347.09	230.66	197.25	183.82	177.70	174.77
20000	462.78	307.54	263.00	245.09	236.94	233.03
25000	578.48	384.42	328.75	306.36	296.17	291.28
30000	694.17	461.31	394.50	367.63	355.40	349.54
35000	809.86	538.19	460.25	428.90	414.64	407.79
40000	952.56	615.07	526.00	490.17	473.87	466.05
45000	1041.25	691.96	591.75	551.44	533.10	524.31
50000	1156.95	768.84	657.50	612.71	592.34	582.56
55000	1272.64	845.72	723.25	673.98	651.57	640.82
60000	1388.34	922.61	789.00	735.25	710.80	699.07
65000	1504.03	999.49	854.75	796.52	770.04	757.33
70000	1619.72	1076.37	920.50	857.79	829.27	815.58
75000	1735.42	1153.26	986.25	919.06	888.50	873.84
80000	1851.11	1230.14	1051.99	980.33	947.74	932.10
85000	1966.81	1307.02	1117.74	1041.60	1006.97	990.35
90000	2082.50	1383.91	1183.49	1102.87	1066.20	1048.61
95000	2198.20	1460.79	1249.24	1164.14	1125.44	1106.86
100000	2313.89	1537.67	1314.99	1225.41	1184.67	1165.12

14.00% Amount	5 Years	10 Years	15 Years	20 Years	25 Years	30 Years
50	1.17	.78	.67	.63	.61	.60
100	2.33	1.56	1.34	1.25	1.21	1.19
500	11.64	7.77	6.66	6.22	6.02	5.93
1000	23.27	15.53	13.32	12.44	12.04	11.85
2000	46.54	31.06	26.64	24.88	24.08	23.70
5000	116.35	77.64	66.59	62.18	60.19	59.25
10000	232.69	155.27	133.18	124.36	120.38	118.49
15000	349.03	232.90	199.77	186.53	180.57	177.74
20000	465.37	310.54	266.35	248.71	240.76	236.98
25000	581.71	388.17	332.94	310.89	300.95	296.22
30000	698.05	465.80	399.53	373.06	361.13	355.47
35000	814.39	543.44	466.11	435.24	421.32	414.71
40000	930.74	621.07	532.70	497.41	481.51	473.95
45000	1047.08	698.70	599.29	559.59	541.70	533.20
50000	1163.42	776.34	665.88	621.77	601.89	592.44
55000	1279.76	853.97	732.46	683.94	662.07	651.68
60000	1396.10	931.60	799.05	746.12	722.26	710.93
65000	1512.44	1009.24	865.64	808.29	782.45	770.17
70000	1628.78	1086.87	932.22	870.47	842.64	829.42
75000	1745.12	1164.50	998.81	932.65	902.83	888.66
80000	1861.47	1242.14	1065.40	994.82	963.01	947.90
85000	1977.81	1319.77	1131.99	1057.00	1023.20	1007.15
90000	2094.15	1397.40	1198.57	1119.17	1083.39	1066.39
95000	2210.49	1475.04	1265.16	1181.35	1143.58	1125.63
100000	2326.83	1552.67	1331.75	1243.53	1203.77	1184.88

14.25% Amount	5 Years	10 Years	15 Years	20 Years	25 Years	30 Years
50	1.17	.79	.68	.64	.62	.61
100	2.34	1.57	1.35	1.27	1.23	1.21
500	11.70	7.84	6.75	6.31	6.12	6.03
1000	23.40	15.68	13.49	12.62	12.23	12.05
2000	46.80	31.36	26.98	25.24	24.46	24.10
5000	117.00	78.39	67.43	63.09	61.15	60.24
10000	233.99	156.78	134.86	126.18	122.30	120.47
15000	350.98	235.16	202.29	189.26	183.44	180.71
20000	467.97	313.55	269.72	252.35	244.59	240.94
25000	584.96	391.94	337.15	315.43	305.74	301.18
30000	701.95	470.32	404.58	378.52	366.88	361.41
35000	818.94	548.71	472.01	441.61	428.03	421.65
40000	935.93	627.10	539.44	504.69	489.18	481.88
45000	1052.92	705.48	606.87	567.78	550.32	542.11
50000	1169.91	783.87	674.29	630.86	611.47	602.35
55000	1286.90	862.26	741.72	693.95	672.62	662.58
60000	1403.89	940.64	809.15	757.04	733.76	722.82
65000	1520.88	1019.03	876.58	820.12	794.91	783.05
70000	1637.87	1097.42	944.01	883.21	856.05	843.29
75000	1754.86	1175.80	1011.44	946.29	917.20	903.52
80000	1871.85	1254.19	1078.87	1009.38	978.35	963.75
85000	1988.84	1332.58	1146.30	1072.47	1039.49	1023.99
90000	2105.83	1410.96	1213.73	1135.55	1100.64	1084.22
95000	2222.82	1489.35	1281.16	1198.64	1161.79	1144.46
100000	2339.81	1567.74	1348.58	1261.72	1222.93	1204.69

14.50% Amount	5 Years	10 Years	15 Years	20 Years	25 Years	30 Years
50	1.18	.80	.69	.64	.63	.62
100	2.36	1.59	1.37	1.28	1.25	1.23
500	11.77	7.92	6.83	6.40	6.22	6.13
1000	23.53	15.83	13.66	12.80	12.43	12.25
2000	47.06	31.66	27.32	25.60	24.85	24.50
5000	117.65	79.15	68.28	64.00	62.11	61.23
10000	235.29	158.29	136.56	128.00	124.22	122.46
15000	352.93	237.44	204.83	192.00	186.33	183.69
20000	470.57	316.58	273.11	256.00	248.44	244.92
25000	588.21	395.72	341.38	320.00	310.55	306.14
30000	705.85	474.87	409.66	384.00	372.65	367.37
35000	823.49	554.01	477.93	448.00	434.76	428.60
40000	941.14	633.15	546.21	512.00	496.87	489.83
45000	1058.78	712.30	614.48	576.00	558.98	551.06
50000	1176.42	791.44	682.76	640.00	621.09	612.28
55000	1294.06	870.58	751.03	704.00	683.19	673.51
60000	1411.70	949.73	819.31	768.00	745.30	734.74
65000	1529.34	1028.87	887.58	832.00	807.41	795.97
70000	1646.98	1108.01	955.86	896.00	869.52	857.19
75000	1764.63	1187.16	1024.13	960.00	931.63	918.42
80000	1882.27	1266.30	1092.41	1024.00	993.74	979.65
85000	1999.91	1345.44	1160.68	1088.00	1055.84	1040.88
90000	2117.55	1424.59	1228.96	1152.00	1117.95	1102.11
95000	2235.19	1503.73	1297.23	1216.00	1180.06	1163.33
100000	2352.83	1582.87	1365.51	1280.00	1242.17	1224.56

14.75% Amount	5 Years	10 Years	15 Years	20 Years	25 Years	30 Years
50	1.19	.80	.70	.65	.64	.63
100	2.37	1.60	1.39	1.30	1.27	1.25
500	11.83	8.00	6.92	6.50	6.31	6.23
1000	23.66	15.99	13.83	12.99	12.62	12.45
2000	47.32	31.97	27.66	25.97	25.23	24.89
5000	118.30	79.91	69.13	64.92	63.08	62.23
10000	236.59	159.81	138.26	129.84	126.15	124.45
15000	354.89	239.72	207.38	194.76	189.22	186.68
20000	473.18	319.62	276.51	259.68	252.30	248.90
25000	591.48	399.52	345.63	324.59	315.37	311.12
30000	709.77	479.43	414.76	389.51	378.44	373.35
35000	828.07	559.33	483.88	454.43	441.52	435.57
40000	946.36	639.23	553.01	519.35	504.59	497.80
45000	1064.66	719.14	622.13	584.26	567.66	560.02
50000	1182.95	799.04	691.26	649.18	630.74	622.24
55000	1301.24	878.95	760.38	714.10	693.81	684.47
60000	1419.54	958.85	829.51	779.02	756.88	746.69
65000	1537.83	1038.75	898.63	843.94	819.96	808.91
70000	1656.13	1118.66	967.76	908.85	883.03	871.14
75000	1774.42	1198.56	1036.88	973.77	946.10	933.36
80000	1892.72	1278.46	1106.01	1038.69	1009.18	995.59
85000	2011.01	1358.37	1175.13	1103.61	1072.25	1057.81
90000	2129.31	1438.27	1244.26	1168.52	1135.32	1120.03
95000	2247.60	1518.18	1313.38	1233.44	1198.40	1182.26
100000	2365.90	1598.08	1382.51	1298.36	1261.47	1244.48

15.00% Amount	5 Years	10 Years	15 Years	20 Years	25 Years	30 Years
50	1.19	.81	.70	.66	.65	.64
100	2.38	1.62	1.40	1.32	1.29	1.27
500	11.90	8.07	7.00	6.59	6.41	6.33
1000	23.79	16.14	14.00	13.17	12.81	12.65
2000	47.58	32.27	28.00	26.34	25.62	25.29
5000	118.95	80.67	69.98	65.84	64.05	63.23
10000	237.90	161.34	139.96	131.68	128.09	126.45
15000	356.85	242.01	209.94	197.52	192.13	189.67
20000	475.80	322.67	279.92	263.36	256.17	252.89
25000	594.75	403.34	349.90	329.20	320.21	316.12
30000	713.70	484.01	419.88	395.04	384.25	379.34
35000	832.65	564.68	489.86	460.88	448.30	442.56
40000	951.60	645.34	559.84	526.72	512.34	505.78
45000	1070.55	726.01	629.82	592.56	576.38	569.00
50000	1189.50	806.68	699.80	658.40	640.42	632.23
55000	1308.45	887.35	769.78	724.24	704.46	695.45
60000	1427.40	968.01	839.76	790.08	768.50	758.67
65000	1546.35	1048.68	909.74	855.92	832.54	821.89
70000	1665.30	1129.35	979.72	921.76	896.59	885.12
75000	1784.25	1210.02	1049.70	987.60	960.63	948.34
80000	1903.20	1290.68	1119.67	1053.44	1024.67	1011.56
85000	2022.15	1371.35	1189.65	1119.28	1088.71	1074.78
90000	2141.10	1452.02	1259.63	1185.12	1152.75	1138.00
95000	2260.05	1532.69	1329.61	1250.96	1216.79	1201.23
100000	2379.00	1613.35	1399.59	1316.79	1280.84	1264.45

15.25% Amount	5 Years	10 Years	15 Years	20 Years	25 Years	30 Years
50	1.20	.82	.71	.67	.66	.65
100	2.40	1.63	1.42	1.34	1.31	1.29
500	11.97	8.15	7.09	6.68	6.51	6.43
1000	23.93	16.29	14.17	13.36	13.01	12.85
2000	47.85	32.58	28.34	26.71	26.01	25.69
5000	119.61	81.44	70.84	66.77	65.02	64.23
10000	239.22	162.87	141.68	133.53	130.03	128.45
15000	358.83	244.31	212.52	200.30	195.04	192.67
20000	478.43	325.74	283.35	267.06	260.06	256.90
25000	598.04	407.18	354.19	333.83	325.07	321.12
30000	717.65	488.61	425.03	400.59	390.08	385.34
35000	837.25	570.05	495.87	467.36	455.10	449.57
40000	956.86	651.48	566.70	534.12	520.11	513.79
45000	1076.47	732.92	637.54	600.89	585.12	578.01
50000	1196.07	814.35	708.38	667.65	650.13	642.23
55000	1315.68	895.79	779.22	734.42	715.15	706.46
60000	1435.29	977.22	850.05	801.18	780.16	770.68
65000	1554.89	1058.66	920.89	867.95	845.17	834.90
70000	1674.50	1140.09	991.73	934.71	910.19	899.13
75000	1794.11	1221.53	1062.57	1001.48	975.20	963.35
80000	1913.71	1302.96	1133.40	1068.24	1040.21	1027.57
85000	2033.32	1384.39	1204.24	1135.01	1105.22	1091.79
90000	2152.93	1465.83	1275.08	1201.77	1170.24	1156.02
95000	2272.53	1547.26	1345.92	1268.54	1235.25	1220.24
100000	2392.14	1628.70	1416.75	1335.30	1300.26	1284.46

15.50% Amount	5 Years	10 Years	15 Years	20 Years	25 Years	30 Years
50	1.21	.83	.72	.68	.66	.66
100	2.41	1.65	1.44	1.36	1.32	1.31
500	12.03	8.23	7.17	6.77	6.60	6.53
1000	24.06	16.45	14.34	13.54	13.20	13.05
2000	48.11	32.89	28.68	27.08	26.40	26.10
5000	120.27	82.21	71.70	67.70	65.99	65.23
10000	240.54	164.42	143.40	135.39	131.98	130.46
15000	360.80	246.62	215.10	203.09	197.97	195.68
20000	481.07	328.83	286.80	270.78	263.95	260.91
25000	601.33	411.03	358.50	338.48	329.94	326.13
30000	721.60	493.24	430.20	406.17	395.93	391.36
35000	841.87	575.44	501.90	473.86	461.92	456.59
40000	962.13	657.65	573.60	541.56	527.90	521.81
45000	1082.40	739.85	645.30	609.25	593.89	587.04
50000	1202.66	822.06	717.00	676.95	659.88	652.26
55000	1322.93	904.26	788.70	744.64	725.86	717.49
60000	1443.20	986.47	860.40	812.33	791.85	782.72
65000	1563.46	1068.67	932.10	880.03	857.84	847.94
70000	1683.73	1150.88	1003.80	947.72	923.83	913.17
75000	1803.99	1233.08	1075.50	1015.42	989.81	978.39
80000	1924.26	1315.29	1147.20	1083.11	1055.80	1043.62
85000	2044.53	1397.49	1218.90	1150.80	1121.79	1108.84
90000	2164.79	1479.70	1290.60	1218.50	1187.78	1174.07
95000	2285.06	1561.91	1362.30	1286.19	1253.76	1239.30
100000	2405.32	1644.11	1434.00	1353.89	1319.75	1304.52

Appendix B
Remaining Balance
Tables

See page 128 for a discussion of Remaining Balance Tables.

8.00%	Age of Loan	5 years	10 years	15 years	20 years	25 years	30 years
	1	83.06	93.19	96.40	97.89	98.69	99.16
	2	64.71	85.82	92.51	95.60	97.27	98.26
	3	44.83	77.84	88.29	93.12	95.74	97.28
	4	23.31	69.20	83.72	90.43	94.07	96.22
	5	0	59.84	78.77	87.53	92.27	95.07
	6		49.70	73.41	84.38	90.32	93.83
	7		38.72	67.60	80.97	88.21	92.48
	8		26.83	61.31	77.27	85.92	91.02
	9		13.95	54.51	73.27	83.45	89.44
	10		0	47.13	68.94	80.76	87.72
	11			39.15	64.25	77.86	85.87
	12			30.50	59.17	74.71	83.86
	13			21.13	53.67	71.30	81.69
	14			10.99	47.71	67.61	79.33
	15			0	41.25	63.61	76.78
	16				34.26	59.29	74.02
	17				26.69	54.60	71.03
	18				18.49	49.52	67.79
	19				9.62	44.02	64.28
	20				0	38.06	60.48
	21					31.62	56.36
	22					24.63	51.91
	23					17.07	47.08
	24					8.87	41.85
	25					0	36.19
	26						30.06
	27						23.42
	28						16.22
	29						8.44
	30						0

8.25%	Age of Loan	5 years	10 years	15 years	20 years	25 years	30 years
	1	83.15	93.28	96.48	97.95	98.74	99.21
	2	64.85	85.99	92.65	95.72	97.38	98.34
	3	44.98	78.07	88.50	93.30	95.89	97.41
	4	23.42	69.47	83.99	90.68	94.28	96.39
	5	0	60.13	79.10	87.83	92.53	95.28
	6		50.00	73.78	84.73	90.64	94.09
	7		39.00	68.01	81.38	88.58	92.78
	8		27.05	61.75	77.73	86.34	91.37
	9		14.08	54.95	73.77	83.91	89.84
	10		0	47.56	69.47	81.27	88.17
	11			39.55	64.80	78.41	86.36
	12			30.85	59.74	75.30	84.40
	13			21.40	54.23	71.93	82.27
	14			11.14	48.26	68.26	79.95
	15			0.	41.78	64.28	77.44
	16				34.74	59.96	74.71
	17				27.09	55.28	71.75
	18				18.79	50.18	68.53
	19				9.78	44.66	65.04
	20				0	38.66	61.25
	21					32.14	57.14
	22					25.07	52.67
	23					17.39	47.82
	24					9.05	42.55
	25					0	36.83
	26						30.63
	27						23.89
	28						16.57
	29						8.62
	30						0

8.50%	Age of Loan	5 years	10 years	15 years	20 years	25 years	30 years
	1	83.24	93.37	96.55	98.01	98.70	99.24
	2	64.99	86.15	92.80	95.84	97.47	98.42
	3	45.14	78.29	88.71	93.49	96.04	97.53
	4	23.52	69.74	84.26	90.92	94.48	96.55
	5	0.	60.43	79.42	88.13	92.79	95.49
	6		50.30	74.16	85.09	90.94	94.34
	7		39.28	68.42	81.78	88.93	93.08
	8		27.28	62.18	78.18	86.74	91.71
	9		14.22	55.39	74.26	84.36	90.22
	10		0	48.00	69.99	81.77	88.60
	11			39.95	65.35	78.95	86.84
	12			31.19	60.30	75.88	84.92
	13			21.66	54.80	72.54	82.83
	14			11.29	48.81	68.90	80.56
	15			0	42.30	64.95	78.08
	16				35.21	60.64	75.39
	17				27.49	55.95	72.46
	18				19.09	50.85	69.27
	19				9.95	45.29	65.80
	20				0	39.25	62.02
	21					32.67	57.90
	22					25.51	53.43
	23					17.71	48.55
	24					9.23	43.25
	25					0	37.48
	26						31.20
	27						24.36
	28						16.92
	29						8.82
	30						0

8.75%	Age of Loan	5 years	10 years	15 years	20 years	25 years	30 years
	1	83.33	93.45	96.62	98.07	98.84	99.28
	2	65.14	86.31	92.94	95.96	97.57	98.50
	3	45.29	78.51	88.92	93.66	96.19	97.64
	4	23.63	70.01	84.53	91.16	94.68	96.71
	5	0	60.73	79.75	88.42	93.03	95.69
	6		50.60	74.53	85.43	91.24	94.58
	7		39.56	68.83	82.18	89.28	93.36
	8		27.50	62.61	78.62	87.14	92.04
	9		14.35	55.83	74.74	84.81	90.60
	10		0	48.43	70.51	82.26	89.02
	11			40.35	65.90	79.48	87.30
	12			31.54	60.86	76.45	85.43
	13			21.93	55.36	73.14	83.38
	14			11.44	49.36	69.54	81.15
	15			0	42.82	65.60	78.71
	16				35.68	61.30	76.06
	17				27.89	56.62	73.16
	18				19.39	51.50	69.99
	19				10.12	45.93	66.54
	20				0	39.84	62.77
	21					33.20	58.66
	22					25.95	54.18
	23					18.04	49.28
	24					9.41	43.95
	25					0	38.12
	26						31.76
	27						24.83
	28						17.26
	29						9.01
	30						0

9.00%

Age of Loan	5 years	10 years	15 years	20 years	25 years	30 years
1	83.42	93.54	96.69	98.13	98.88	99.32
2	65.28	86.47	93.08	96.08	97.66	98.57
3	45.44	78.73	89.12	93.84	96.33	97.75
4	23.74	70.28	84.80	91.39	94.87	96.86
5	0	61.02	80.07	88.71	93.27	95.88
6		50.90	74.89	85.77	91.53	94.81
7		39.84	69.23	82.57	89.62	93.64
8		27.73	63.04	79.06	87.53	92.36
9		14.49	56.27	75.22	85.24	90.96
10		0	48.86	71.03	82.74	89.43
11			40.76	66.44	80.00	87.75
12			31.90	61.41	77.01	85.92
13			22.20	55.92	73.74	83.92
14			11.60	49.91	70.16	81.73
15			0	43.34	66.25	79.33
16				36.16	61.97	76.71
17				28.29	57.28	73.84
18				19.69	52.16	70.70
19				10.29	46.56	67.27
20				0	40.43	63.52
21					33.72	59.41
22					26.39	54.92
23					18.37	50.01
24					9.60	44.64
25					0	38.76
26						32.33
27						25.30
28						17.61
29						9.20
30						0

9.25%

Age of Loan	5 years	10 years	15 years	20 years	25 years	30 years
1	83.51	93.62	96.76	98.18	98.93	99.35
2	65.42	86.62	93.22	96.19	97.75	98.64
3	45.59	78.95	89.33	94.01	96.47	97.86
4	23.84	70.54	85.06	91.61	95.05	97.00
5	0	61.32	80.39	88.99	93.51	96.06
6		51.21	75.26	86.11	91.81	95.04
7		40.12	69.63	82.95	89.94	93.91
8		27.96	63.47	79.49	87.90	92.67
9		14.62	56.71	75.70	85.66	91.31
10		0	49.29	71.53	83.21	89.82
11			41.16	66.97	80.52	88.19
12			32.25	61.97	77.57	86.40
13			22.47	56.48	74.33	84.44
14			11.75	50.46	70.78	82.29
15			0	43.86	66.89	79.93
16				36.63	62.62	77.35
17				28.70	57.94	74.51
18				20.00	52.81	71.40
19				10.46	47.18	67.99
20				0	41.01	64.26
21					34.25	60.16
22					26.83	55.66
23					18.70	50.73
24					9.78	45.33
25					0	39.40
26						32.90
27						25.78
28						17.96
29						9.39
30						0

9.50%

Age of Loan	5 years	10 years	15 years	20 years	25 years	30 years
1	83.60	93.70	96.83	98.24	98.97	99.38
2	65.56	86.78	93.35	96.30	97.84	98.71
3	45.74	79.17	89.53	94.18	96.60	97.96
4	23.95	70.81	85.32	91.84	95.23	97.14
5	0	61.61	80.70	89.27	93.73	96.24
6		51.51	75.62	86.44	92.08	95.25
7		40.40	70.03	83.33	90.27	94.16
8		28.18	63.89	79.92	88.27	92.97
9		14.76	57.14	76.16	86.08	91.65
10		0	49.72	72.04	83.67	90.21
11			41.56	67.50	81.02	88.62
12			32.60	62.51	78.11	86.87
13			22.74	57.03	74.91	84.95
14			11.91	51.01	71.39	82.84
15			0	44.38	67.52	80.52
16				37.10	63.27	77.97
17				29.10	58.59	75.17
18				20.30	53.46	72.09
19				10.63	47.81	68.70
20				0	41.60	64.98
21					34.78	60.89
22					27.27	56.39
23					19.03	51.45
24					9.96	46.01
25					0	40.04
26						33.47
27						26.25
28						18.31
29						9.59
30						0

9.75%

Age of Loan	5 years	10 years	15 years	20 years	25 years	30 years
1	83.68	93.78	96.90	98.29	99.01	99.41
2	68.71	86.94	93.49	96.41	97.93	98.77
3	45.89	79.39	89.72	94.34	96.73	98.06
4	24.06	71.07	85.58	92.05	95.41	97.27
5	0	61.91	81.01	89.54	93.95	96.41
6		51.81	75.97	86.76	92.35	95.46
7		40.68	70.43	83.71	90.58	94.41
8		28.41	64.31	80.34	88.63	93.26
9		14.89	57.57	76.62	86.49	91.98
10		0	50.15	72.53	84.12	90.58
11			41.97	68.02	81.51	89.03
12			32.95	63.06	78.64	87.33
13			23.01	57.58	75.48	85.45
14			12.07	51.55	71.99	83.38
15			0	44.90	68.15	81.10
16				37.58	63.91	78.59
17				29.50	59.24	75.82
18				20.61	54.10	72.77
19				10.80	48.43	69.41
20				0	42.19	65.70
21					35.30	61.62
22					27.72	57.12
23					19.36	52.16
24					10.15	46.69
25					0	40.67
26						34.04
27						26.72
28						18.67
29						9.79
30						0

10.00%	Age of Loan	5 years	10 years	15 years	20 years	25 years	30 years
	1	83.77	93.87	96.97	98.35	99.05	99.44
	2	65.85	87.09	93.62	96.52	98.01	98.83
	3	46.04	79.60	89.92	94.50	96.85	98.15
	4	24.17	71.33	85.83	92.27	95.57	97.40
	5	0	62.20	81.32	89.80	94.16	96.57
	6		52.10	76.33	87.08	92.61	95.66
	7		40.96	70.82	84.07	90.88	94.65
	8		28.64	64.73	80.75	88.98	93.53
	9		15.03	58.01	77.08	86.88	92.30
	10		0	50.58	73.02	84.56	90.94
	11			42.37	68.54	82.00	89.43
	12			33.30	63.60	79.17	87.77
	13			23.29	58.13	76.04	85.93
	14			12.22	52.09	72.58	83.91
	15			0	45.42	68.76	81.66
	16				38.05	64.54	79.19
	17				29.91	59.88	76.45
	18				20.91	54.74	73.43
	19				10.98	49.05	70.09
	20				0	42.77	66.41
	21					35.83	62.33
	22					28.16	57.83
	23					19.69	52.86
	24					10.34	47.37
	25					0	41.30
	26						34.60
	27						27.20
	28						19.02
	29						9.98
	30						0

10.25%	Age of Loan	5 years	10 years	15 years	20 years	25 years	30 years
	1	83.86	93.95	97.03	98.40	99.09	99.47
	2	65.99	87.24	93.75	96.62	98.09	98.89
	3	46.20	79.82	90.11	94.65	96.97	98.24
	4	24.28	71.59	86.08	92.48	95.74	97.52
	5	0	62.49	81.62	90.06	94.37	96.73
	6		52.40	76.68	87.39	92.86	95.85
	7		41.24	71.21	84.43	91.18	94.88
	8		28.87	65.15	81.16	89.33	93.80
	9		15.17	58.44	77.53	87.27	92.61
	10		0	51.00	73.51	84.99	91.29
	11			42.77	69.06	82.47	89.82
	12			33.66	64.13	79.68	88.20
	13			23.56	58.67	76.59	86.41
	14			12.38	52.63	73.16	84.42
	15			0	45.94	69.37	82.21
	16				38.52	65.17	79.78
	17				30.31	60.52	77.08
	18				21.22	55.37	74.08
	19				11.15	49.67	70.77
	20				0	43.35	67.10
	21					36.35	63.04
	22					28.61	58.54
	23					20.03	53.56
	24					10.52	48.04
	25					0	41.93
	26						35.16
	27						27.67
	28						19.37
	29						10.18
	30						0

10.50%

Age of Loan	5 years	10 years	15 years	20 years	25 years	30 years
1	83.95	94.03	97.10	98.45	99.13	99.50
2	66.13	87.39	93.88	96.72	98.16	98.94
3	46.35	80.03	90.30	94.81	97.09	98.33
4	24.38	71.85	86.33	92.68	95.90	97.64
5	0	62.78	81.92	90.32	94.57	96.88
6		52.70	77.03	87.70	93.10	96.04
7		41.52	71.59	84.79	91.47	95.10
8		29.10	65.56	81.56	89.66	94.06
9		15.31	58.86	77.97	87.65	92.90
10		0	51.43	73.99	85.42	91.62
11			43.17	69.57	82.94	90.20
12			34.01	64.66	80.19	88.62
13			23.84	59.21	77.13	86.86
14			12.54	53.16	73.74	84.91
15			0	46.45	69.97	82.75
16				38.99	65.79	80.35
17				30.72	61.15	77.68
18				21.53	56.00	74.73
19				11.33	50.28	71.44
20				0	43.93	67.79
21					36.88	63.74
22					29.05	59.24
23					20.36	54.25
24					10.71	48.71
25					0	42.56
26						35.73
27						28.14
28						19.72
29						10.38
30						0

10.75%

Age of Loan	5 years	10 years	15 years	20 years	25 years	30 years
1	84.04	94.10	97.16	98.49	99.16	99.53
2	66.27	87.54	94.00	96.82	98.23	99.00
3	46.50	80.24	90.49	94.95	97.20	98.41
4	24.49	72.11	86.57	92.88	96.05	97.75
5	0	63.07	82.22	90.57	94.77	97.03
6		53.00	77.37	88.00	93.34	96.22
7		41.80	71.98	85.14	91.75	95.31
8		29.33	65.97	81.95	89.98	94.31
9		15.45	59.29	78.41	88.02	93.19
10		0	51.85	74.46	85.83	91.95
11			43.58	70.07	83.39	90.56
12			34.36	65.19	80.68	89.02
13			24.11	59.75	77.66	87.31
14			12.70	53.70	74.30	85.40
15			0	46.96	70.57	83.28
16				39.47	66.41	80.91
17				31.12	61.78	78.28
18				21.84	56.62	75.35
19				11.50	50.89	72.09
20				0	44.50	68.47
21					37.40	64.43
22					29.49	59.94
23					20.69	54.94
24					10.90	49.37
25					0	43.18
26						36.29
27						28.62
28						20.08
29						10.58
30						0

11.00%	Age of Loan	5 years	10 years	15 years	20 years	25 years	30 years
	1	84.12	94.18	97.22	98.54	99.20	99.55
	2	66.41	87.69	94.13	96.91	98.31	99.05
	3	46.65	80.45	90.67	95.10	97.31	98.49
	4	24.60	72.37	86.81	93.07	96.20	97.86
	5	0	63.36	82.51	90.81	94.95	97.16
	6		53.30	77.71	88.29	93.57	96.39
	7		42.08	72.36	85.48	92.03	95.52
	8		29.56	66.38	82.34	90.30	94.55
	9		15.59	59.71	78.84	88.38	93.47
	10		0	52.28	74.93	86.23	92.26
	11			43.98	70.57	83.84	90.92
	12			34.72	65.71	81.17	89.42
	13			24.39	60.28	78.19	87.74
	14			12.86	54.23	74.86	85.87
	15			0	47.47	71.15	83.79
	16				39.94	67.01	81.46
	17				31.53	62.39	78.87
	18				22.15	57.24	75.97
	19				11.68	51.49	72.74
	20				0	45.08	69.13
	21					37.92	65.11
	22					29.94	60.63
	23					21.03	55.62
	24					11.09	50.03
	25					0	43.80
	26						36.85
	27						29.09
	28						20.43
	29						10.78
	30						0

11.25%	Age of Loan	5 years	10 years	15 years	20 years	25 years	30 years
	1	84.21	94.26	97.28	98.59	99.23	99.57
	2	66.55	87.84	94.25	97.01	98.37	99.10
	3	46.80	80.66	90.85	95.24	97.41	98.56
	4	24.71	72.63	87.05	93.26	96.34	97.97
	5	0	63.64	82.80	91.05	95.14	97.30
	6		53.59	78.05	88.58	93.79	96.55
	7		42.36	72.73	85.82	92.29	95.72
	8		29.79	66.79	82.72	90.61	94.78
	9		15.73	60.14	79.26	88.73	93.74
	10		0	52.70	75.39	86.63	92.57
	11			44.38	71.07	84.27	91.26
	12			35.07	66.23	81.64	89.80
	13			24.66	60.81	78.70	88.16
	14			13.02	54.76	75.41	86.33
	15			0	47.98	71.73	84.29
	16				40.41	67.61	82.00
	17				31.93	63.01	79.44
	18				22.46	57.85	76.57
	19				11.86	52.09	73.37
	20				0	45.65	69.79
	21					38.44	65.78
	22					30.38	61.30
	23					21.36	56.29
	24					11.28	50.69
	25					0	44.42
	26						37.40
	27						29.56
	28						20.79
	29						10.97
	30						0

11.50%

Age of Loan	5 years	10 years	15 years	20 years	25 years	30 years
1	84.30	94.34	97.34	98.63	99.26	99.60
2	66.69	87.99	94.37	97.10	98.44	99.14
3	46.95	80.86	91.03	95.38	97.51	98.63
4	24.82	72.88	87.29	93.45	96.48	98.06
5	0	63.93	83.09	91.29	95.32	97.42
6		53.89	78.38	88.87	94.01	96.71
7		42.64	73.11	86.15	92.55	95.90
8		30.02	67.19	83.10	90.91	95.00
9		15.87	60.56	79.68	89.07	93.99
10		0	53.12	75.85	87.01	92.86
11			44.78	71.55	84.70	91.59
12			35.43	66.74	82.11	90.17
13			24.94	61.34	79.21	88.57
14			13.18	55.28	75.95	86.78
15			0	48.49	72.30	84.77
16				40.88	68.20	82.52
17				32.34	63.61	80.00
18				22.77	58.46	77.17
19				12.03	52.69	73.99
20				0	46.22	70.44
21					38.96	66.45
22					30.82	61.97
23					21.70	56.96
24					11.47	51.33
25					0	45.03
26						37.96
27						30.03
28						21.14
29						11.18
30						0

11.75%

Age of Loan	5 years	10 years	15 years	20 years	25 years	30 years
1	84.38	94.41	97.40	98.68	99.30	99.62
2	66.83	88.13	94.49	97.19	98.50	99.19
3	47.10	81.07	91.20	95.51	97.61	98.70
4	24.93	73.13	87.52	93.63	96.61	98.16
5	0	64.21	83.37	91.52	95.49	97.55
6		54.19	78.71	89.14	94.22	96.86
7		42.92	73.48	86.47	92.80	96.09
8		30.25	67.59	83.47	91.20	95.22
9		16.01	60.97	80.09	89.41	94.24
10		0	53.54	76.30	87.39	93.14
11			45.18	72.04	85.12	91.91
12			35.78	67.25	82.57	90.52
13			25.22	61.86	79.70	88.97
14			13.35	55.80	76.48	87.21
15			0	49.00	72.86	85.24
16				41.35	68.79	83.03
17				32.75	64.21	80.54
18				23.08	59.07	77.75
19				12.21	53.28	74.60
20				0	46.78	71.07
21					39.48	67.10
22					31.27	62.63
23					22.04	57.62
24					11.66	51.98
25					0	45.64
26						38.51
27						30.50
28						21.50
29						11.38
30						0

12.00%	Age of Loan	5 years	10 years	15 years	20 years	25 years	30 years
	1	84.47	94.49	97.46	98.72	99.32	99.64
	2	66.97	88.27	94.60	97.27	98.56	99.23
	3	47.25	81.27	91.38	95.65	97.71	98.77
	4	25.04	73.39	87.75	93.81	96.74	98.25
	5	0	64.50	83.65	91.74	95.65	97.66
	6		54.48	79.04	89.42	94.43	97.00
	7		43.20	73.84	86.79	93.05	96.26
	8		30.48	67.99	83.83	91.49	95.42
	9		16.15	61.39	80.50	89.73	94.48
	10		0	53.95	76.75	87.76	93.42
	11			45.58	72.52	85.53	92.22
	12			36.13	67.75	83.02	90.87
	13			25.50	62.37	80.19	89.35
	14			13.51	56.32	77.00	87.64
	15			0	49.50	73.41	85.71
	16				41.81	69.36	83.53
	17				33.15	64.80	81.08
	18				23.39	59.66	78.32
	19				12.39	53.87	75.20
	20				0	47.35	71.69
	21					40.00	67.74
	22					31.71	63.29
	23					22.37	58.27
	24					11.85	52.61
	25					0	46.24
	26						39.06
	27						30.97
	28						21.85
	29						11.58
	30						0

12.25%	Age of Loan	5 years	10 years	15 years	20 years	25 years	30 years
	1	84.56	94.56	97.52	98.76	99.35	99.66
	2	67.11	88.42	94.71	97.36	98.62	99.27
	3	47.41	81.48	91.55	95.77	97.80	98.83
	4	25.15	73.64	87.97	93.99	96.87	98.33
	5	0	64.78	83.93	91.96	95.81	97.77
	6		54.78	79.36	89.68	94.63	97.14
	7		43.48	74.21	87.10	93.28	96.43
	8		30.71	68.38	84.19	91.76	95.62
	9		16.29	61.80	80.90	90.05	94.71
	10		0	54.37	77.19	88.12	93.68
	11			45.97	72.99	85.93	92.52
	12			36.49	68.24	83.46	91.21
	13			25.77	62.89	80.67	89.72
	14			13.67	56.84	77.52	88.05
	15			0	50.00	73.95	86.15
	16				42.28	69.93	84.02
	17				33.56	65.39	81.60
	18				23.70	60.26	78.87
	19				12.57	54.46	75.79
	20				0	47.91	72.31
	21					40.51	68.38
	22					32.15	63.93
	23					22.71	58.91
	24					12.05	53.25
	25					0	46.84
	26						39.61
	27						31.44
	28						22.21
	29						11.78
	30						0

12.50%	Age of Loan	5 years	10 years	15 years	20 years	25 years	30 years
	1	84.64	94.63	97.57	98.80	99.38	99.67
	2	67.25	88.56	94.83	97.44	98.68	99.31
	3	47.56	81.68	91.72	95.90	97.89	98.89
	4	25.26	73.89	88.19	94.16	96.99	98.42
	5	0	65.06	84.20	92.18	95.97	97.88
	6		55.07	79.68	89.94	94.82	97.28
	7		43.75	74.57	87.41	93.51	96.59
	8		30.94	68.77	84.54	92.03	95.81
	9		16.43	62.21	81.30	90.36	94.93
	10		0	54.78	77.62	88.47	93.94
	11			46.37	73.45	86.32	92.81
	12			36.84	68.74	83.89	91.53
	13			26.05	63.40	81.14	90.08
	14			13.84	57.35	78.02	88.45
	15			0	50.50	74.49	86.59
	16				42.74	70.49	84.49
	17				33.96	65.97	82.11
	18				24.02	60.84	79.42
	19				12.75	55.04	76.37
	20				0	48.46	72.91
	21					41.02	69.00
	22					32.59	64.57
	23					23.05	59.55
	24					12.24	53.87
	25					0	47.44
	26						40.15
	27						31.90
	28						22.56
	29						11.98
	30						0

12.75%	Age of Loan	5 years	10 years	15 years	20 years	25 years	30 years
	1	84.73	94.71	97.63	98.84	99.41	99.69
	2	67.39	88.70	94.94	97.52	98.73	99.34
	3	47.71	81.88	91.88	96.02	97.97	98.95
	4	25.36	74.13	88.41	94.32	97.10	98.50
	5	0	65.34	84.47	92.39	96.12	97.98
	6		55.36	80.00	90.20	95.00	97.40
	7		44.03	74.93	87.71	93.74	96.74
	8		31.17	69.16	84.89	92.30	96.00
	9		16.57	62.62	81.68	90.66	95.15
	10		0	55.20	78.04	88.81	94.18
	11			46.77	73.91	86.70	93.09
	12			37.20	69.22	84.31	91.85
	13			26.33	63.90	81.60	90.44
	14			14.00	57.86	78.51	88.83
	15			0	51.00	75.02	87.02
	16				43.21	71.05	84.95
	17				34.37	66.54	82.61
	18				24.33	61.42	79.95
	19				12.94	55.61	76.93
	20				0	49.02	73.50
	21					41.53	69.61
	22					33.03	65.20
	23					23.39	60.18
	24					12.43	54.49
	25					0	48.03
	26						40.69
	27						32.37
	28						22.91
	29						12.18
	30						0

13.00%	Age of Loan	5 years	10 years	15 years	20 years	25 years	30 years
	1	84.81	94.78	97.68	98.88	99.43	99.71
	2	67.53	88.84	95.04	97.60	98.79	99.38
	3	47.86	82.08	92.04	96.14	98.05	99.00
	4	25.47	74.38	88.63	94.48	97.22	98.57
	5	0	65.62	84.74	92.60	96.27	98.08
	6		55.66	80.31	90.45	95.18	97.53
	7		44.31	75.28	88.01	93.95	96.89
	8		31.41	69.55	85.23	92.55	96.17
	9		16.72	63.03	82.07	90.96	95.35
	10		0	55.61	78.47	89.14	94.42
	11			47.16	74.37	87.07	93.36
	12			37.55	69.71	84.72	92.15
	13			26.61	64.40	82.05	90.78
	14			14.17	58.36	79.00	89.21
	15			0	51.49	75.54	87.43
	16				43.67	71.59	85.40
	17				34.77	67.10	83.10
	18				24.64	62.00	80.47
	19				13.12	56.18	77.49
	20				0	49.57	74.09
	21					42.04	70.22
	22					33.47	65.82
	23					23.72	60.81
	24					12.63	55.11
	25					0	48.62
	26						41.23
	27						32.83
	28						23.27
	29						12.39
	30						0

13.25%	Age of Loan	5 years	10 years	15 years	20 years	25 years	30 years
	1	84.90	94.85	97.73	98.91	99.46	99.72
	2	67.67	88.97	95.15	97.67	98.84	99.41
	3	48.01	82.27	92.20	96.26	98.13	99.05
	4	25.58	74.62	88.84	94.64	97.33	98.64
	5	0	65.90	85.00	92.80	96.41	98.18
	6		55.95	80.62	90.70	95.36	97.64
	7		44.59	75.63	88.30	94.16	97.03
	8		31.64	69.93	85.56	92.80	96.34
	9		16.86	63.43	82.44	91.24	95.55
	10		0	56.02	78.88	89.46	94.65
	11			47.56	74.82	87.44	93.62
	12			37.90	70.18	85.13	92.44
	13			26.89	64.90	82.49	91.10
	14			14.33	58.86	79.48	89.58
	15			0	51.98	76.05	87.83
	16				44.13	72.13	85.84
	17				35.18	67.66	83.57
	18				24.96	62.56	80.98
	19				13.30	56.75	78.03
	20				0	50.12	74.66
	21					42.55	70.81
	22					33.91	66.43
	23					24.06	61.42
	24					12.82	55.71
	25					0	49.20
	26						41.77
	27						33.29
	28						23.62
	29						12.59
	30						0

13.50%	Age of Loan	5 years	10 years	15 years	20 years	25 years	30 years
	1	84.98	94.92	97.79	98.95	99.48	99.74
	2	67.81	89.11	95.26	97.74	98.89	99.44
	3	48.16	82.47	92.36	96.37	98.21	99.10
	4	25.69	74.87	89.05	94.80	97.43	98.71
	5	0	66.18	85.26	93.00	96.54	98.26
	6		56.24	80.93	90.94	95.53	97.75
	7		44.87	75.98	88.58	94.37	97.17
	8		31.87	70.31	85.89	93.04	96.50
	9		17.00	63.83	82.81	91.52	95.74
	10		0	56.42	79.29	89.78	94.87
	11			47.95	75.26	87.79	93.87
	12			38.26	70.66	85.52	92.73
	13			27.17	65.39	82.92	91.42
	14			14.50	59.36	79.95	89.93
	15			0	52.47	76.55	88.22
	16				44.59	72.66	86.27
	17				35.58	68.21	84.04
	18				25.27	63.13	81.48
	19				13.48	57.31	78.56
	20				0	50.66	75.22
	21					43.05	71.40
	22					34.35	67.03
	23					24.40	62.03
	24					13.02	56.32
	25					0	49.78
	26						42.30
	27						33.75
	28						23.97
	29						12.79
	30						0

13.75%	Age of Loan	5 years	10 years	15 years	20 years	25 years	30 years
	1	85.07	94.99	97.84	98.98	99.50	99.75
	2	67.94	89.25	95.36	97.82	98.93	99.47
	3	48.31	82.66	92.51	96.48	98.28	99.15
	4	25.80	75.11	89.26	94.95	97.53	98.78
	5	0	66.45	85.52	93.19	96.68	98.35
	6		56.53	81.23	91.17	95.69	97.86
	7		45.15	76.32	88.86	94.56	97.30
	8		32.11	70.69	86.21	93.27	96.66
	9		17.15	64.23	83.17	91.79	95.92
	10		0	56.83	79.69	90.09	95.08
	11			48.34	75.70	88.14	94.11
	12			38.61	71.12	85.91	93.00
	13			27.46	65.87	83.35	91.73
	14			14.66	59.86	80.41	90.27
	15			0	52.96	77.04	88.60
	16				45.05	73.18	86.69
	17				35.98	68.76	84.49
	18				25.59	63.68	81.97
	19				13.67	57.87	79.08
	20				0	51.20	75.77
	21					43.55	71.98
	22					34.79	67.62
	23					24.73	62.63
	24					13.21	56.91
	25					0	50.35
	26						42.83
	27						34.21
	28						24.33
	29						12.99
	30						0

14.00%	Age of Loan	5 years	10 years	15 years	20 years	25 years	30 years
	1	85.15	95.06	97.89	99.02	99.53	99.77
	2	68.08	89.38	95.46	97.89	98.98	99.50
	3	48.46	82.85	92.67	96.59	98.35	99.19
	4	25.91	75.35	89.46	95.09	97.63	98.84
	5	0	66.73	85.77	93.38	96.80	98.43
	6		56.82	81.53	91.40	95.85	97.96
	7		45.43	76.66	89.13	94.76	97.43
	8		32.34	71.06	86.53	93.50	96.81
	9		17.29	64.63	83.53	92.05	96.10
	10		0	57.23	80.09	90.39	95.28
	11			48.73	76.13	88.48	94.35
	12			38.97	71.58	86.28	93.27
	13			27.74	66.36	83.76	92.03
	14			14.83	60.35	80.86	90.61
	15			0	53.44	77.53	88.97
	16				45.51	73.70	87.09
	17				36.38	69.30	84.93
	18				25.90	64.23	82.45
	19				13.85	58.42	79.59
	20				0	51.73	76.31
	21					44.05	72.54
	22					35.22	68.21
	23					25.07	63.23
	24					13.41	57.50
	25					0	50.92
	26						43.36
	27						34.67
	28						24.68
	29						13.20
	30						0

14.25%	Age of Loan	5 years	10 years	15 years	20 years	25 years	30 years
	1	85.23	95.13	97.94	99.05	99.55	99.78
	2	68.22	89.51	95.56	97.95	99.02	99.53
	3	48.61	83.04	92.82	96.69	98.42	99.23
	4	26.03	75.59	89.66	95.24	97.73	98.90
	5	0	67.00	86.02	93.56	96.93	98.51
	6		57.11	81.83	91.63	96.00	98.06
	7		45.71	77.00	89.40	94.94	97.55
	8		32.57	71.44	86.84	93.72	96.95
	9		17.44	65.02	83.88	92.31	96.27
	10		0	57.64	80.48	90.68	95.48
	11			49.12	76.56	88.81	94.57
	12			39.32	72.04	86.65	93.53
	13			28.02	66.83	84.17	92.32
	14			15.00	60.84	81.31	90.93
	15			0	53.92	78.01	89.33
	16				45.96	74.21	87.49
	17				36.79	69.83	85.36
	18				26.21	64.78	82.91
	19				14.03	58.97	80.09
	20				0	52.27	76.84
	21					44.55	73.10
	22					35.65	68.78
	23					25.41	63.81
	24					13.60	58.09
	25					0	51.49
	26						43.88
	27						35.12
	28						25.03
	29						13.40
	30						0

14.50%	Age of Loan	5 years	10 years	15 years	20 years	25 years	30 years
	1	85.32	95.19	97.98	99.08	99.57	99.79
	2	68.35	89.64	95.65	98.02	99.06	99.55
	3	48.76	83.23	92.96	96.79	98.49	99.27
	4	26.14	75.83	89.86	95.37	97.82	98.95
	5	0	67.28	86.27	93.74	97.04	98.58
	6		57.40	82.12	91.85	96.15	98.15
	7		45.99	77.33	89.66	95.12	97.66
	8		32.81	71.80	87.14	93.93	97.09
	9		17.58	65.42	84.23	92.56	96.43
	10		0	58.04	80.87	90.97	95.67
	11			49.51	76.98	89.13	94.79
	12			39.67	72.49	87.01	93.77
	13			28.30	67.31	84.57	92.60
	14			15.17	61.32	81.74	91.24
	15			0	54.40	78.48	89.68
	16				46.41	74.70	87.87
	17				37.19	70.35	85.78
	18				26.53	65.32	83.37
	19				14.22	59.51	80.58
	20				0	52.79	77.36
	21					45.04	73.65
	22					36.09	69.35
	23					25.74	64.39
	24					13.80	58.66
	25					0	52.05
	26						44.40
	27						35.58
	28						25.38
	29						13.60
	30						0

14.75%	Age of Loan	5 years	10 years	15 years	20 years	25 years	30 years
	1	85.40	95.26	98.03	99.11	99.59	99.80
	2	68.49	89.77	95.75	98.08	99.10	99.58
	3	48.91	83.42	93.11	96.89	98.55	99.31
	4	26.25	76.06	90.05	95.51	97.90	99.01
	5	0	67.55	86.51	93.91	97.16	98.65
	6		57.68	82.41	92.06	96.30	98.24
	7		46.26	77.66	89.92	95.30	97.77
	8		33.04	72.17	87.44	94.14	97.22
	9		17.73	65.80	84.57	92.80	96.59
	10		0	58.43	81.24	91.24	95.85
	11			49.90	77.39	89.45	95.00
	12			40.02	72.94	87.37	94.01
	13			28.58	67.78	84.96	92.87
	14			15.34	61.80	82.17	91.55
	15			0	54.88	78.94	90.02
	16				46.86	75.20	88.24
	17				37.59	70.86	86.19
	18				26.84	65.85	83.81
	19				14.40	60.04	81.06
	20				0	53.32	77.87
	21					45.53	74.18
	22					36.52	69.91
	23					26.08	64.96
	24					13.99	59.23
	25					0	52.60
	26						44.92
	27						36.03
	28						25.73
	29						13.81
	30						0

15.00%	Age of Loan	5 years	10 years	15 years	20 years	25 years	30 years
	1	85.48	95.33	98.08	99.14	99.60	99.81
	2	68.63	89.90	95.84	98.14	99.14	99.60
	3	49.06	83.61	93.25	96.99	98.61	99.35
	4	26.36	76.30	90.24	95.64	97.99	99.06
	5	0	67.82	86.75	94.08	97.27	98.72
	6		57.97	82.70	92.27	96.43	98.33
	7		46.54	77.99	90.17	95.46	97.87
	8		33.27	72.53	87.73	94.34	97.35
	9		17.87	66.19	84.90	93.03	96.74
	10		0	58.83	81.62	91.51	96.02
	11			50.29	77.80	89.75	95.20
	12			40.37	73.38	87.71	94.24
	13			28.87	68.24	85.34	93.13
	14			15.51	62.27	82.59	91.84
	15			0	55.35	79.39	90.34
	16				47.31	75.68	88.61
	17				37.99	71.37	86.59
	18				27.16	66.38	84.25
	19				14.59	60.57	81.53
	20				0	53.84	78.37
	21					46.02	74.71
	22					36.95	70.46
	23					26.42	65.53
	24					14.19	59.80
	25					0	53.15
	26						45.43
	27						36.48
	28						26.08
	29						14.01
	30						0

15.25%	Age of Loan	5 years	10 years	15 years	20 years	25 years	30 years
	1	85.56	95.39	98.12	99.17	99.62	99.82
	2	68.76	90.03	95.94	98.20	99.18	99.62
	3	49.22	83.79	93.39	97.08	98.67	99.38
	4	26.47	76.53	90.43	95.77	98.07	99.11
	5	0	68.09	86.99	94.25	97.38	98.78
	6		58.26	82.98	92.48	96.57	98.41
	7		46.82	78.32	90.42	95.63	97.98
	8		33.51	72.89	88.02	94.53	97.47
	9		18.02	66.57	85.23	93.26	96.88
	10		0	59.23	81.99	91.78	96.19
	11			50.67	78.21	90.05	95.39
	12			40.73	73.81	88.05	94.47
	13			29.15	68.70	85.71	93.38
	14			15.68	62.75	83.00	92.13
	15			0	55.82	79.83	90.66
	16				47.76	76.16	88.96
	17				38.38	71.88	86.98
	18				27.47	66.90	84.67
	19				14.77	61.10	81.99
	20				0	54.36	78.86
	21					46.51	75.23
	22					37.38	71.00
	23					26.75	66.08
	24					14.39	60.36
	25					0	53.70
	26						45.94
	27						36.92
	28						26.43
	29						14.21
	30						0

15.50%	Age of Loan	5 years	10 years	15 years	20 years	25 years	30 years
	1	85.64	95.46	98.17	99.20	99.64	99.83
	2	68.90	90.16	96.03	98.26	99.22	99.64
	3	49.37	83.98	93.53	97.17	98.72	99.42
	4	26.58	76.76	90.62	95.90	98.15	99.15
	5	0	68.35	87.22	94.41	97.48	98.85
	6		58.54	83.26	92.68	96.70	98.49
	7		47.09	78.64	90.66	95.79	98.07
	8		33.74	73.24	88.30	94.72	97.58
	9		18.17	66.95	85.55	93.48	97.02
	10		0	59.62	82.35	92.03	96.35
	11			51.06	78.61	90.34	95.58
	12			41.08	74.24	88.38	94.68
	13			29.43	69.15	86.08	93.63
	14			15.85	63.21	83.40	92.40
	15			0	56.29	80.27	90.97
	16				48.21	76.62	89.30
	17				38.78	72.37	87.36
	18				27.79	67.41	85.08
	19				14.96	61.62	82.44
	20				0	54.87	79.35
	21					46.99	75.74
	22					37.80	71.54
	23					27.09	66.63
	24					14.58	60.91
	25					0	54.23
	26						46.45
	27						37.37
	28						26.77
	29						14.42
	30						0

Glossary

adjustable-rate mortgage (ARM)   a mortgage in which the effective interest rate may change from time to time. As a result of such changes, the monthly payment will change as well. The ARM contract specifies the frequency of change as well as the maximum interest rate that can be applied during the life of the contract.

amortization   the process by which a loan is paid off. During the early years, most of the monthly payment goes toward interest; during the later years, the reverse is true, and the loan is amortized more rapidly.

amortization table   a table used for calculating the monthly payment required to retire a loan. The table specifies the annual interest rate and the compounding method. It then lists rows for each year or for amounts borrowed, and columns for the years involved.

assumable loan   a loan that can be taken over by a buyer at the time the borrower sells his or her house.

balloon mortgage   a mortgage that provides for interest-only or very low principal payments for a number of months or years. The full outstanding principal balance is due at the end of the term, usually 3 to 5 years.

basic interest formula   the formula used to calculate interest. It involves four elements: the principal amount, the interest rate, the time involved, and a compounding method. Time involved could be a matter of a few weeks or months, or 30 years; and the compounding method will affect the total of interest to be paid.

biweekly mortgage   a repayment arrangement in which one extra payment is made per year. One-half of the monthly payment is made every two weeks. Because there are 52 weeks in the year, 26 half-payments are made. The extra payment is applied toward principal, as a method for accelerating the mortgage.

breakeven point   the number of months needed to break even after refinancing. To calculate, divide the total costs of refinancing by the amount of monthly savings on the loan payment. The result is the breakeven point, or the months required to cover the costs. For example, you can reduce your monthly payment by $65 if you refinance now. However, closing costs will be about $1,700. It will take you about 26 months to reach the breakeven point. If you plan to sell your home within the next 26 months, it would not make sense to refinance today.

buy-down mortgage   terms offered by a builder or developer, to make it easier to sell new property, or by a lender, in a slow market. The interest is prepaid for the borrower, so initial payments are lower. The interest rate increases over a specified period of time (often 1 to 3 years), as prepaid interest is applied to the outstanding balance at the beginning of each year.

callable feature   a feature, in some loans, that allows the lender to demand full payment at a specified point. For example, a loan might be amortized over a 30-year term, but it may contain a 5-year call feature. The lender may demand payment of the entire outstanding balance at that time.

cap   the maximum amount of increase that can be applied in an adjustable-rate mortgage. For example, a contract might begin with an interest rate of 9 percent, with two types of caps. The annual cap specifies that the interest rate may not be increased by more than 1 percent; the lifetime cap specifies that the interest may never be increased by more than 6 percent above the original rate.

cash flow   the amount of cash available each month to pay expenses. The term is used to describe investments made with borrowed funds. For example, an investor might borrow money to buy a rental house, hoping to make mortgage payments from rent receipts. If the house remains vacant, the cash flow will not be adequate to make mortgage payments.

Cash flow might be quite different from profit. For example, a mortgage payment includes principal, which is not an expense. Thus, it is possible to show a net profit while experiencing negative cash flow. And, because depreciation, a noncash expense, is allowed on investment property, it is also possible to show a net loss while experiencing positive cash flow.

compound interest a charge for interest that occurs more often than once per year. In most mortgage contracts, interest is compounded monthly, meaning that one-twelfth of the annual interest rate is applied against each month's outstanding loan balance. Other methods of compounding include quarterly, semiannually, or daily.

convertible mortgage a loan that includes a provision for conversion from one set of terms to another. Most common is the adjustable-rate loan that, at the borrower's option, can be converted to a fixed-rate loan. The convertible loan usually specifies a limited number of years during which the conversion can be made.

creative financing a term generally used to describe any terms and conditions other than those associated with conventional borrowing; methods used to allow people to qualify for loans when the lender's normal terms would otherwise preclude them.

debt consolidation a process of borrowing money to pay off existing debts, and extending the repayment term with lower, more affordable payments. The strategy often does not work, however, because the borrower replaces the same debts within a short period of time. The result: Higher debts and greater budgetary strain.

depreciation the gradual deduction, or writing off, of an investment or business property. Investors in real estate are allowed to depreciate residential property over 27.5 years, and commercial property over 31.5 years. Land cannot be depreciated.

effective monthly rate the rate of interest applied to each month, computed by dividing the annual rate by 12. The effective monthly rate is applied to each month's outstanding loan balance.

effective tax rate   the rate of income tax paid on taxable income each year.

emergency reserve fund   a fund set up in a highly liquid account, such as a savings account, to be used in case of emergencies. Such a fund should be established before beginning a program of mortgage acceleration, which is a very illiquid investment.

equity   ownership; or, the portion of a house representing net worth. For example, a house has a current market value of $100,000 and the mortgage balance is $60,000. Equity is $40,000, the difference.

equity line of credit   a line of credit secured by the equity in real property. For example, a lender will allow a homeowner to draw up to 80 percent of current market value through a line of credit. The home-owner is charged interest only on the balance actually drawn. In comparison, a loan is subject to interest on the full amount, even if it is not needed at the time the loan is granted.

FHA loan   a loan guaranteed by the Federal Housing Administration (FHA). Such loans are granted only for owner-occupied residential purchases. Borrowers are asked to put up minimum down payments, and borrowers are guaranteed repayment.

fixed cost   an attribute of a long-term fixed mortgage. Because the monthly payment does not vary for the entire term, the cost is fixed for the entire life of the contract.

fixed-rate mortgage (FRM)   a mortgage in which the monthly payment does not vary over the entire lifetime of the contract. Although the breakdown between interest and principal changes, the payment does not.

graduated payment mortgage   financing in which a schedule of gradually increasing payments is agreed on in advance by borrower and lender. Interest rates usually remain constant; principal is gradually accelerated over time.

growing equity mortgage   a prescheduled form of mortgage acceleration in which a specified amount of payment is applied toward the principal balance, and the overall monthly payment increases over time.

home equity loan   a loan secured by home equity as collateral. The lender is entitled to payments until the loan is repaid. If the borrower does not make those payments, the lender may foreclose and seize the equity in the home as satisfaction of the debt.

interest   the cost of borrowing money. In most mortgage contracts, interest is compounded monthly. This means that the stated annual rate is divided by 12 to find the effective monthly rate. The effective monthly rate is then multiplied by the previous loan balance. The result is the amount of interest for that month's mortgage payment.

interpolation   an estimate of the monthly payment or factor. This is used when an interest rate falls in between available tables. For example, your loan might be at 9.625 percent; and a book of tables might provide information only for 9.50 and 9.75 percent. By calculating the average of the lower and higher rates, you may interpolate the required information at your rate of interest.

line of credit   a form of lending in which the borrower is allowed to draw up to a maximum amount. Unlike a loan, the draw may be made at the borrower's convenience, and interest is charged only on the amount drawn.

liquidity   the availability of cash. A savings account, for example, is highly liquid, because money can be easily and quickly withdrawn. Mortgage acceleration is a profitable but very illiquid investment. Money can be taken back out only by borrowing with equity as security, or by selling the property.

loan commitment   a document, given to a borrower by a lender, stating that a loan will be granted based on the borrower's credit history and financial strength. This is a useful document for home buyers seeking a preapproval as a means of eliminating a financing contingency. The commitment specifies a maximum amount and imposes a time limit, and usually also locks in an interest rate.

monthly compounding   a method of compounding interest by dividing the annual rate by 12. The result is then applied to the outstanding balance of the loan.

mortgage acceleration   the process of speeding up the repayment of a loan by paying more to principal than is required by the loan terms. This reduces all future interest and, as a result, takes time off the required repayment term.

negative amortization   a situation in which the monthly payment is not enough to cover the current month's interest expense. As a consequence, the loan balance increases each month rather than declining. This could occur in an adjustable-rate mortgage when the monthly payment amount is not increased enough to cover interest expenses.

net interest   the interest actually paid on a mortgage, after reducing the amount for the tax benefits derived. The calculation is useful in estimating the true cost of housing. For example, a 10 percent mortgage is reduced by the effective tax rate being paid. At the 28 percent level, net interest would be 7.2 percent.

points   charges assessed by lenders as part of the cost of borrowing money. Each point is equal to one percent of the loan amount. For example, if the loan is $80,000 and the lender charges two points, the borrower will be expected to pay $1,600 as part of the closing costs, to obtain that loan.

principal   that portion of a loan payment applied to the balance of the loan. The remainder is considered as interest, or the cost of borrowing money.

purchase money mortgage   a loan for the entire amount to be financed, less the down payment, with the financing often provided entirely by the seller.

refinancing   the replacement of one loan with another, often involving a higher loan amount and a taking-out of cash; or, replacement of a relatively high interest rate with a relatively low one. Refinancing may be undertaken as a way of paying for home improvements or other expenses.

remaining balance table   a table that shows the percentage of a loan's balance remaining unpaid at the end of each year. The table specifies the interest rate and the repayment term. The percentages shown in each column and row are multiplied by the original loan amount, to calculate the amount unpaid after each year.

repayment term   the number of months or years that will be required to repay a loan, assuming that only the required monthly payment is made. The most common repayment terms for mortgages are 15-year and 30-year loans.

rollover mortgage   a mortgage set on a long-term schedule of amortization, but with the provision that the terms of the loan will be renegotiated, or rolled over, every few years. This means the lender can apply a new rate of interest or, in some instances, demand payment in full of the principal amount.

sale–leaseback   an arrangement, usually between family members, in which property is sold by one person to another and then leased back. For example, an elderly parent may have a lot of equity in a house and a need for continued shelter, but may also need more cash flow. By selling the house to a younger relative, the elderly parent may have a home as well as additional monthly income. For the younger relative, the transaction represents a wise investment as well as tax benefits.

second mortgage   a mortgage secured by real property, but with a lower priority in the event of a default. In such a case, the first mortgage holder is repaid first and, if adequate equity remains, the second mortgage holder is then repaid.

seller financing   any form of loan in which the seller provides all or part of the financing.

shared appreciation mortgage   a mortgage offered well below prevailing market rates. The lender is entitled to a share in future market value, as part of the conditions for the loan. This may occur upon sale or at the end of a specified period of time.

shared equity mortgage   an agreement entered into between a resident homeowner and an investor. Each owns part of the equity and contributes to the down payment, the monthly payment, or both.

straight-line depreciation   depreciation that is claimed at the same level each year. For example, residential real estate used as investment property can be depreciated over 27.5 years, using the straight-line method, which means that the value of the building (but not the land) is divided by 27.5. The result is the amount allowed each year as depreciation expense.

VA loan   a loan in which repayment is guaranteed to the lender by the Veterans Administration (VA). An owner-occupant who is a veteran or the spouse of a veteran can qualify for a VA loan, which requires little or nothing in the way of a down payment.

wraparound mortgage   a mortgage involving a buyer's assumption of an existing loan, coupled with additional financing provided by the seller or an outside lender. The total of payments is wrapped together and made in a single payment, usually to the seller, who then makes payments to the original lender and/or the new lender, or keeps the portion representing seller financing.

Index